WELCOME TO THE RASPBERRY PI

Discover how to get the most from your Pi with a variety of hands-on projects suitable for any user. Follow our plain English, step-by-step instructions, and before long you'll be a Pi pro!

The Raspberry Pi has been nothing short of a revolution: since its launch in 2012, the credit card-sized single-board computer has sold more than two million units in almost every country in the world, revitalised interest in UK high-tech manufacturing, and been the catalyst for a ground-up reform in how computing is taught in the UK.

The Pi has proven a real winner in the hobbyist electronic community, powering devices from high-altitude balloons that send back images from near space to miniature arcade machines, from home-made laser cutters to souse-vide cookers, but getting started can be daunting. From the bare circuit board design of the Pi to the use of Linux, still unfamiliar to many, as its operating system, it's easy to be overwhelmed by the Pi and fail to make use of its true potential.

That's where this guide comes in. Within its pages, you'll learn how to take control of the Pi and use it in a variety of hands-on projects. From an absolute beginner unpacking a Pi for the first time to a hacker looking to make the jump from rival platforms, you'll find something of interest to get your teeth into within its pages, with clear, plain English instructions for each step along the way – and soon you'll be a Pi professional.

PRODUCTIVITY

Despite its low cost and power-sipping processor, the Pi has serious potential as a productivity-enhancing machine. From running your own personal web server to boosting its performance through overclocking, and even beating the spies with an encrypted privacy-enhancing router, this software-based chapter is a great introduction to the Pi and its Linux operating system.

ENTERTAINMENT

The Pi's processor features a powerful multimedia chip, the Broadcom VideoCore-IV, which makes it an excellent device for home entertainment. In this chapter, you'll transform the Pi into everything from a retro gaming system to an internet radio receiver, and learn how it can bring Smart TV functionality to even the oldest set.

PLUG-IN HARDWARE

Like building blocks, the Pi becomes more fun when you add a few extras. Using the tutorials in this chapter, you'll learn how to build a security system that posts images to Twitter, a powerful yet compact digital photo frame, how to use the Pi to mine the infamous Bitcoin cryptocurrency, and even how to extend its capabilities with the open hardware Arduino project.

DIY & ADVANCED

The Pi's true potential only becomes apparent when you begin to make use of its General-Purpose Input-Output (GPIO) connectivity. For those willing to pick up a soldering iron, regardless of experience, this chapter demonstrates how the GPIO header can be used to drive motors, simulate a traffic light, create an internet-connected doorbell, or even an Internet of Things (IoT) printer. For the gamers, there's even a guide to building a customised arcade control stick.

Put simply, if you want to get the most out of your Pi – or to see what the headline-grabbing gadget can do before taking the plunge and placing an order – this is the guide for you.

Gareth Halfacree

CONTENTS

CHAPTER 4:
PLUG-IN HARDWARE

CHAPTER 5:
DIY & ADVANCED

CONCLUSION:
NEXT STEPS

WHAT IS THE RASPBERRY PI?

Developed in the UK by the Raspberry Pi Foundation, this low-cost single-board computer is now into its third year and going from strength to strength

Although those involved in its creation didn't know it at the time, the launch of the Raspberry Pi was the catalyst for an explosion of interest in computing education. A trigger for the UK government's placing of computing on the national curriculum, the low-cost single-board computer has found a home in everything from balloons hovering at the edge of space to brew houses eager to monitor their latest batches.

With 512MB of memory, a 700MHz processor and just two USB ports, it's true that the Pi can't rival a modern desktop or laptop in raw power. However, with its flexible general-purpose input-output (GPIO) port at the top-left and a power-sipping design that allows it to run from a mobile phone charger, the Pi has proven a stellar success with the maker, hacker and tinkerer communities.

The first question that faces any new Pi owner is: just what can I do with it? The flexibility of the Pi, arguably its biggest selling point, can prove a downfall here: it would be easer to create a list of what you can't do with a Pi and a desire to learn.

This MagBook is designed as a handy reference guide containing some interesting, fun, productive and unique projects suitable for any Pi owner. Far from an exhaustive list, it offers step-by-step walkthroughs in plain English, which can turn the bare board of the Raspberry Pi into everything from the heart of a Smart TV setup to a device designed to mine the infamous Bitcoin cryptocurrency. No knowledge of programming, electronics or even the Pi itself is required. Just grab your keyboard, mouse and tools, and set about learning just what a good investment you made in the Pi.

A LITTLE HISTORY

The Raspberry Pi, as it was originally conceived, was a tool for engineers and hackers. Its first production run, which took place in China thanks to a lack of interest from UK manufacturers, comprised just 1,500 units. A figure its creators believed would easily accommodate early adopters keen to try out the device.

When the Pi went on sale, demand was high enough to crash the websites of companies that chose to stock the device. The initial stock of 1,500 units sold out in minutes, and for months following the Pi remained difficult to buy for anyone who wasn't willing to sit and refresh retailers' stock pages in their browsers.

That surge of demand proved that the Pi's creators, a group of educators and engineers from the traditional home of British computing Cambridge, had something major on their hands. Suddenly, manufacturers were clamouring for their business. The Pi is now manufactured in a facility in Wales, with the freshly formed not-for-profit Raspberry Pi Foundation overseeing proceedings.

The Pi has also undergone something of a transformation since its launch. Restrictive features, such as having just 256MB of memory and fuses on its USB ports that prevent the use of certain accessories, have been upgraded and modified. The original Model B, which follows the naming convention of Acorn's classic BBC microcomputers of the 1980s, has also been joined by an even lower-cost Model A. While it lacks the network port and 512MB memory of the latest Model B revision, it draws

The Model B Revision 1 (left) lacks a P5 connector.

The Model B Revision 2 is currently the most popular model.

less power, making it a great choice for battery-operated projects.

Now into its third year, the Raspberry Pi project is going from strength to strength and, thanks to educational materials developed by examination board OCR and funding from advertising giant Google, the device looks set to continue that trend well into the future.

IDENTIFYING YOUR PI

Although it has only been available to the public for just over two years, the Pi has undergone significant changes over that time. Although most of those changes don't affect the Pi's suitability for the projects outlined in this MagBook, they can trip you up when you least expect it. If you already own a Pi but you're not sure which model, you'll learn how to identify it here. If you haven't yet taken the plunge, read this section first as a handy pre-purchase guide to ensure you get the right model.

The Model A is the newest and cheapest Raspberry Pi.

THE MODEL A

Despite its model name putting it firmly at the start of the alphabet, the Model A is actually the newest Raspberry Pi. Designed to reduce the cost of the already bargain-basement Pi even further and to eke the most life out of batteries in embedded projects, the Model A is immediately recognisable by a gap at the right of the printed circuit board (PCB) where you'd normally find the Ethernet network port. The other physical change is in the USB ports, where the two ports of the more expensive Model B have been replaced by a single port.

The Model A is capable of running almost all the same software as the Model B, and includes the same general-purpose input-output (GPIO) header. Its lack of a network port can also be overcome by connecting a USB network adapter – either wired or wireless – to its single USB port. A bigger drawback, however, is in its lack of memory: like the original Model B, detailed below, it has just 256MB, making it less suited to certain complex programs like games.

THE MODEL B

The Model B costs more than the Model A, but you get a lot for your money. As well as a doubling of the RAM from 256MB to 512MB, the Model B includes a wired networking port at the right-hand side of the PCB, along with two USB ports for accessories and peripherals. These features do come at the cost of power draw, however. Those planning on long-life battery-based or solar-powered projects would do well to consider whether the additional features of the Model B are really necessary.

There are two versions of the Model B, only one of which is available for sale today. The first, known as the Model B Revision 1, was the original design to go on sale. It can be distinguished by its lack of a P5 connector, seen on a Model B Revision 2 below the GPIO connector at the top-left of the board, and by having only 256MB of memory like a Model A.

The newer version, on sale today, is the Model B Revision 2. This is the most popular model, and if your Pi was purchased within the last year is almost certainly the version you have. Unlike the original Model B, it features a full 512MB of memory, and is identified by the presence of the P5 connector. ●

WHAT YOU NEED TO GET STARTED

To get your Pi up and running, you'll need a few basic components. Here we look at some of the essentials that every new user will require

Although not strictly necessary, a USB hub is handy.

The Raspberry Pi is supplied as a plain, uncased circuit board. Unlike a desktop or a laptop, it's not ready to use out of the box, so you'll need to gather some additional accessories before you can attempt any of the projects in this MagBook. The good news is that none of these are expensive, and many – such as a monitor, keyboard and mouse – you're likely to have already.

It's also possible to buy the Pi as a starter kit from various retailers. These kits typically come with everything you need to get started with the software-based projects in this MagBook, but lack the extra hardware needed for some of the later projects. They also cost slightly more than buying the parts individually from the cheapest sources.

However you decide to buy the parts, you'll need the following to build the projects in this book:

A RASPBERRY PI

The projects in this MagBook were written and tested using a Raspberry Pi Model B Revision 2, the most modern version of the device. In every case, however, the projects will work just fine on an original Raspberry Pi Model B Revision 1; where certain features have changed, it will be noted. It's also possible to use the cheaper Model A for any project, although for many you'll also need to connect a USB network adapter – either wired or wireless – through a USB hub, thanks to the Model A's single USB port and lack of onboard networking. That aside, however, having a Model A won't restrict your ability to complete any of the projects.

A POWER ADAPTER

The Raspberry Pi doesn't include a power supply, but the chances are you've already got one lying around. The Pi takes its power from a small micro-USB connector on the left-hand side of the board. This is the same connector used by the majority of smartphones, tablets and e-readers, meaning it should be possible to take an existing charger and use it with the Pi.

Not all chargers will work, however. The Raspberry Pi Model A can draw up to 800mA of power, which is more than the 500mA of a regular USB port. This means you can't connect the Pi to a desktop or laptop computer for power, and it also means that cheaper or older USB power supplies may not work or cause the Pi to behave erratically or crash.

To be sure a power supply is adequate for the Pi, check the output markings on the label. If it reads "5V 500mA", it may not be powerful enough. For the most stable performance, use a supply rated at 1A (1,000mA) or higher.

AN SD CARD

The Raspberry Pi doesn't use a hard drive like a desktop computer, but stores all its files – including the operating system – on an SecureDigital (SD) card, the same type of memory card used by many digital cameras. You can buy SD cards with the operating system pre-loaded from many sources, although it typically works out cheaper to buy a blank card and install the operating system – available for free download from the

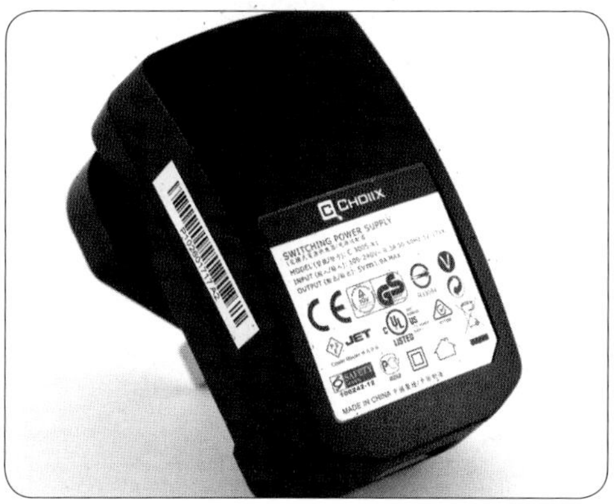

Many of you are likely to have most of these essentials already.

Raspberry Pi Foundation – yourself.

In either case, make sure that the card is at least 8GB in capacity. Any smaller and you won't be able to use the New Out Of Box Software (NOOBS), a tool released by the Foundation to make it easy to install new operating systems and recover the Pi's SD card in the event of corruption or user error. Also look for cards that offer at least Class 10 performance. The lower the class, the slower the card and this can have a serious knock-on effect on the Pi's overall usability.

A KEYBOARD AND MOUSE

Unless the Pi is your first computer, or you're a dedicated laptop or tablet user, you've almost certainly got a keyboard and mouse suitable for use with the Pi. The Pi requires its peripherals to use a USB connector, rather than the older round PS/2 connector, and certain high-power models – in particular those with backlit keys – may not work correctly. If you find that the keyboard starts repeating letters as though a key was held down, but works fine when connected to a desktop or laptop, this is a sign it's demanding too much power from the Pi.

To make the most of the Pi's limited USB ports, it's worth looking for combined keyboard and mouse units that use a single port. These can take the form of a keyboard with built-in trackpad, like a laptop, or separate wireless keyboards and mice with a unified receiver dongle.

A DISPLAY

The Raspberry Pi has two main video outputs, designed for different display types: an analogue composite connection, the yellow port on the top of the board, and a digital High Definition Multimedia Interface (HDMI) connection, the silver port on the bottom of the board. The HDMI port offers the highest quality, and connects directly to a modern HDTV set. It can also be used with a Digital Video Interface (DVI) monitor with a low-cost HDMI-to-DVI adapter cable. A more expensive active adapter cable can be used to convert the HDMI port to a Video Graphics Array (VGA) port, as found on older monitors or labelled as a "PC Input" on some HDTVs.

If you have no HDMI, DVI or VGA displays around, you can use the composite video connector to connect the Pi to a TV set. Doing so results in a less detailed picture, but makes good use of an outdated TV that would otherwise be destined for landfill.

A POWERED USB HUB

You don't strictly need a USB hub to use a Pi, but it can certainly come in handy. The Pi's USB ports are underpowered compared to those of a desktop or laptop, and some high-power devices – such as the ASIC used in the Bitcoin Mining project later on – won't work correctly unless connected to a powered hub. The hub also extends the number of USB ports available to the Pi and can be used to power the Pi itself instead of a dedicated power adapter, removing the need to find two power sockets.

Having the above to hand will stand you in good stead for attacking the projects in this MagBook, but it's not an exhaustive list. When you move onto the hardware-based projects, you'll need additional devices ranging from special add-on boards that provide a display or buttons to electronic components such as switches and LEDs. These parts, unique to each project, are detailed at the start of each project. If you're reading this in the newsagent with a view to buying what you need while you're in town, make sure you look at the projects you're planning to build before getting the bus home. ●

SETTING UP YOUR PI READY FOR USE

You have a little work to do before you can connect your tiny, new computer to a display and boot it up. Just follow our simple steps to get started

Unlike a normal desktop or laptop computer, the Raspberry Pi is supplied as standard without any accessories – without even a case, in fact. Although the credit card-sized board can seem daunting at first glance, the Pi is a relatively simple device and can be quickly set up ready for use. If you're an absolute Pi beginner, you'll find what you need to know here. If you've already set up your Pi and had a play, feel free to skip ahead to the chapter on Productivity and get started with the first of the projects.

UNBOXING THE PI

The Raspberry Pi is supplied as a bare circuit board, wrapped in a metallised plastic bag inside a small cardboard box. Looking at the size of the box, it's hard to imagine that there's a fully functional general-purpose computer inside, but the Pi's size belies its flexibility. Its unprotected nature does, however, require a little more careful handling than that of a traditional desktop or laptop.

After opening the box, remove the bag containing the Pi. This bag is treated with a layer of metal designed to dissipate electrostatic energy. This is the electricity that builds up in your body as you move around, and is responsible for the sharp crack and sting you get if you prod a metal door handle with your finger after rubbing your feet on a nylon carpet. That shock is known as an electrostatic discharge, or ESD, and it can be fatal to electronics. What gives you a sharp shock is enough energy to destroy sensitive electronic components, such as those used to make the Pi.

Before removing the Pi from the bag, touch a grounded metal surface such as the case of your desktop PC or a radiator. This will discharge any static electricity currently built up in your body before it can damage the Pi. If you plan to use the Pi without a case while building hardware-based projects, it's a good idea to invest in an anti-static wrist-strap (£6.99, maplin.co.uk). This keeps you in contact with a grounded metal surface at all times, ensuring static can't build up.

When removing the Pi from the bag, always hold it by the edges of the printed circuit board. Never touch the exposed pins at the top-left of the board. These are the General Purpose Input-Output (GPIO) pins, and are connected directly to the Pi's processor. A static discharge to the GPIO pins can destroy a Pi. They're also relatively easy to bend, and a short caused by bent pins touching each other is equally damaging.

If you're not placing the Pi in a case, put it on a non-conductive surface. You shouldn't lay it on the bag in which it came, as the metal layer makes that conductive and can short out the Pi's components. A wooden or glass desk is fine, as is a foam mouse-mat. Make sure it's not going to get in your way, but that you can easily reach its various ports with your cables.

POPULAR PI OPERATING SYSTEMS

The most popular operating systems for the Raspberry Pi are:

- **Raspbian** The OS officially recommended by the Raspberry Pi Foundation. Based on the Debian Linux distribution, it offers a good mix of performance and flexibility, and is the basis for the projects in this MagBook.
- **Pidora** A version of the Fedora Linux operating system customised for the Pi; more attractive than Raspbian, but with less support.
- **OpenElec** A specialist operating system designed to convert a Pi into a home theatre system; an alternative to Raspbmc.
- **Raspbmc** A specialist operating system designed to convert a Pi into a home theatre system; an alternative to OpenElec.
- **Arch Linux** A port of the Linux distribution of the same name; designed for those with good knowledge of Linux, and not very accessible to beginners.
- **RISC OS** Originally developed by Acorn for the Archimedes range of home computers. RISC OS is fast and flexible, and the only operating system commonly used on the Pi that isn't based on Linux.

A TOUR OF THE BOARD

The exposed nature of the Raspberry Pi's design makes it a great way to learn more about how computers are built. Although it may seem dramatically different to a desktop or laptop, it contains all of the same components.

The heart of the Raspberry Pi is the Broadcom BCM2835 system-on-chip (SoC) processor. Originally developed for multimedia set-top boxes, the BCM2835 contains a relatively slow ARM central processing unit (CPU) alongside a significantly more powerful graphics processing unit (GPU). Almost everything on the Raspberry Pi, from the GPIO pins to the HDMI video output, is driven directly from the BCM2835. The only exceptions are the Ethernet and USB ports of the Model B, which we'll discuss later.

If you're looking for the BCM2835 on the Pi, you won't find it. The chip is hidden underneath the square chip at the centre of the board, usually marked Samsung or Hynix, depending on manufacturer. This chip is the Pi's random access memory (RAM), either 256MB or 512MB, depending on model. To save space on the board, the RAM module is attached to the surface of the BCM2835 in what is known as a package-on-package (PoP) configuration. If you hold the Pi up and look at the side of the chip, you'll see that it's actually two chips sandwiched together.

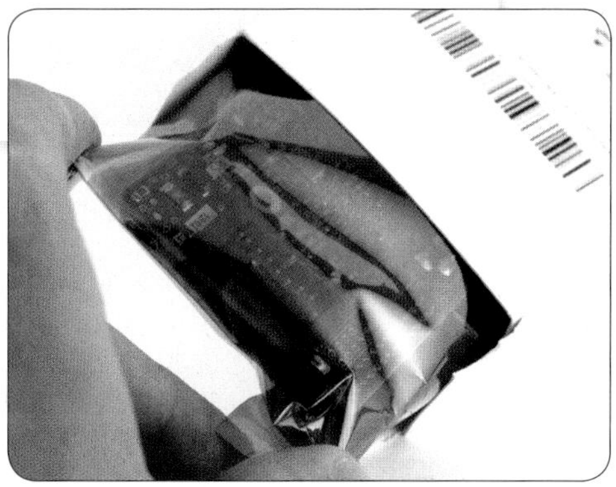

Hold the Pi by the edges when removing it from its bag.

The Raspberry Pi Model B has an additional, smaller chip at the right-hand side of the board, just below the 3.5mm audio jack. This chip expands the capabilities of the BCM2835 with the ability to drive a wired Ethernet network socket and an additional USB port. The chip isn't present on the Model A, which has only a single USB port and no Ethernet connectivity. The Model B's Ethernet port and two USB ports actually appear to the BCM2835 to be connected over a single USB channel. This can cause some performance bottlenecks if you're accessing USB storage devices over the network.

The exposed nature of the Pi's design makes it a great way to learn more about how computers are built

The exposed pins at the top-left of the board are the Pi's General Purpose Input-Output (GPIO) connector. This provides a means for the Pi to communicate with external hardware components, and is used in several of the projects to add to the Pi's capabilities without tying up the USB ports. It provides much of the Pi's flexibility, and is the biggest differentiator between the Pi and a traditional PC.

The other two interesting areas found on the top of the board look identical: the Camera Serial Interface (CSI) connector on the right; and the Display Serial Interface (DSI) connector on the left. The CSI connector accepts a ribbon cable from the Raspberry Pi Camera Module to record video or capture pictures in high definition. The DSI connector accepts a ribbon cable from a dedicated display of the type usually found in tablets and smartphones, but is rarely used thanks to the presence of an HDMI port on the bottom edge of the board.

The various ports of the Raspberry Pi can be found along its edges. The left-hand edge features a micro-USB connector for power. This draws more power than a PC's USB ports can provide, so it's important that you always connect this to a USB power adapter. This edge also houses the SD card slot, which is the Pi's equivalent of a hard drive. The mechanism of the

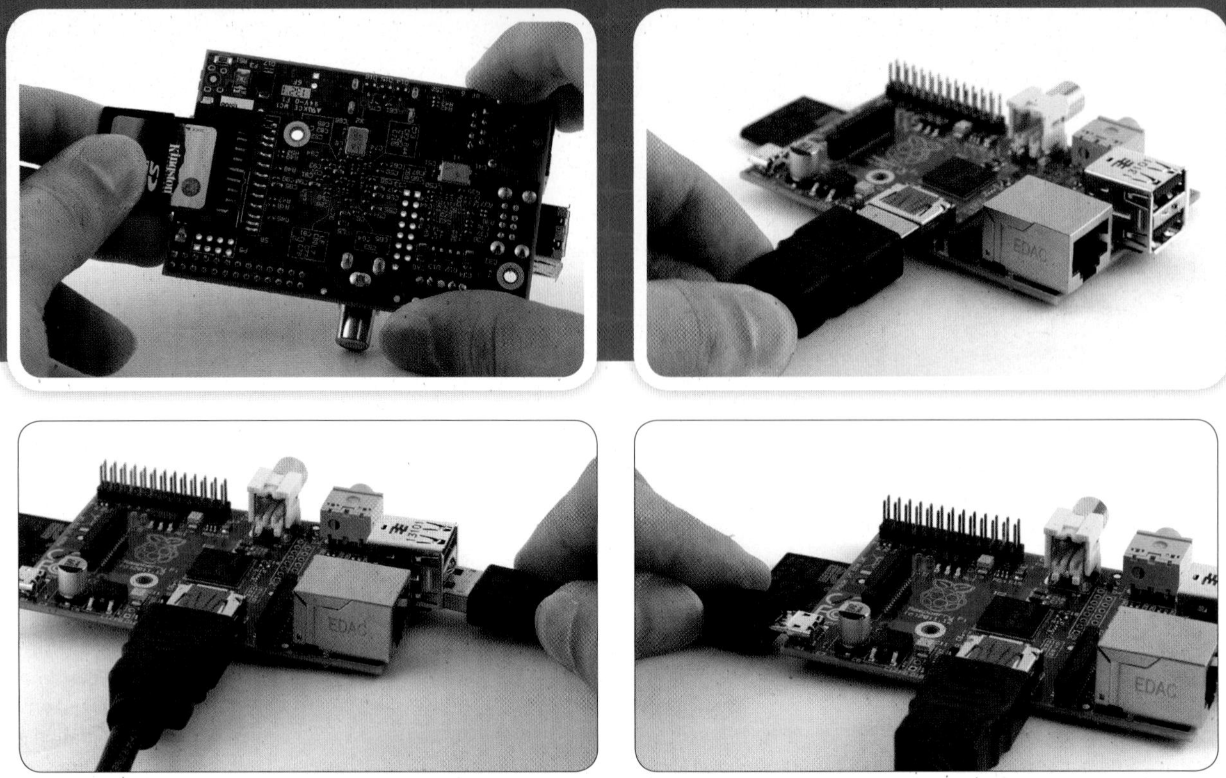

Take care when connecting the Pi to its peripherals.

slot itself can be seen by turning the board upside down.

The bottom edge houses the High Definition Multimedia Interface (HDMI) port, which provides the Pi with connectivity to a display. The HDMI port carries both video and audio signals, and is compatible with any monitor or TV featuring an HDMI input. Adapter cables can be used to add support for DVI or VGA monitors. The top edge houses a composite video connector and a 3.5mm analogue audio output. These can be used in place of the HDMI port to connect the Pi to an older TV that doesn't support digital video, but the quality is much lower than the digital signal available from the HDMI port.

Finally, the right-hand edge of the board varies, depending on the model of Raspberry Pi you own. The most popular Raspberry Pi Model B variant includes two USB ports and a single wired Ethernet connection. The lower-cost Model A variant has only a single USB port and no Ethernet port. It's possible to add wired or wireless networking to the Model A using a USB dongle. More information is available in the Running the Pi wirelessly project in the Plug-In Hardware chapter.

CHOOSING AN OPERATING SYSTEM

As you might expect from a barebones board, the Raspberry Pi doesn't come bundled with an operating system. Instead, it's up to the user to choose the operating system that best suits their needs and install it on an SD card. Alternatively, you can buy SD cards with Pi-compatible operating systems pre-loaded from many sources, including the Raspberry Pi Foundation at **raspberrypi.org**.

The beauty of the Raspberry Pi is that it makes it easy to experiment. All of the operating systems designed for use with the Pi are provided free of charge, meaning you can download one, try it and, if you decide it's not for you, easily start again with a different operating system.

For beginners, however, Raspbian is the recommended operating system. Based on the Debian Linux distribution, Raspbian is designed to be as user-friendly as possible and has been heavily enhanced to make the most of the Pi's somewhat limited processing power. It comes bundled with a range of applications, from web browsers to a free version of the Wolfram Language programming system, and is the version most commonly used for tutorials found online. It's also the basis for the projects in this MagBook. Using a different operating system is possible, but not recommended until you're comfortable with how the Pi works.

Traditionally, the only way to install an operating system on an SD card for a Pi was to download a pre-made image. Recently, the Raspberry Pi Foundation released a tool called New Out Of Box Software (NOOBS). This is provided as an archive that can be quickly copied onto a blank SD card of 8GB of larger. When inserted into a Raspberry Pi and booted, NOOBS will provide a menu from which you can choose the operating system – or systems, if you want the option to boot into more than one – you want to install directly on the Pi. It's a much more convenient system, although the old SD card images are still available from **raspberrypi.org/download** for manual installation.

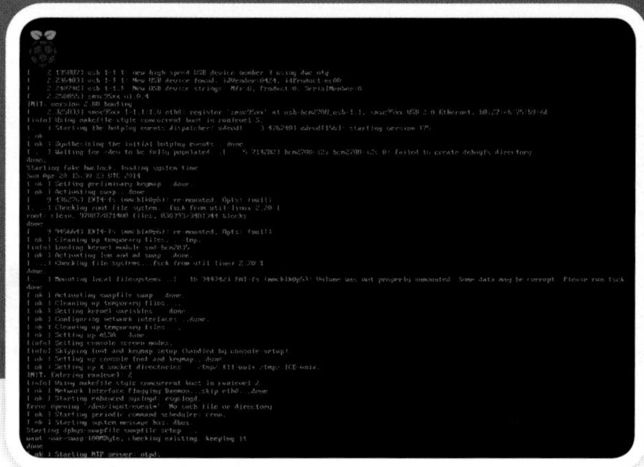

When the Pi first boots, follow onscreen instructions.

CONNECTING THE PI

When you've chosen an operating system and prepared an SD card, insert it into the slot on the left-hand side of the Pi. You might find it easiest to turn the Pi upside down for this, inserting the card into the slot with the gold contacts facing down and forwards and the label facing you. You don't need to push the card in too firmly. If it doesn't appear to be sliding home smoothly, check that it's the right way around and that both sides are under the lips of the slot. The SD card slot is one of the more fragile parts of the Pi, so always be careful when inserting or removing cards.

Next, you can connect the Pi up to its peripherals. At the very least, you'll need a keyboard and a monitor to get started; ideally, you want a mouse as well. If you're using a Model A, this isn't possible unless you get a wired or wireless keyboard and mouse combination set that uses a single USB port or use an external USB hub. For the Model B, you can connect a keyboard and mouse simultaneously.

Try to use the Pi's HDMI port for video output, if you can. The quality of video you can get from the HDMI port is vastly superior to the composite video port. Using the composite port will result in a very low-resolution picture, leaving you little room onscreen for windows or text. It is, however, a good way to make use of an otherwise outdated TV, as detailed in the Entertainment chapter's Smart TV project.

With your display, keyboard and mouse connected, you can finally connect power to the Pi using the micro-USB connector. Unlike a desktop or laptop PC, the Pi has no power button. Once you insert the micro-USB cable, the Pi will boot into the operating system – or NOOBS, if you've installed it on the SD card. There's also no button to turn the Pi off; instead, it's achieved at the command line, known as the terminal or console.

FIRST STEPS

When the Pi first boots, you'll need to follow the onscreen instructions using the keyboard. Eventually, you'll be presented with a login prompt. If you've installed Raspbian, the details you need are:

```
Username: pi
Password: raspberry
```

If you've installed a different operating system, you'll need to consult the documentation on its website for the correct login details. When you've logged in, you'll be dropped to a command-line session. If you're not used to Linux, it can take a while to get used to its commands and syntax. ●

COMMON LINUX COMMANDS

Here's a list of the most common Linux commands you'll need to get started

- **ls** Lists the files in the current directory; equivalent to the Windows dir command.
- **nano** A command-line text editor; save files with Ctrl+O and exit with Ctrl+X.
- **sudo** Runs a command as the super-user, or root, account; gives full access to the system, and is usually required when a program accesses the GPIO pins.
- **apt-get** The Apt package manager; used with update, upgrade and install commands to download new software.
- **startx** Loads the X Windows graphical user interface; provides a mouse-based control system and access to pre-loaded software.
- **exit** Logs out of the current session.
- **halt** Shuts down the Pi safely and allows you to remove the power cable; needs to be run using sudo.
- **reboot** Restarts the Pi to apply changes you've made to the system; needs to be run using sudo.
- **rm** Removes a file; equivalent to the del command in Windows.
- **mv** Moves a file; specify the name of the file and the new location, or the new name if using it to rename a file.
- **cp** Copies a file; equivalent to the copy command in Windows.
- **cd** Change directory; can be used without the name of a directory to return you to the home directory for your user.

CHAPTER TWO

PRODUCTIVITY

The Raspberry Pi may not seem like the most obvious choice for a productivity-enhancing device. Its tiny size compared to a desktop or laptop computer leads many to believe it's little more than a toy, a first impression often reinforced by many of the more famous projects being related to gaming and education.

At its heart, however, the Pi has a powerful processor – the Broadcom BCM2835 – which can perform any task required of a PC. Although it's not as high performance as the processors commonly found in desktops and laptops, it makes up for that by being significantly cheaper both to buy and run. The Pi sips, rather than chugs, electricity, and it does so completely silently with no moving parts.

In this chapter, you'll learn how the Pi can be used to augment – or even replace – your existing computer systems.

2

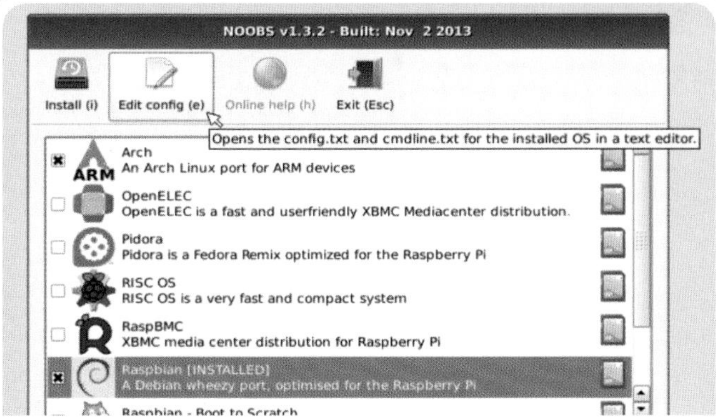

NOOBS v1.3.2 - Built: Nov 2 2013
Install (i)
Edit config (e)
Online help (h)
Exit (Esc)
Opens the config.txt and cmdline.txt for the installed OS in a text editor.
Arch
An Arch Linux port for ARM devices
OpenELEC
OpenELEC is a fast and userfriendly XBMC Mediacenter distribution.
Pidora
Pidora is a Fedora Remix optimized for the Raspberry Pi
RISC OS
RISC OS is a very fast and compact system
RaspBMC
XBMC media center distribution for Raspberry Pi
Raspbian [INSTALLED]
A Debian wheezy port, optimised for the Raspberry Pi

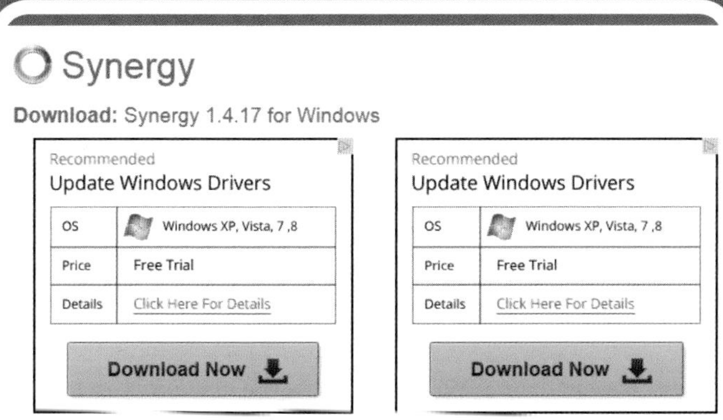

Synergy
Download: Synergy 1.4.17 for Windows
Recommended
Update Windows Drivers
OS
Windows XP, Vista, 7 ,8
Price
Free Trial
Details
Click Here For Details
Download Now
Recommended
Update Windows Drivers
OS
Windows XP, Vista, 7 ,8
Price
Free Trial
Details
Click Here For Details
Download Now

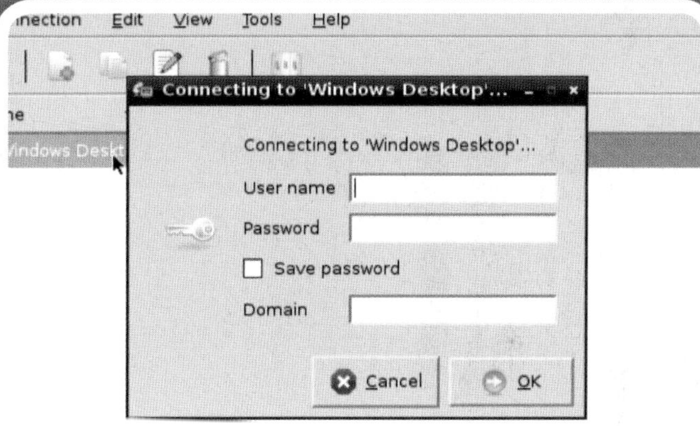

Edit
View
Tools
Help
Connecting to 'Windows Desktop'...
Connecting to 'Windows Desktop'...
User name
Password
Save password
Domain
Cancel
OK

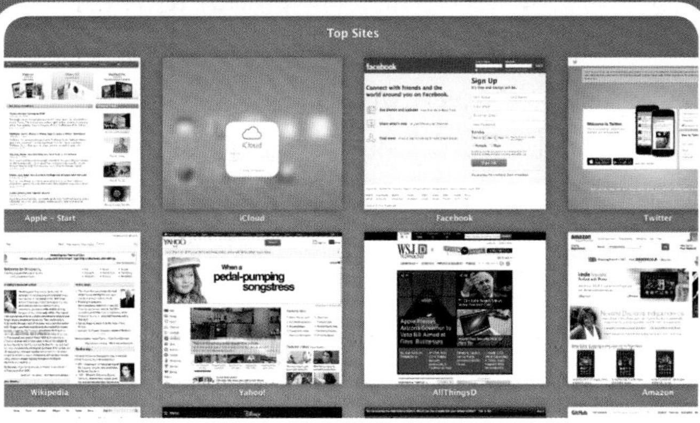

Top Sites
Apple - Start
iCloud
Facebook
Twitter
Wikipedia
Yahoo!
AllThingsD
Amazon

WordPress
Success!
WordPress has been installed. Were you expecting more steps? Sorry to disappoint.
Username
Gareth
Password
Your chosen password.

INSTALLING AN OS WITH NOOBS

Discover how NOOBS makes it much easier to set up a Pi for the first time. We also look at the more advanced features it offers post-install

The New Out Of Box Software (NOOBS) was introduced in response to the hassle of switching between different operating systems when using the Raspberry Pi. Previously, users had to find compatible operating systems – not all of which were listed on the official Raspberry Pi Foundation download page – and download a card image manually, then write the image to an SD card using a somewhat user-unfriendly tool that wipes any existing content on the card.

NOOBS is a distinctly different method. Once installed onto an SD card, NOOBS loads before any other operating system and allows you to pick from a list of compatible operating systems that are downloaded and installed on demand. Once an operating system is installed, NOOBS can be triggered again to install a different operating system or edit the configuration files of an existing installation – a very useful trick if something has gone wrong with an existing installation.

If you're new to the Pi, NOOBS is a great introduction to the device. And if you're an old hand used to the manual install method, it's a tool well worth learning. In either case, you'll benefit considerably from knowing not just how to use it to install your operating system but also how to trigger it post-install and access its more advanced features.

INSTALLING NOOBS

Although some retailers have begun selling SD cards with the NOOBS software pre-loaded, the preferred method is to install it yourself. As well as costing less than buying a pre-loaded card – especially if you have an 8GB or larger SD card spare from a digital camera or similar – installing the software yourself ensures that you always have the very latest version. It also means that if anything happens to your SD card, you know how to get it back into a working state or, failing that, make a fresh copy.

The first step to installing NOOBS on an SD card is to download the latest version of the software from the Raspberry Pi Foundation's official

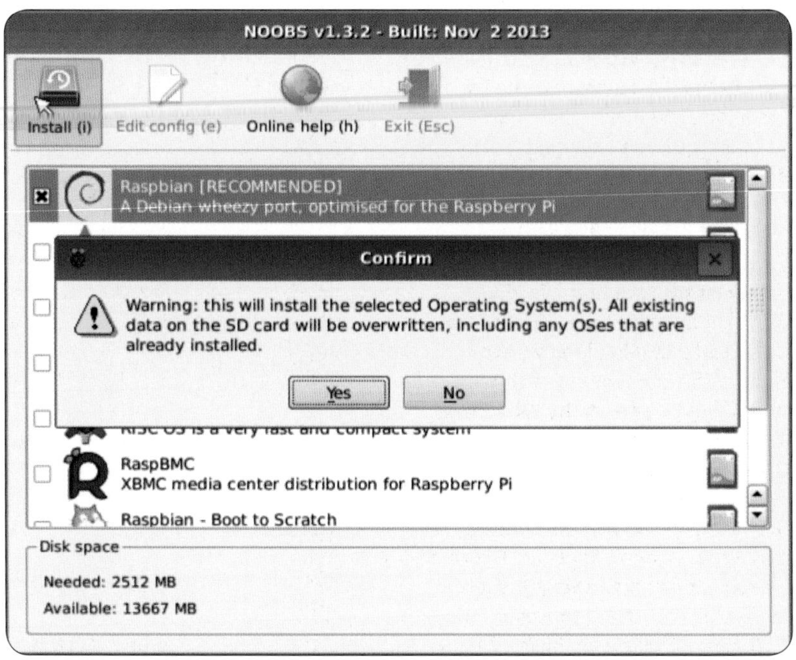

NOOBS lets you select which OSes you want to install.

WHAT YOU'LL NEED

In addition to the materials detailed at the start of this MagBook, to install NOOBS on a fresh SD card you'll need a laptop or desktop computer with an active internet connection, a blank SD card – or a card you don't mind overwriting – of at least 8GB capacity, and an SD card reader. Many laptops include an SD card reader; desktop users may need to buy a USB-connected SD card reader, such as the Integral SD Single-Slot Reader (£3, amazon.co.uk).

Welcome to your Raspberry Pi
We're currently setting up your SD card but don't worry, you'll be able to start programming very soo
Raspbian: Extracting filesystem
0%
0 MB of 1963 MB written (0.0 MB/sec)

Installing the software yourself ensures you always have the latest version.

website. Point your web browser of choice at **www.raspberrypi.org/downloads** and download one of the two NOOBS installers listed. The first, labelled as "offline and network install", is a large download that works with Raspberry Pis that aren't connected to the internet and contains a copy of the operating system. The second, labelled as "network install only", is a much smaller download, but requires that the Pi be connected to the internet when installing the operating system. As you'll need to download at least one operating system in either case, most users will be best off choosing the offline installer.

The installer is designed to be extracted to a blank SD card. If you're reusing an existing card, or want to wipe a broken NOOBS install from your card and start again, you'll need to format the card first. Windows users should insert the SD card into their reader and load the Windows Explorer file manager by clicking its icon or holding down the Windows Key and pressing E on the keyboard. Once loaded, find the SD card in the list of drives, right-click and choose the Format option. In the window that appears, make sure Quick Format is ticked and click the Start button to begin the formatting process.

If you're a Mac user, insert the SD card and load Disk Utility from the Utilities menu. Find the SD card in the list of drives connected to your Mac and click Erase. When prompted, choose MS-DOS (FAT) as the partition type.

For recovery mode, hold Shift

The process of installing Raspbian takes ten minutes.

If you're a Linux user, either format the SD card using your distribution's disk manager, or open a terminal and list the disks connected to the system with the command:

```
sudo fdisk -l
```

When you've found the SD card, make a note of the letter that follows "/dev/sd" and format the drive using the following command:

```
sudo mkfs.msdos /dev/sdX
```

where X is the letter you noted earlier. Be careful when doing this; Linux will quite happily overwrite any drive in the system with a new, empty partition if you get the letter wrong!

When you've got a fresh, empty SD card, you need to extract the contents of the NOOBS Zip Archive onto the card. In most operating systems, this is as simple as opening the SD card in one file manager window and double-clicking the Zip Archive in another. Highlight all the files in the archive, and drag them to the SD card window. If you've selected the offline installer, the process of copying the files may take some time to complete. Make sure the process has finished by using the eject or unmount function of your operating system before removing the card.

INSTALLING AN OS VIA NOOBS

When you've finished installing NOOBS on your SD card, it still doesn't have any operating systems ready for you to use, even if you chose the offline installer option. These need to be installed directly on the Pi before they can be used, a process that takes around ten minutes to complete.

Start by inserting the SD card into the slot on the underside of the Raspberry Pi, label facing away from the board. Be gentle; it doesn't require much force to seat, and the connectors are somewhat fragile. When the SD card is inserted, you can connect the keyboard, mouse, display, network cable – unless you're using a Model A – and finally the power cable.

After a few seconds, a light-grey screen with a menu at the centre will appear. If not, you may need to adjust your display settings. If you're using

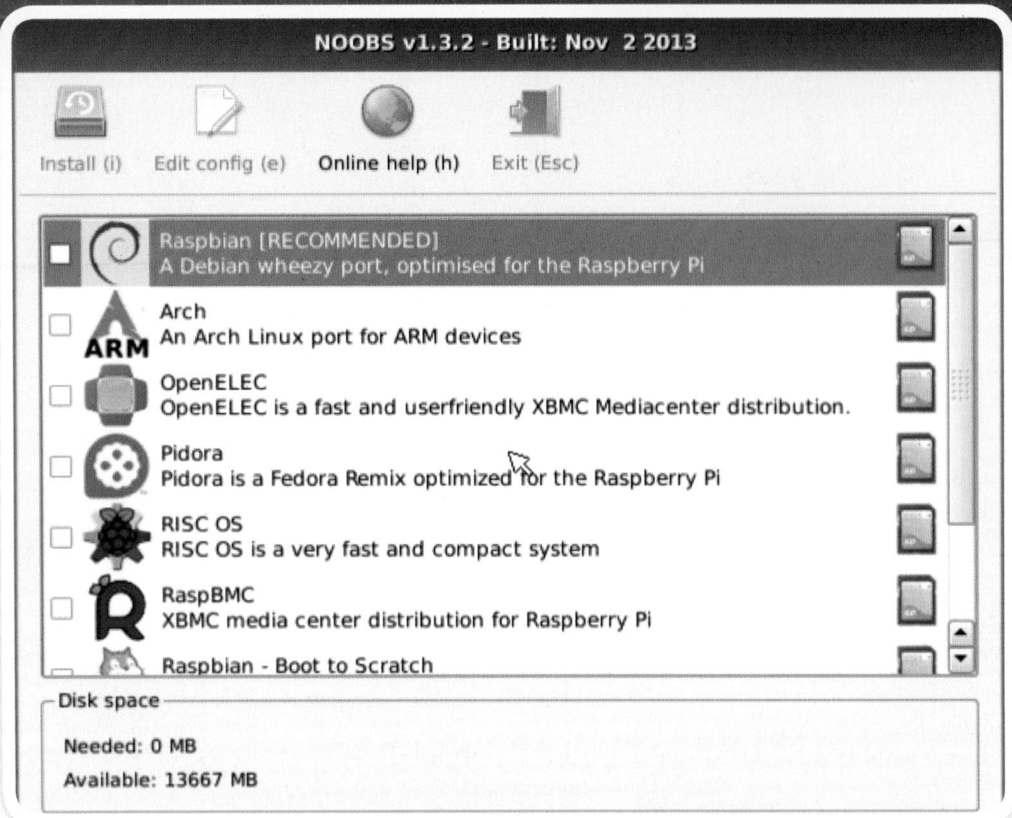

Raspbian is labelled as "RECOMMENDED" at the top of the list.

For many users, the only time they see NOOBS is when they're first installing an operating system on the Pi

the composite video connector, press the number 3 on your keyboard for UK-style PAL mode or 4 for US-style NTSC mode. If you're using the HDMI connection – even if through a DVI or VGA converter – and there's still no picture, press 2 to switch from the default video mode to a low-resolution "safe" mode that should work with almost any monitor or TV.

The NOOBS menu offers various choices, some of which aren't available until at least one operating system is installed. At this point, the key feature is the list of operating systems in the centre of the screen. Each operating system listed can be installed from NOOBS, and it's even possible to install more than one to create a multiboot system ideal for experimentation. The most commonly used operating system, and the one on which most of the projects in this book are based, is Raspbian – labelled as "RECOMMENDED" at the top of the list. Other notable entries in the list include Arch, a distribution aimed at proficient Linux users, and RISC OS, originally developed for the Acorn computers of the 1980s and 1990s – the processor technology of which became ARM, and powers the Pi along with the overwhelming majority of smartphones and tablets today.

For now, you should just tick the box to the left of Raspbian at the top of the list and click the Install button at the top-left of the window. This will prompt you to make sure you're happy with wiping any existing data on the card, then begin the process of installing Raspbian, which takes around ten minutes. If you chose the network install version of NOOBS, the process may take considerably longer, as it has to download the operating system as it's being installed, rather than just loading it from saved files on the SD card. When the process has finished, press the OK button to reboot the Pi and load the new operating system.

ADVANCED NOOBS FEATURES

For many users, the only time they see NOOBS is when they're first installing an operating system on the Pi. When the installation has finished, however, NOOBS doesn't go away; it stays on the SD card in case you need it in the future, hidden but accessible to those who know the trick.

When you first turn on a Pi with NOOBS, it will briefly load the familiar NOOBS interface before handing off to the host operating system. At this point, NOOBS can be loaded by pressing the Shift key on the keyboard. The easiest way to get the timing right is to hold down the Shift key, insert the microSD power cable, and only release the Shift key when you see the NOOBS interface appear. When NOOBS is loaded in this way, you'll gain access to a previously unavailable icon on the top menu, Edit Config, which can also be accessed through the E key on the keyboard.

Traditional desktop and laptop computers use a special chip known as the Basic Input-Output System (BIOS) to hold their settings, such as what processor and memory is installed, and at what speed they should be run. The Pi, by contrast, holds its settings in a pair of text files on the SD card: config.txt and cmdline.txt. Without an SD card loaded, a Pi won't do anything when power is applied because it can't find either of these files. And if these files

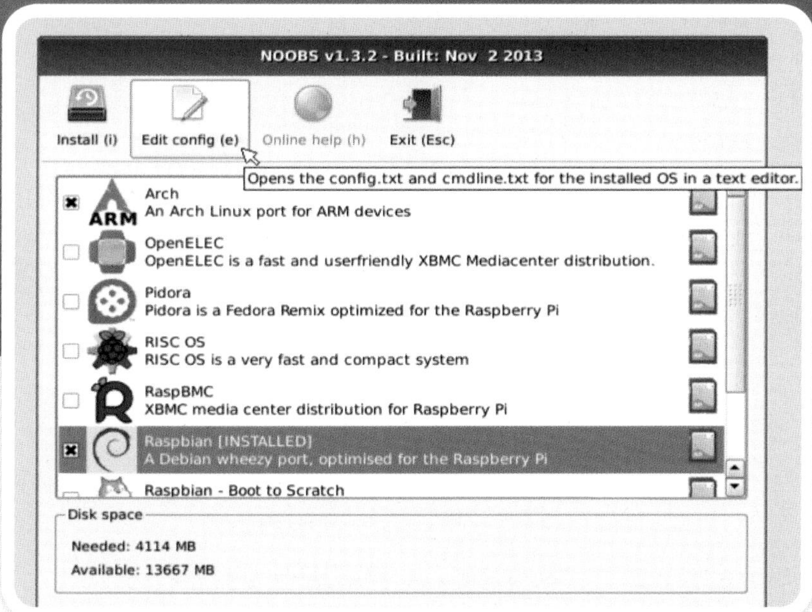

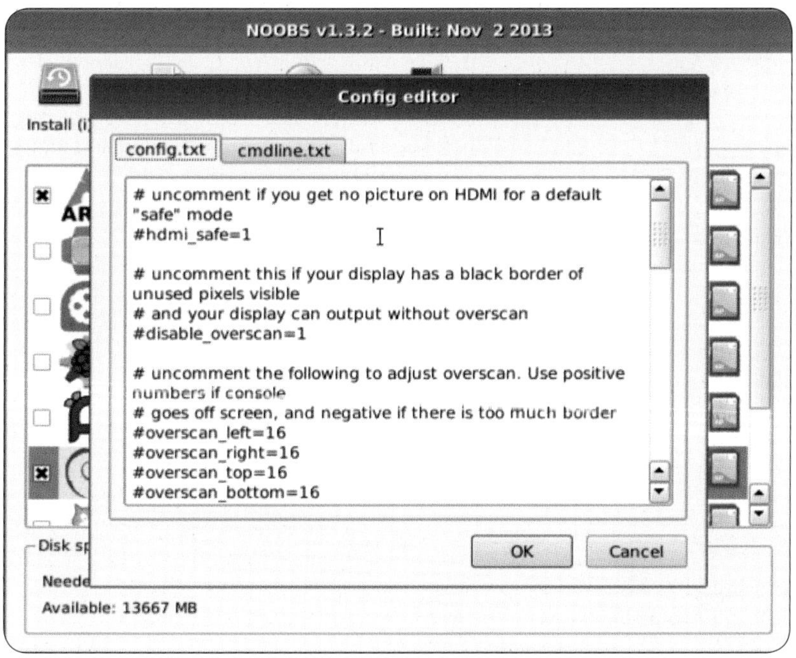

are missing, corrupt or have invalid values, the Pi is likely to fail to boot.

Clicking an installed operating system in the list followed by the Edit Config option in NOOBS will load both files into a built-in text editor. It's an extremely handy ability to have, as changes to these files can make the main operating system fail to load correctly – a problem that previously could only be resolved by inserting the Pi's SD card into another computer and editing the files there.

Time spent learning how these files work and how to edit them in NOOBS is time you won't have to spend when something has gone wrong. Note that each operating system has its own independent copies of these files. If you want to change the behaviour of multiple operating systems, you'll have to edit each system's files individually.

The configuration editor in NOOBS works the same as any other text editor. The flashing cursor indicates where your typed instructions will appear, and can be moved with the arrow keys on the keyboard or by clicking with the mouse. Any changes you make will be saved when you click the OK button. If you've made a mistake, click Cancel to close the editor without saving any changes then click the Edit Config button to reload the files from the SD card.

Edit Config can also be accessed through the E key.

EDITING CONFIG.TXT

The config.txt file contains various settings that control the hardware of the Pi. These settings can be used to change how the picture appears on the screen, control the speed of the Pi's processor or memory, or alter how much of the Pi's RAM is reserved for use by the graphics processor. It's also one of the more common causes for a Pi to fail to boot. Editing the file to speed up the Pi's processor by overclocking – a topic dealt with in a less error-prone manner later on – can result in invalid values, causing the Pi to hang as it tries to load.

Config.txt contains various settings that control the Pi's hardware.

One important feature of config.txt is that every entry has a default, which it will use in the absence of further instructions. By default, many of the settings listed in the file are preceded by a hash (#) symbol. This indicates that the entry will be ignored by the system. Many of the tips contained in the file – which are themselves preceded by a hash, to prevent the system attempting to read them as settings that should be applied – will advise you to uncomment a particular setting. This simply means removing the hash symbol at the start of the line.

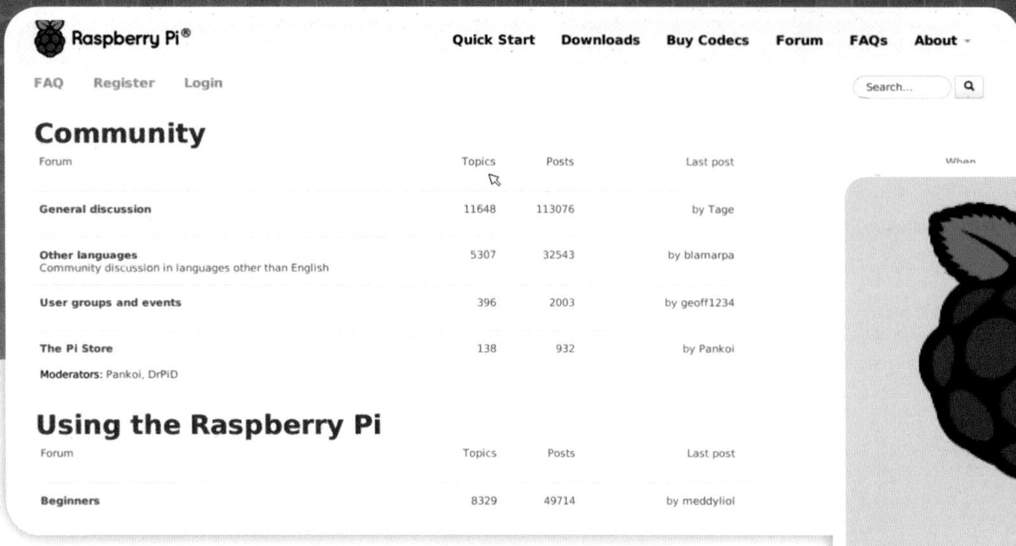

The Online Help button gives access to the Raspberry Pi Foundation's official forums.

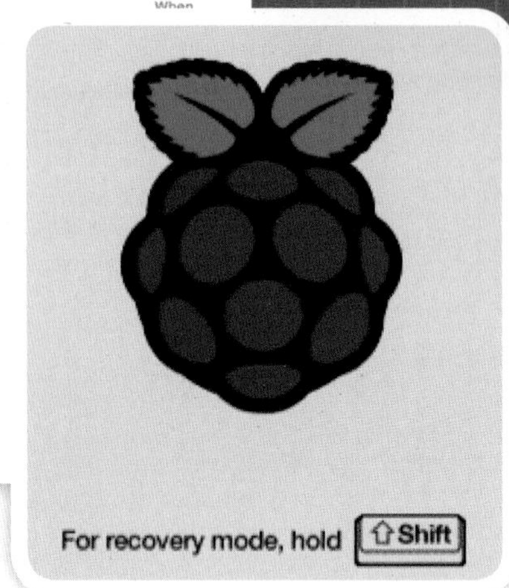

You can switch into recovery mode by pressing the up arrow and Shift.

The settings that need most common adjustment in config.txt relate to how the Pi handles the connected display. Although compatibility is typically good, some display types – in particular, monitors connected using an HDMI-to-DVI cable – can fail to be properly detected by the Pi, resulting in a distorted image or no picture.

If you're having display trouble, try adjusting the following settings, remembering to remove the hash symbol from the start of the line if it's present, and ensuring that the name of the setting and its value are separated by an equals symbol.

The config.txt file also includes options for increasing the performance of the Broadcom BCM2835 processor through a process known as overclocking. Doing so through config.txt isn't recommended, however, as there's a simpler and safer method known as Turbo Mode. This is detailed later in this chapter, alongside the advanced method for the adventurous.

The final portion of the config.txt file you may want to edit concerns the memory split. Although the Pi has either 256MB or 512MB of memory, depending on model, not all of it is available to the system. A chunk of the memory is reserved for use by the graphics processor, just like how a graphics card in a desktop PC has its own dedicated memory. For uses like high-definition video playback, gaming, or using the Raspberry Pi Camera Module, keeping a large chunk reserved for the graphics processor is a must. When using the Pi on embedded projects where a display may not even be connected, however, it's a waste of memory the system could put to better use.

The memory split is controlled using a setting called gpu_mem. This sets the amount of memory, from a minimum of 16MB to a maximum of 128MB, that the Pi reserves for the graphics processor. Values need to be a multiple of 16MB for the option to be recognised. This is an especially important setting to adjust on the Model A and original Model B Revision 1 Pis, which have only 256MB of memory in total.

EDITING CMDLINE.TXT

The second setting file that can be edited through NOOBS, by clicking on its labelled tab, is cmdline.txt. This file contains the instructions passed to the operating system's kernel when it boots, and shouldn't normally be altered. Mistakes made in this file can cause the operating system to fail to load, so always double-check your changes before hitting the OK button to save them,

The settings that need most common adjustment in config.txt relate to how the Pi handles the connected display

The most common reason to modify cmdline.txt is to disable the serial console on the GPIO pins. By default, the Pi uses the serial pins of the GPIO header to provide a Linux terminal to a connected system. It's a handy way of controlling an embedded Pi from a laptop without needing a monitor or keyboard, but it also means the serial channel can't be used for anything else. Some add-on devices, such as the Ciseco Pi-Lite board, are designed to use the serial connection themselves, so the serial console needs to be disabled.

Editing the cmdline.txt file and removing the entries console=ttyAMA0,115200 kgdboc=ttyAMA0,115200 without touching any other portion of the file will disable the serial console. It may also be necessary to edit the /etc/inittabb file, which needs to be done from inside the operating system. If this is the case, the installation instructions that came with your add-on board will tell you what to do.

EDITING CONFIG.TXT

- **disable_overscan** By default, the Pi uses a feature called "overscan" to ensure that none of the image is lost to the edges of the TV. It's a relatively old-fashioned feature originally introduced for cathode-ray tube televisions, and when used on a modern sets results in the Pi's image appearing in a black box in the centre of the screen. Setting this to 1 disables overscan completely, while the default value of 0 switches it on.
- **overscan_left/right/top/bottom** These settings control the amount of overscan used on the image, measured in pixels. Fine-tuning these settings can be a trial-and-error process, but if you want to reduce or increase the amount of overscan – increasing and reducing the size of the image at the centre, respectively – you can set manual values here. The default is 16 pixels of overscan on all sides.
- **hdmi_mode** This controls the resolution and refresh rate of the video output from the Pi's HDMI port. Normally, this will be configured for the optimal picture quality for your connected display. In rare cases, however, this isn't detected correctly and needs to be set manually. A full list of settings is available at **elinux.org/RPiconfig#Video_mode_options**, while the most commonly used settings are:
  1 – 640 × 480, also known as VGA
  16 – 1080p Full HD Progressive video at 60Hz
  4 – 720p HD Progressive video at 60Hz
  20 – 1080i Full HD Interlaced video at 50Hz
- **config_hdmi_boost** Some monitors require that the signal from the HDMI port be more powerful than others, especially when used with longer cables or adapters. If you find your picture looks snowy or dim, you can boost the power level using a number from 1 to 7 here.
- **sdtv_mode** The most common reason for the composite video connector to fail to work is for the video standard it's outputting to be for the wrong country. Changing the values of this option will set the video standard accordingly, with the following being valid choices:
  0 – NTSC, the standard for North America
  1 – NTSC-J, the standard for Japan
  2 – PAL, the standard for the UK, Europe and Australia
  3 – PAL-M, the standard for Brazil
- **sdtv_aspect** If your picture looks squashed or stretched, it's almost certain that the Pi is using the wrong aspect ratio. Unlike the HDMI output, where this is corrected by choosing a different value for hdmi_mode and directly altering the resolution, aspect ratio for the composite video connector is controlled using this special setting and one of three values:
  1 – Selects a 4:3 aspect ratio
  2 – Selects a 14:9 aspect ratio
  3 – Selects a 16:9 aspect ratio
- **hdmi_safe** The nuclear option for display problems, hdmi_safe sets the HDMI output to a low-resolution, high-power mode, which should be compatible with almost any monitor or HDTV.

INSTALLING A NEW OS

The final thing you may want to do with NOOBS is install a new operating system, or even multiple operating systems. By entering NOOBS before the installed OS loads, you can pick any entry from the list to try a different operating system, or reinstall your existing operating system if it's got corrupted. It's even possible to install more than one operating system at once. Simply tick multiple boxes before clicking the Install button, and each operating system will be installed in its own dedicated partition. When the Pi is next booted, NOOBS will present a menu, allowing you to choose which of the installed operating systems you want to load.

Installing a new operating system, or reinstalling an existing operating system, wipes all existing data on the SD card bar from NOOBS itself. This includes your documents, saved files, bookmarks and any customisations you've made to the OS, including the addition of new users. It's literally like starting from scratch. As a result, make sure that you've copied all the files you wish to keep onto an external storage device such as a USB flash drive or hard drive before clicking the Install button.

GETTING HELP

The final feature of NOOBS is accessed using the Online Help button, or pressing the H key on the keyboard. This loads a small, lightweight web browser that provides access to the Raspberry Pi Foundation's official forums. Here, you can browse threads offering advice and help on using the Pi and its software, follow educational projects, and register for an account to make a post of your own if you need help.

The Raspberry Pi forums are maintained by the Foundation, but driven by the community. It's not an official support channel, and shouldn't be used if you're looking to get a faulty Pi replaced under warranty; for that, contact the shop from where it was purchased. They still act as an extremely handy education resource, and if you're having problems getting your operating system working, a post from NOOBS – combined with patience, while you wait for the community to read your question and respond – can get you back on track.

As the Online Help button launches a web browser, it's only available on the Raspberry Pi Model B. NOOBS loaded on a Model A, or the Model B with no network cable connected and active, will show the button greyed out. When you've finished using the browser, just hit the cross in the top corner to return to the main NOOBS menu.

OVERCLOCKING THE RASPBERRY PI

Overclocking is a great way to get extra performance out of your Pi at no cost. Turbo Mode is tried and tested, and won't invalidate your warranty

The Pi is built around a Broadcom BCM2835 system-on-chip (SoC) processor, which combines a surprisingly powerful VideoCore graphics processor – roughly on par with the graphical performance of the original Microsoft Xbox – with a weaker ARM general-purpose processor. It was developed by Broadcom for use in multimedia set-top boxes, hence its 3D capabilities and integrated high-definition video playback support. This also explains the relatively weedy CPU, which was never designed to run similar software to a desktop machine.

That's not to say the Pi can't do so, of course, and it's possible to eke even more power out of the Pi by increasing the speed at which the processor runs, through overclocking. When the Pi launched, it came with a strict warning from the Foundation: overclocking is dangerous, and will void your warranty. Later, safer methods of boosting the speed of the processor were found and the overclocking process split in two: Turbo Mode, an officially sanctioned and relatively trouble-free method; and manual overclocking, which can have better results, but comes with the threat of a loss of warranty.

A heatsink will allow the Pi to radiate its heat more effectively.

Overclocking is a great way to get a little extra performance out of your Pi at no cost, but be aware that it doesn't always work. Differences in the tolerance of the components used to build a Pi, and even microscopic positioning differences during the manufacturing process, mean that some Pis overclock to extreme speeds, while others struggle with even a mild overclock. This is, unfortunately, just the luck of the draw. There's no way to know whether a Pi will overclock well at the time of purchase.

USING TURBO MODE

Before trying the manual overclocking method, it's worth investigating Turbo Mode. Introduced into the Raspbian operating system to boost performance, Turbo Mode is a series of tried-and-testing overclocks, which are known to be safe for the overwhelming majority of Raspberry Pi models. These offer improvements very close to the best that you'll get through manual overclocking, and carry no risk. The Pi's warranty will

WHAT YOU'LL NEED

Overclocking takes place entirely in software, modifying the Pi's configuration files to force the processor to run at a different speed. Doing so can also cause it to generate more heat, especially when the higher settings – which include an increased voltage to the processor, to help it reach higher speeds – are used.

Thankfully, the Pi's processor is designed to run with passive cooling and at high temperatures without harm. If you're using the Pi in a case, in a high ambient temperature, or you want to achieve the highest speed possible, it may be worthwhile buying a heatsink. These are blocks of metal, typically aluminium or copper, which stick to the Pi's processor – the square chip in the centre, which also houses the memory module – using a sticky thermal transfer material and increase its surface area, allowing it to radiate its heat more effectively. Many retailers carry cheap heatsink kits (from £2.50, ebay.co.uk), which include additional heatsinks for the voltage regulator at the bottom-left of the board and the small USB and Ethernet chip at the right-hand side.

It's also possible to buy active heatsinks, which include a fan to force air over the surface. These have significantly better cooling, but are typically unnecessary even at the highest levels of overclocking. They can also be annoyingly loud, the small size of the fan resulting in a high-pitched whine.

The heatsink sticks to the Pi's processor using a thermal transfer material.

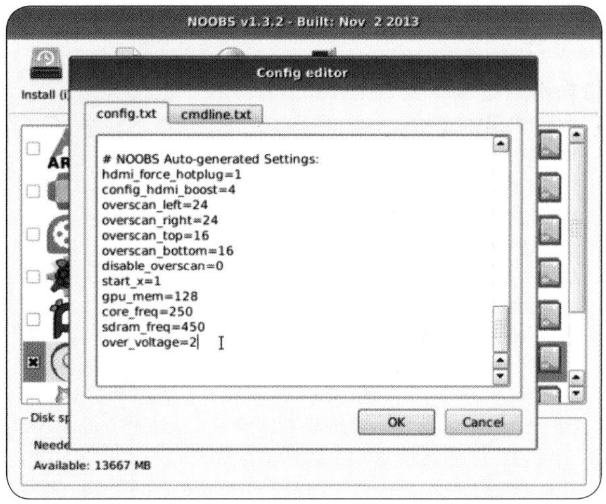

To easily adjust the settings manually, boot into NOOBS.

remain intact even when running on the highest setting.

Turbo Mode is accessed using a utility called the Raspberry Pi Software Configuration Tool, or raspi-config. At present, this is only officially supported in the Raspbian operating system. Work is ongoing to port it, or develop an alternative with the same features, for other operating systems. Among various other settings – some of which are explored later in this MagBook – is the option to adjust the speed of the Pi. To access these, you'll need to be at the command-line interface known as the terminal. This is the default state for a freshly installed copy of Raspbian: simply log in using the username "pi" and the password "raspberry" and you're at the terminal. If you've modified Raspbian to boot into the graphical user interface by default, you can either press the Ctrl, Alt and F2 keys to access a separate terminal, or load the lxterm software terminal from the Accessories menu.

When you're at the terminal, load raspi-config by typing:

```
sudo raspi-config
```

The first part of the command, sudo, tells the system that you want to run the following program with super-user permissions. This is a requirement of making system-wide changes such as overclocking. The second part is the program that should be loaded; in this case, raspi-config.

The Raspberry Pi Software Configuration Tool provides a handy text-based menu for adjusting various settings on the Pi. The overclocking settings are towards the bottom of the list, labelled as "7 Overclock". Use the cursor keys followed by Enter to choose the option, which will immediately result in a warning about potential instability. Read the warning carefully, then press Enter again to continue.

The pre-set Turbo Mode configurations are split into four levels, each of which controls three portions of the Pi's hardware: the CPU, labelled as ARM; the GPU, labelled as core; and the memory, labelled as SDRAM. Additionally, higher-performance settings increase the voltage provided to the BCM2835, to improve stability at higher speeds; this is labelled as overvolt. The options are:

- **None** This is the default setting, and runs the CPU at 700MHz, the GPU at 250MHz and the memory at 400MHz. If you've previously overclocked your Pi and want to reverse the effects, choose this option.
- **Modest** A mild overclock that boosts the CPU to 800MHz, while leaving the GPU and memory the same. This should be compatible with all Pis and rarely results in heat problems or instability.
- **Medium** The most commonly used overclock, this preset boosts the CPU to 900MHz and the memory to 450MHz, while leaving the GPU alone. It's also the first overclock to use the overvolt setting to increase the voltage provided to the BCM2835, which causes temperatures to rise and can result in instability. If you have problems at this level, drop back to Modest.
- **High** This preset bumps the CPU speed up to 950MHz, leaving the GPU and memory set as with Medium, but requires a considerable boost in voltage to do so. This preset should be used with caution unless you have a heatsink connected to the Pi.

SHARING A KEYBOARD AND MOUSE

Discover how to share one mouse and keyboard between multiple PCs over the network using free, open-source software called Synergy

Although it's possible to use a Pi with a keyboard and mouse directly connected, this isn't always convenient. With only two USB ports, the Pi quickly fills up, requiring the use of a USB hub to expand the number of available ports for peripherals. Simply connecting a standard wired keyboard and mouse is enough to fill a Model B, and with the Model A having only a single USB port the user is left swapping between the two unless a hub is used.

There is an alternative, however: sharing the keyboard and mouse of a desktop or laptop computer. Although the Pi still needs its own dedicated display, this frees up the USB ports for other peripherals, and saves valuable desk space to boot.

Make sure you select the right version for your OS.

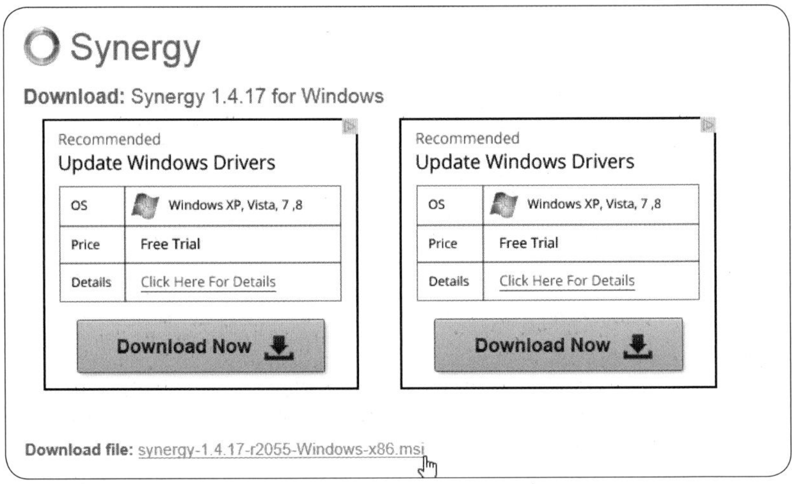

INSTALLING SYNERGY SERVER

Sharing a keyboard and mouse over the network is easily achieved using a free, open-source software package called Synergy. This takes the input from one machine and transfers it to another, acting as though the two were directly connected. If you've ever used a PC with multiple monitors, you'll be familiar with the experience of moving the mouse off the edge of one monitor and having it appear on the other. Synergy works in exactly the same way, except the second monitor is actually an entirely different computer.

Synergy is available for Windows, OS X and Linux operating systems, and can be downloaded for free from **synergy-foss.org**. Make sure you select the right version for your operating system. Synergy is available in 64-bit and 32-bit variants, matched to the host operating system.

Installing and configuring Synergy is very similar on all operating systems, with the Windows version shown in these screenshots. When you click on the download link on the webpage – ignoring the adverts exhorting you to update your drivers – choose Run to start the installation process. Click the Install button, then accept the User Account Control warning regarding change being made if it appears. If you're prompted to restart Windows Explorer, choose Yes.

Partway through the installation process, Synergy will ask you whether you're installing it as a Server or a Client system. The server is the computer that has the keyboard and mouse connected; the clients are systems, including the Raspberry Pi, that you wish to control. You're installing the server portion here, so choose Server before clicking Next to

WHAT YOU'LL NEED

Sharing a keyboard and mouse from a desktop or laptop computer to a Raspberry Pi takes place over the network, so you'll need a Model B with an active network connection or a Model A with a USB network adapter connected. The Pi should be connected to the same network as the desktop or laptop, and if using a wireless network you need to make sure that "Client Isolation" is switched off on your router or access point; otherwise, the Pi and PC won't be able to communicate.

Lastly, you'll also need a keyboard and mouse for the Pi to perform the initial setup. Once the software is installed and configured, you can disconnect these and control the Pi purely using the shared keyboard and mouse.

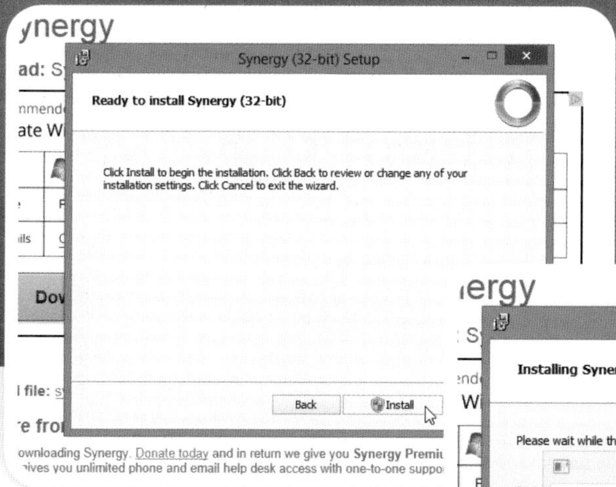

Installing and configuring Synergy is very similar on all OSes.

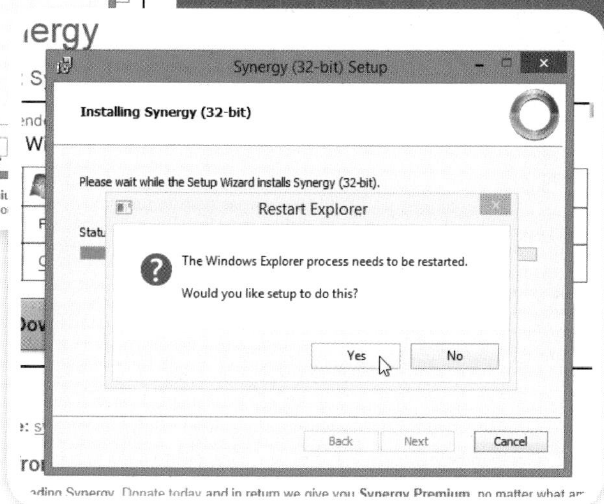

If prompted to restart Windows Explorer, choose Yes.

continue the installation process. The latest versions of Synergy include the option to encrypt traffic as it flows over the network. In most cases, this isn't necessary and you can simply skip the option by clicking Finish.

CONFIGURING SYNERGY SERVER

When the installation process is complete, Synergy will automatically load. Don't worry about the watchdog error that appears in the log at the bottom of the window; that just means that the server portion hasn't loaded yet. First, you'll need to configure its settings by clicking the Configure Server button to load the layout window.

Synergy works by treating its client systems as separate displays. The layout screen allows you to adjust how these displays relate to each other by dragging and dropping their images onto the grid. At the centre is the existing server system, and at present no other systems are configured. To add a new client, drag the monitor icon from the top-right onto an empty space in the grid. Where you drop it depends on how your desk is laid out. If the Pi's monitor or TV is to the right of the server, drop the monitor icon to the right. If it's to the left, drop it to the left. You can keep doing this for as many clients as you have. For now, though, leave it at one.

When you've positioned the monitor icon, double-click it to change its settings. Almost everything in the window that appears can be left at its defaults, except for the screen name. Change this to read RaspberryPi – don't try to put any spaces in, as Synergy won't let you – and press OK followed by OK again on the configuration screen to return to the main Synergy window.

With the server configured, you can click on the Start button at the bottom right of the window to load the server itself. When you do, you should see the log start to scroll status messages ending in "watchdog status: ok". This message lets you know that the server is up and running, and ready to accept clients. Make a note of the IP address, printed in bold in the Server section of the window, and you can begin configuring your Raspberry Pi.

INSTALLING SYNERGY CLIENT

Installing Synergy on the Raspberry Pi is considerably easier than installing it on Windows or OS X, thanks to its built-in package manager. In a Raspbian terminal, type the following commands:

```
sudo apt-get update
sudo apt-get upgrade
sudo apt-get install synergy
```

The first command tells Apt, the package manager used by Raspbian, to update its list of available software. The second tells it to use that list to find any software on the system that has an upgrade available, download said upgrade and install it. It's always a good idea to start any Raspberry Pi project with these two commands, as attempting to work with outdated software – especially if you're trying to compile another package from its source code – can result in errors and instability.

The third command tells Apt to find and install Synergy. Although the first two can take a few minutes to complete – especially on a slower internet connection – the installation process is fast, thanks to Synergy's small size. When the process has finished, you can check to see if it has installed correctly by typing the following command:

```
synergyc --version
```

If Synergy returns its version number, it has installed successfully; if not, check your commands for typos or other mistakes.

RUNNING SYNERGY CLIENT

Synergy is only useful when you're running a graphical user interface on the Pi. If you've been using the text-only console up to now, you'll need to load the graphical user interface. If you've been using a terminal within the graphical user interface, skip this step. To load the graphical user interface, type:

```
startx
```

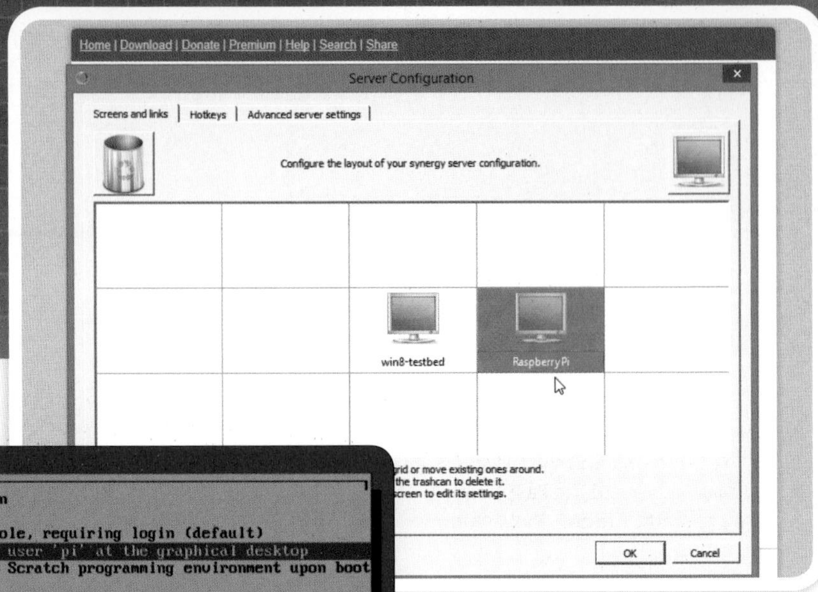

Synergy works by treating its client systems as separate displays.

When the desktop has loaded, double-click on the LXTerminal icon to load a terminal. Unlike the server-side version of Synergy, the client software needs no advanced configuration. Instead, it's possible to set the software entirely on the command line. All you need to know is the layout of icons you configured in the server and the name you gave to the icon that corresponds to the Raspberry Pi, which, if you followed these instructions, should be RaspberryPi. Type the following command:

```
synergyc -n RaspberryPi
ipaddress
```

where ipaddress is the IP address of the server, which you noted down earlier. If you've forgotten the address, go back to your desktop or laptop and look at the Synergy window, where the IP address will be shown in bold.

It's normal for Synergy to load silently, so don't worry if no messages appear at the terminal. At this point, you can disconnect the keyboard and mouse from the Pi and take control using the peripherals connected to your desktop or laptop computer instead. If you return to the Synergy server window, you should see a new entry in the log: "client 'RaspberryPi' has connected". This tells you that

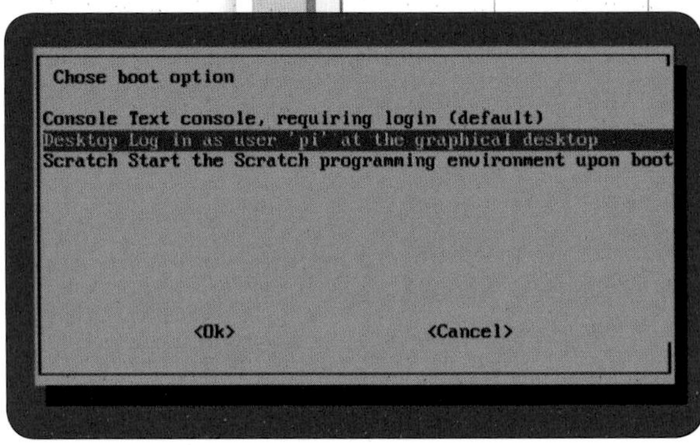

Set up the Pi to load Synergy on boot automatically.

the Raspberry Pi's Synergy client has correctly found the server running on your desktop or laptop.

If you now move your mouse cursor to the edge of the monitor next to the Pi's display – the right-hand edge, in this example configuration – it will vanish, and the message "leaving screen" will appear in the Synergy server log. If you look at the Raspberry Pi's monitor, you should see that the Pi's cursor has moved from wherever you left it to the left-hand edge of the display. It's now under the control of the mouse connected to your desktop or laptop computer.

You can move the mouse cursor around in exactly the same way as you would if a physical mouse were connected to the Pi; you can even play games without difficulty. The keyboard, too, is now connected to the Pi over the network. Anything you type will appear in the Pi's applications just the same as if the keyboard were physically connected.

To return to your desktop or laptop, simply move the mouse cursor off the edge of the screen once again and it will reappear on its original display. The message "entering screen" will appear in the Synergy server log to confirm that control has passed back to the host system. There's no limit to how many times you can do this; moving back and forth between controlling the two systems is as easy as moving the mouse.

Synergy comes with a hidden extra in the form of a shared clipboard. Any text you copy from one system will be available to the other, and vice-versa. You can test this by typing something into Notepad on your desktop and copying it before moving your mouse off the edge of the screen. On the Pi, load LeafPad from the Accessories menu and press Ctrl+V to paste the text. This works for any application; try copying the address of a website from the browser on one system to the browser on the other.

LOADING SYNERGY ON BOOT

Running Synergy manually is fine for now, but it can get annoying to have to plug in a physical keyboard and mouse every time you reboot the Pi. Thankfully, the process can be automated such that Synergy loads whenever the Pi starts up, meaning you'll never need to connect a keyboard and mouse to the Pi again.

First, you'll need to configure Raspbian to load the graphical user interface whenever the Pi is started,

Synergy is available for Windows, OS X and Linux operating systems, and can be downloaded for free

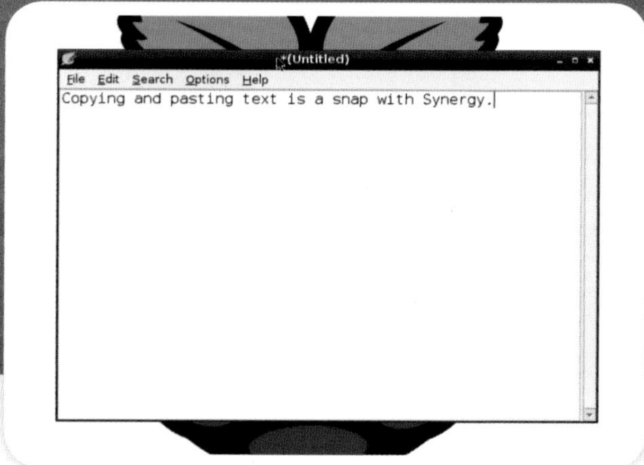

Synergy comes with a hidden extra in the form of a shared clipboard.

in place of the default where the user logs into the console and the GUI is loaded manually. Load the Raspberry Pi Software Configuration Tool using the command:

```
sudo raspi-config
```

Using the cursor keys, highlight option 3, labelled "Boot to Desktop/Scratch", and press Enter. In the menu that appears, choose the second option. This automatically logs the default user Pi into the system and starts the graphical user interface. Press Enter to confirm, then press Tab twice to highlight Finish, followed by Enter. You'll be prompted to reboot; we haven't quite finished yet, so choose No with the cursor keys and press Enter.

Loading the graphical user interface at startup is half the battle, but you still need to have Synergy load and connect to the server without having to type on a keyboard connected to the Pi. At the terminal, type the following command:

```
mkdir /home/pi/.config/
lxsession /home/pi/.config/
lxsession/LXDE
```

Make sure there's a space after "lxsession" and before the second "/home" or the command will fail. This creates two directories, which, among other things, can be used to make software start as soon as the Pi user logs into the graphical user interface, which you've already automated using the Raspberry Pi Software Configuration Tool.

Next, you need to create a file called "autostart" with the command – or commands – you want to load automatically each time the system starts. In this case, you're looking to load the Synergy client and connect it to the server. Type the following commands to automatically create a suitable file:

```
echo "synergyc -n
RaspberryPi ipaddress" >> /
home/pi/.config/lxsession/
LXDE/autostart
chmod +x /home/pi/.config/
lxsession/LXDE/autostart
```

The first command creates the autostart file, and fills it with with the command to load the Synergy client. Remember to swap out ipaddress for the IP address of your desktop or laptop. The second command tells Raspbian that this file is executable, like a program. If you forget that command, the file will be ignored and you'll still have to start Synergy manually.

To reboot the Pi, and to test the autostart file, type:

```
sudo reboot
```

When the Pi reboots, it should automatically load the graphical user interface and Synergy. Watch the Synergy server log on your desktop and laptop for the message telling you that the client RaspberryPi has connected. If it never appears, plug a keyboard and mouse back into the Pi, and double-check your autostart file for typos or mistakes.

This process expects the IP address of the machine Synergy is connecting to never change. If you find that it fails over a period of days or weeks, it's likely because your desktop or laptop is changing its IP address. The Pi doesn't know about the change, so it still tries to connect to the old IP. Look in the manual for your network router for instructions on setting manual IP addresses, and give the machine running the Synergy server a permanent IP address to avoid this. ●

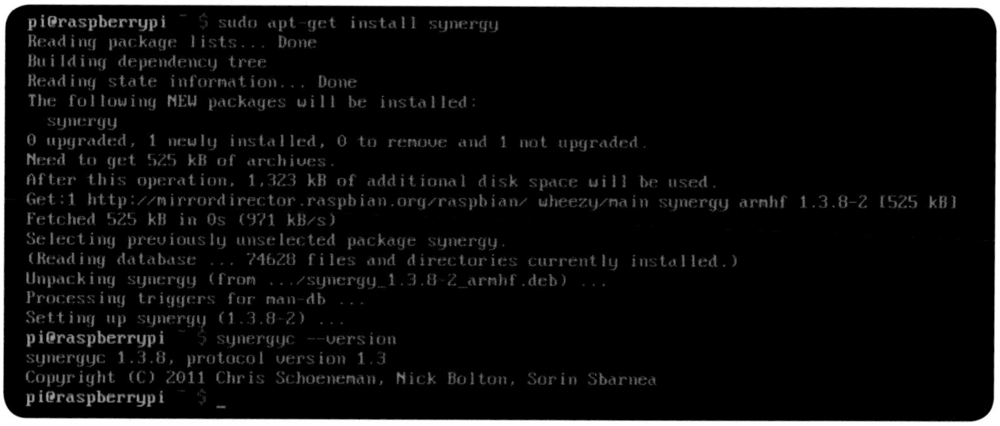

pi@raspberrypi ~ $ sudo apt-get install synergy
Reading package lists... Done
Building dependency tree
Reading state information... Done
The following NEW packages will be installed:
synergy
0 upgraded, 1 newly installed, 0 to remove and 1 not upgraded.
Need to get 525 kB of archives.
After this operation, 1,323 kB of additional disk space will be used.
Get:1 http://mirrordirector.raspbian.org/raspbian/ wheezy/main synergy armhf 1.3.8-2 [525 kB]
Fetched 525 kB in 0s (971 kB/s)
Selecting previously unselected package synergy.
(Reading database ... 74628 files and directories currently installed.)
Unpacking synergy (from .../synergy_1.3.8-2_armhf.deb) ...
Processing triggers for man-db ...
Setting up synergy (1.3.8-2) ...
pi@raspberrypi ~ $ synergyc --version
synergyc 1.3.8, protocol version 1.3
Copyright (C) 2011 Chris Schoeneman, Nick Bolton, Sorin Sbarnea
pi@raspberrypi ~ $ _

If Synergy returns its version number, it has installed OK.

TURNING THE PI INTO A THIN CLIENT

The Pi's silent running and low power draw make it an ideal choice as a low-cost thin client. Follow our simple guide to enabling a remote desktop

One of the biggest attractions of the Pi as a computing platform is its low power draw. Where a desktop computer might draw upwards of 500W under load, and a laptop as high as 100W, the Pi sits well under 5W. That's not just good news for the environment and your electricity bill; the low power draw of the Pi means that it generates correspondingly less heat. Unlike a desktop computer that typically requires a series of noisy fans, the Pi operates entirely silently, making it a great way to extend computing into quieter areas of the home or office without raising any eyebrows, by creating what's known as a thin client.

WHAT YOU'LL NEED

Turning a Pi into a thin client is a software-based project, so you'll need little more than the Pi itself and a keyboard, mouse and monitor. If you're planning on making the Pi thin client a permanent installation, however, it's a good idea to buy an inexpensive case (from £2.50, ebay.co.uk). The GPIO pins of the Pi are reasonably fragile and prone to being shorted out if something metallic falls across them.

You'll also need a system to act as the server for the thin client; this would normally be your existing Windows, OS X or Linux desktop. You can also use a laptop, but as they often run quietly when not playing games, it's a little harder to see the benefits of using the Pi.

ENABLING REMOTE DESKTOP ON WINDOWS

Microsoft Windows has a built-in server designed to allow a remote system to view the screen and take control of the keyboard and mouse, known as Remote Desktop. It's often used in corporate environments to allow the IT department to troubleshoot an issue without leaving their desks, but here you'll be using it to virtually transport your computer into another room without having to move the heavy, noisy base unit.

First, load the Windows Control Panel from the Start Screen by typing "control panel" and clicking on the icon that appears. When Control Panel loads, click System and Security, then find the entry labelled System in the list. Find Allow Remote Access, and click on the blue text. This will load a System Properties window at the Remote tab. Under Remote Desktop, at the bottom-half of the window, click the radio button next to Allow Remote Connections to This Computer. You'll also need to untick the box that restricts connections to machines with Network Level Authentication. Finally, press OK to save your changes.

Enabling Remote Desktop can be considered a minor security risk, as it allows others to view your screen and type or click on your behalf. In order to do so, the theoretical attacker would need to know your username and password, and be on the same private network. When connected to a public network, Windows Firewall

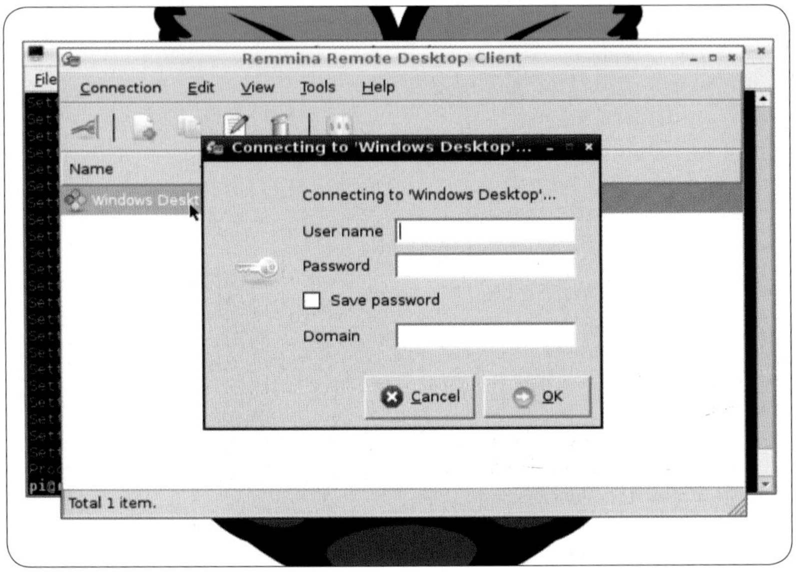

When connecting over the RDP, you'll be asked for your password.

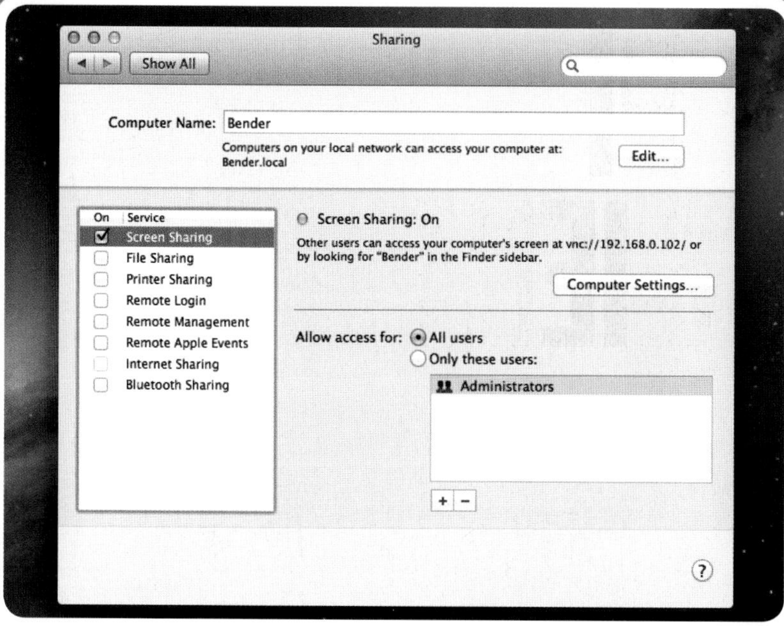

Enable Apple Remote Desktop by clicking Screen Sharing.

automatically disallows Remote Desktop sessions.

ENABLING REMOTE DESKTOP ON OS X

Like Windows, Apple's OS X includes a built-in server designed to allow remote systems to view the screen and take control of the keyboard and mouse. Known as Apple Remote Desktop, it's a standard feature with any version of OS X. There's no need to be running the very latest version in order to make use of the remote desktop functionality.

As with Remote Desktop on Windows, Apple Remote Desktop is disabled by default. To enable it, load the System Preferences app from the Apple menu at the top-left of the screen. Click on the Sharing icon, in the shape of a folder with a road-sign showing a walking man, then find the Screen Sharing service in the list on the left-hand side and tick the box under On. This enables Apple Remote Desktop, but not in a way that will allow the Raspberry Pi to connect.

On the same screen, click the radio button marked Allow Access For: All Users. Next, click the Computer Settings button above and tick both the boxes that appear in the pop-down menu. You'll also need to enter a password, which offers a

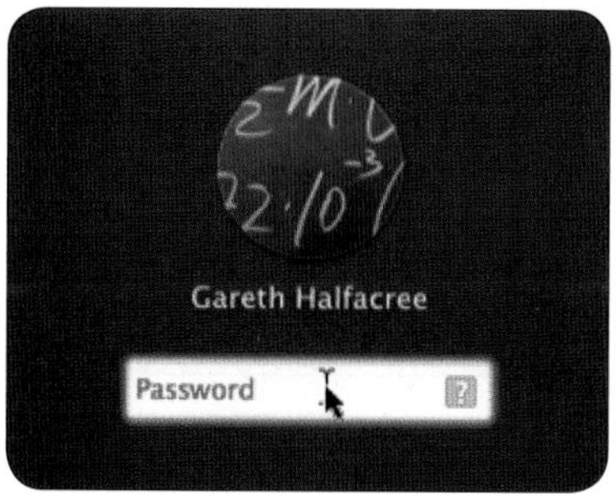

secondary level of protection against unwanted intrusion. This should be around eight characters long, and different to the password set on your user account, which you'll also need when you come to connect from the Raspberry Pi. Click OK to confirm your changes, then you're free to close the Sharing options window.

ENABLING REMOTE DESKTOP ON LINUX

There are various remote desktop server packages for Linux, and which one you should use depends largely on which distribution you're using. Canonical Ubuntu, one of the most popular Linux distributions, comes with a preinstalled remote desktop server called Desktop Sharing. To enable it, click the Ubuntu icon at the top of the Launcher bar and type "desktop sharing" to find the application. Click on the Desktop

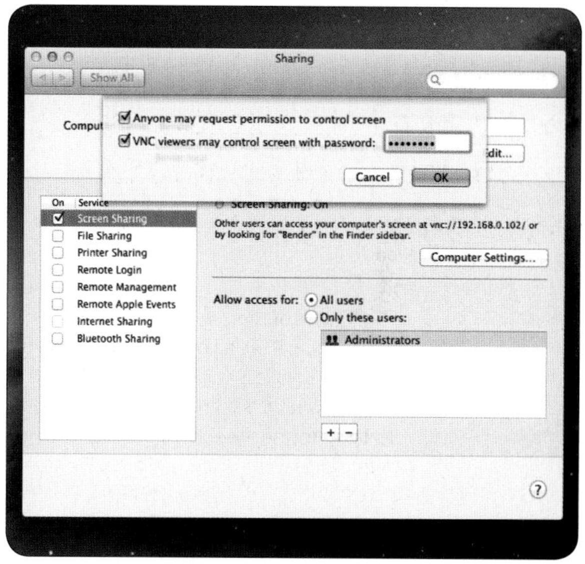

Sharing icon to load the settings window.

Desktop Sharing is disabled by default on Ubuntu, but can be quickly enabled by ticking the box marked Allow Other Users to View Your Desktop. This also ticks the box below, which gives users who connect via Desktop Sharing the ability to also control the machine through the keyboard and mouse; you want to leave this enabled.

For security reasons, Ubuntu normally asks for permission before allowing a remote desktop client to view the display. If you were using Desktop Sharing for troubleshooting or demonstrations that would be fine, but it's a pain to have to go into the room with the desktop and click OK on a pop-up window every time you try to use the Pi thin client. Untick the box marked You Must Confirm Each Access to This Machine, and instead

A password, offers a secondary level of protection.

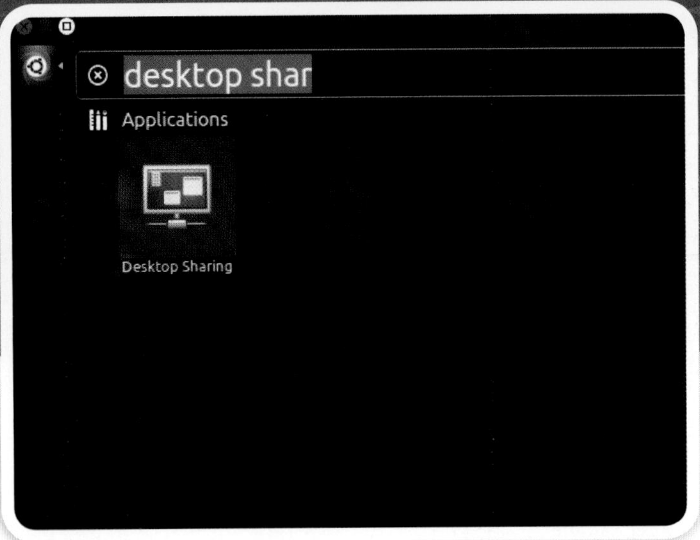

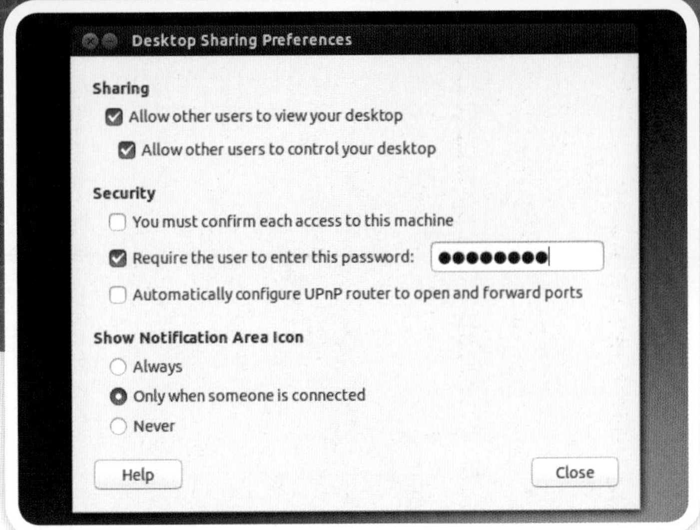

Desktop Sharing is disabled by default on Ubuntu.

tick the box below marked Require The User to Enter This Password. Fill in an eight-character password – again, this should be different to the password used on your user account – and click the Close button to save your changes.

If you use a different Linux distribution, consult the help files or website for information on which desktop sharing system it uses and how to configure it.

INSTALLING A REMOTE DESKTOP CLIENT

Like Synergy, remote desktop systems work on a client-server basis. You've already enabled the server, which is your desktop computer, and now you need to enable the Raspberry Pi as a client. You'll need to be running the graphical user interface for this, so if you're at the text-only console load the GUI by typing:

```
startx
```

By default, Raspbian doesn't come with a remote desktop client installed. To install a universal client that's capable of connecting to Windows, OS X or Linux desktop sharing servers, double-click the LXTerminal icon and type the following commands:

```
sudo apt-get update
sudo apt-get upgrade
sudo apt-get install remmina
```

The first two commands, as when you installed Synergy, ensure that the Pi has its software list up to date and upgrades any packages that aren't the latest available version. The third finds the Remmina package, which acts as a client for several different types of remote desktop server, and installs it along with several other packages on which it depends. You'll be asked to confirm that you're happy for all the listed packages to be installed, after which installation takes about a minute.

Once installed, you can find Remmina in the internet menu accessible by clicking the menu button at the bottom-left of the screen. Click Remmina in this menu to load the configuration screen, then click the New icon – shaped like a blank sheet of paper with a plus overlaid on the bottom-right corner – to start configuring the connection to the server.

How you configure the server depends on which operating system the server is running. All three have their commonalities, though. Enter a friendly name, such as Apple Laptop or Windows Desktop, in the Name field, and the IP address of the computer in the Server field. If you're connecting to a Windows machine, you can leave the Protocol option at its default of RDP – Remote Desktop Protocol. If you're connecting to either OS X or Linux, click the dropdown arrow and change the Protocol to VNC – Virtual Network Computing.

By default, Remmina only receives 256 colours from the server, which makes images look washed-out and strange. To boost the quality, click on the dropdown box next to Colour Depth and choose High Colour or higher. The further down the list you choose, the higher quality the image will be. Higher colour depths require more power from the Pi, however, and may slow down the responsiveness of the connection.

Click the Save button, and your server will be entered into the list on the main Remmina screen. You can do this for as many servers as you like. If you have more than one computer you'd like to be able to control from the Pi, just click the New icon again and enter that computer's details.

When connecting to a Windows system over the Remote Desktop Protocol, you'll be asked for your username and password. This is the account you use on Windows, not the account you use on the Pi.

Anything you do in Remmina occurs on the remote computer, not the Pi, so will work a lot faster

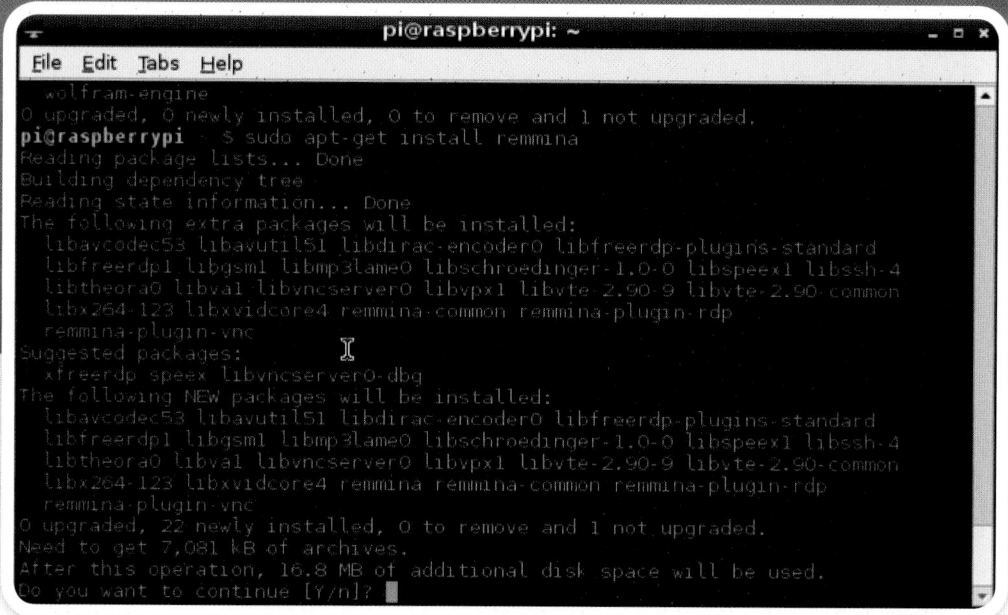

Remmina acts as a client for remote desktop servers.

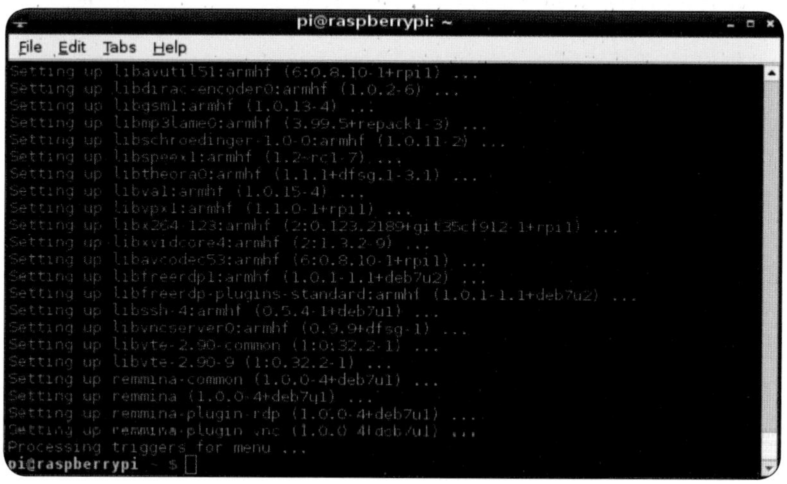

Anything you do in Remmina occurs on the remote PC.

You'll also be asked to confirm the security certificate used to encrypt the connection; just click OK on both the dialogs that appear. Your Windows desktop will then appear on the Raspberry Pi, complete with any applications you already had open.

When connecting to an OS X system over the VNC protocol, you'll be asked for the password you entered into the Sharing menu earlier. Enter this, then when you've connected you'll be asked for the password for your OS X user account. Enter this, and you'll have full control over the OS X system. The same applies to connections to Linux systems, which use the same VNC protocol.

USING REMMINA

Once you have Remmina successfully connecting to your remote system, you can start exploring its functionality. The icons along the top of the Remmina window provide tooltips when you hover your mouse cursor over the top. For now, you can disguise the fact that you're using a remote desktop client at all by hitting the Fullscreen icon – second along from the left, shaped like a window with arrows appearing from it – to make the remote desktop session fill the screen.

Using Remmina in full-screen mode is like physically being at the computer, although it does have its disadvantages. Because everything you do is being digitised and sent over the network, playing games or video can be akin to watching a slideshow. For productivity work, however, it's absolutely fine. It's also a handy way of having access to more computing power. Anything you do in Remmina occurs on the remote computer, not the Pi, so will work a lot faster.

To leave full-screen mode, move the mouse cursor to the top-middle of the screen, and a menu will appear. Just click the Fullscreen icon again to return Remmina to windowed mode and give you the Raspberry Pi desktop again.

Remote Desktop on Windows usually adjusts the resolution to match that of the connecting systems, but not all remote desktop servers do the same. If you find that you're missing parts of your remote desktop off the edge of the screen, click the Scaling icon in the shape of a window with an overlaid magnifying glass. This will shrink the image to fit in the window, which results in a slight blurriness. Pressing the icon again will disable Scaling.

The last icon to be aware of is at the far right of the menu, shaped like a plug coming out of a socket: the Disconnect icon. As its name suggests, this disconnects your Pi from the remote system. Because remote desktops are usually – but not always – shared, you should get into the habit of disconnecting your thin client from the remote server when it's not in use. Otherwise, you may find that someone nudging the mouse on the thin client makes the cursor you're trying to use on your desktop move wildly.

PRIVACY-BOOSTING ROUTER

Want to protect your privacy and security on the internet? Learn how you can set up the Raspberry Pi to run as a TOR proxy service

Electronic privacy is a hot-button topic today. Revelations confirming long-suspected beliefs that world governments snoop and spy into every aspect of a user's digital life have many looking for ways to combat such intrusive behaviour. Some turn to protests and lobbying to get the laws that allow governments to perform such mass monitoring overturned or, where they already hold such activity illegal, enforced. Others turn to technology, arguably the very thing that made it so easy for mass surveillance to take place, for a more immediate fix.

One of the most popular tools in the privacy enthusiast's kit is The Onion Router (TOR), an encrypted network originally developed by the US Navy. Using TOR, a user's network traffic is scrambled and shuffled through a network of computers in various countries before emerging from a system somewhere else entirely. It's used for everything from bypassing state censorship to ensuring the privacy of human rights activists and whistle-blowers, although it has recently entered the public eye thanks to the closure of a notorious underground black-market site known as the Silk Road, which used TOR to protect its customers.

The most common way to use TOR is to install it directly on the system that it will be protecting, but this isn't always possible. With increasing numbers of people switching to mobile devices like smartphones and tablets, where TOR software isn't available, alternatives are needed. Alternatives, in fact, like a Raspberry Pi-powered TOR proxy, which accepts traffic from any device and routes it over the TOR network with no individual configuration required.

WHAT YOU'LL NEED

Setting up a Pi to act as a TOR proxy is a purely software-based project, but it does require a Pi with a network connection to operate. Thankfully, it's reasonably light in its memory requirements; a Model A with USB network adapter, wired or wireless, is easily capable of running TOR and its associated software.

Unlike a true router, which bridges two physical networks such as your home network and the internet, TOR acts as a proxy. As a result, you only need a single network connection on your Pi for it to operate.

INSTALLING TOR

In the early days of the Raspberry Pi, any non-core software had to be downloaded in source-code form and compiled into its executable binary format. Doing so on the Pi is a slow and laborious process, but while it's unavoidable for certain rarer packages it's thankfully becoming an increasingly uncommon requirement.

Where once you'd have needed to download and install a range of development packages and libraries, and compile TOR from source, installing the required software on Raspbian is as easy as opening a terminal and using the following commands:

```
sudo apt-get update
sudo apt-get upgrade
sudo apt-get install tor
lighttpd
```

The first two instructions tell the Pi to download the latest list of available software packages, and upgrade any existing packages that are out of date. As always, it's a good idea to start any Pi project with these commands so as to avoid the problems that running outdated software can cause.

The third instruction uses the Apt package manager to install

WARNING

Although TOR encrypts your network traffic, the data is unencrypted when it leaves the network via systems known as exit nodes. These nodes have, in the past, been used to gather data that, while its source is anonymised, can contain personally identifiable information such as usernames and passwords. Using TOR is no substitute for good practices. Don't submit usernames and passwords over unencrypted connections. Always enable encryption on your email client or webmail system, and if in doubt use a non-TOR connection.

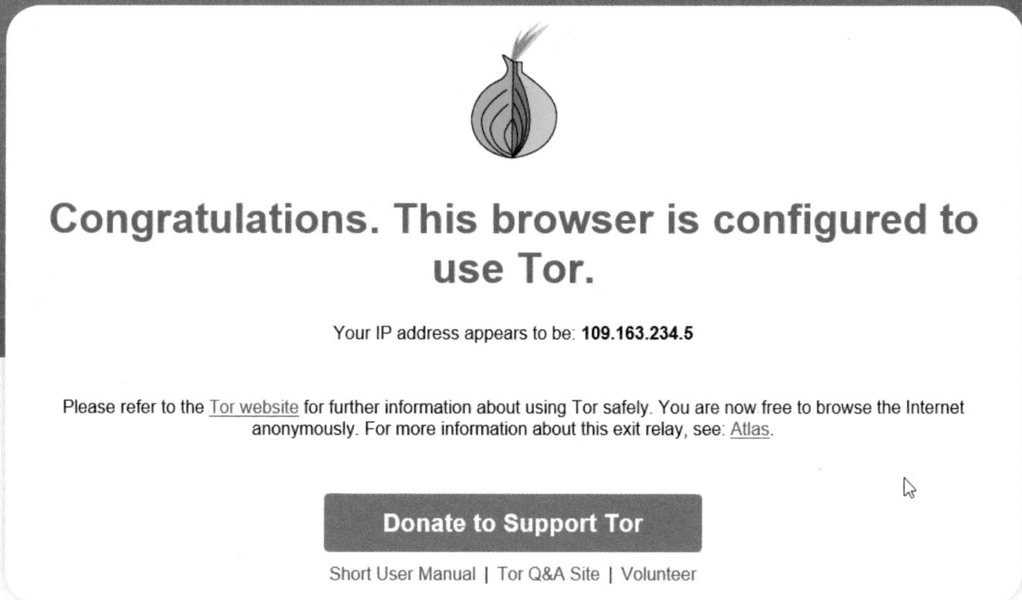

Congratulations. This browser is configured to use Tor.
Your IP address appears to be: 109.163.234.5
Please refer to the Tor website for further information about using Tor safely. You are now free to browse the Internet anonymously. For more information about this exit relay, see: Atlas.
Donate to Support Tor
Short User Manual | Tor Q&A Site | Volunteer

The TOR installation process will take a few minutes.

two software packages: TOR itself, and a lightweight web server called Lighttpd. You'll use the latter to serve an automatic proxy configuration file, used to make setting up client machines to use TOR quick and easy, even where the direct configuration of proxy settings isn't available, such as in certain Apple iOS releases.

The installation process should take no more than a few minutes to complete, after which you'll need to configure TOR to act as a proxy for devices on your network. First, however, you'll want to make sure the Pi doesn't change its IP address.

SETTING A STATIC IP

Most home networks are controlled by a router or gateway that runs the Dynamic Host Configuration Protocol (DHCP), a networking system designed to make it easy to connect new client devices. When a system connects to a network controlled by DHCP, it requests an internet Protocol (IP) address on that network. The DHCP server looks for the first available address and assigns it to the new system.

It's a system that works well, but it's ill-suited to running servers. Because an IP address assigned by DHCP can change, the address can't be relied upon for accessing the server in the future. The solution to this is to set a static IP, either on the router or directly on the client device.

Setting up static IP addresses on the router is the preferred option. The client device can continue to use DHCP to receive other network settings, but it will always be given the same address, which will be made unavailable for use by any other device. Configuring your router or gateway for a static client varies, depending on the make and model. Look in the manual or help file for reference to "static reservations", "static IP" or "DHCP reservations". You'll most likely need to know the Media Access Control (MAC) address of the device you're reserving. You can find this out quickly by typing the following command on the Pi:

```
ifconfig | grep HWaddr
```

If your router doesn't support static IP reservations, the alternative is to set a static address on the Pi itself. This is somewhat less ideal, as if done incorrectly can result in collisions, where the Pi and another device try to use the same address, but it's better than having to find out what IP address the Pi received each time you try to use the proxy server.

To set a static IP, you'll need to know the address of your network, the network mask, the address of your router, and where the DHCP scope – the range of addresses it's configured to give out – begins and ends. All this information can be found on your router's configuration pages. With that information in hand, load the Pi's network configuration file in Nano with the following terminal command:

```
sudo nano /etc/network/
interfaces
```

Find the line that reads "iface etho inet dhcp" and alter it so it reads:

```
iface eth0 inet static
```

Then add these lines beneath:

```
address ip-address
netmask netmask
gateway router-ip
```

where "address" is the static IP you want to assign to the Pi, which should be either above or below the DHCP scope and not in use by any other device; "netmask" is the network mask for your home network – typically, 255.255.255.0; and "gateway" the IP address of your router. Double-check the settings, then save them with Ctrl+O. Exit Nano with

It's possible to set a static address on the Pi itself.

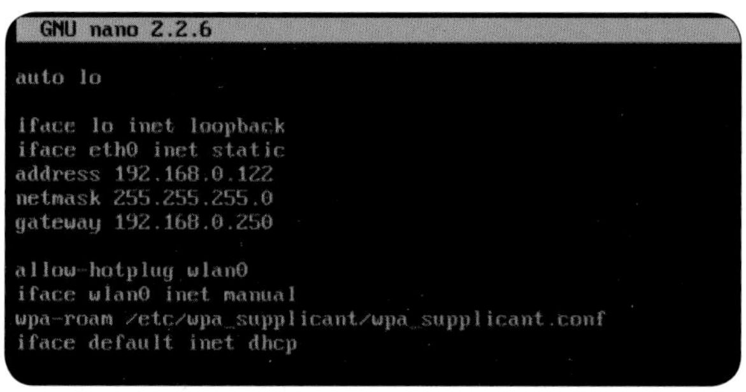

GNU nano 2.2.6
auto lo
iface lo inet loopback
iface eth0 inet static
address 192.168.0.122
netmask 255.255.255.0
gateway 192.168.0.250
allow-hotplug wlan0
iface wlan0 inet manual
wpa-roam /etc/wpa_supplicant/wpa_supplicant.conf
iface default inet dhcp

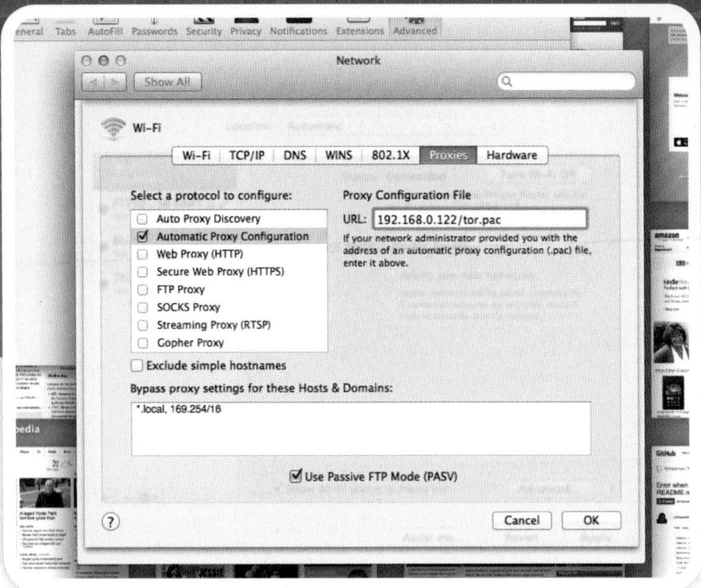

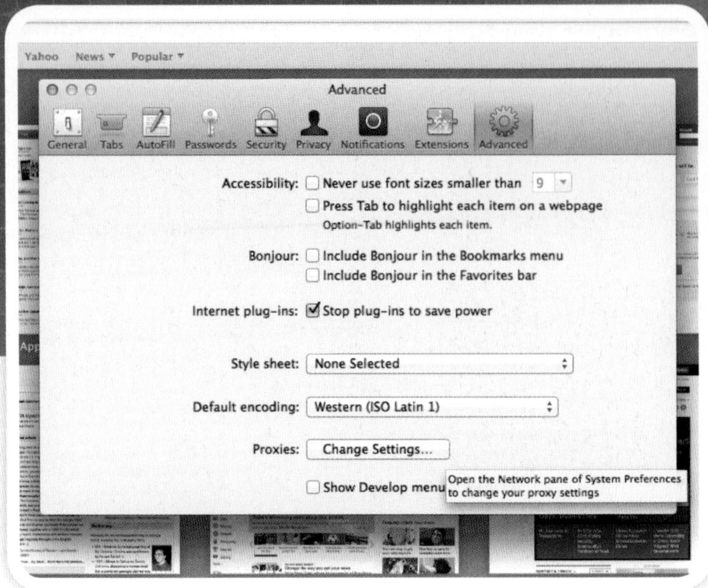

Ctrl+X to return to the terminal.

While the Pi has its new network settings stored, it won't use them until the next time it's rebooted or the networking stack is reloaded. Force the latter with the following command to use the new settings immediately, but be aware that if you're connected remotely via SSH, VNC or similar, you'll lose your connection and need to reconnect using the new address:

```
sudo service networking
restart
```

CONFIGURING TOR

The default behaviour for TOR is to accept traffic only from the local computer, which is fine when you're happy to install a copy of the TOR software on every machine on your network. To make the copy installed on your Pi operate as a proxy for any computer in the network, you'll need to edit its configuration file. Open this file in the Nano text editor with the following command:

```
sudo nano /etc/tor/torrc
```

The first part of the command, sudo, gives you the permissions you need to make system-wide changes by editing the file, while the second loads the TOR configuration file in Nano. If you end up with an empty file, check your command for typos; it's likely there's a mistake in the address of the file.

Safari doesn't have any dedicated proxy settings.

Firefox maintains its own proxy settings.

The TOR configuration file is reasonably complex, although well documented. Each section includes a comment section detailing how it affects the operation of TOR, along with commented-out examples you can tailor to your needs. It's a good idea to read through these comments – prefixed with a hash symbol (#) so TOR knows to ignore them when reading the configuration file – before going any further, to get an idea of what TOR can and can't do.

To configure TOR as a proxy,

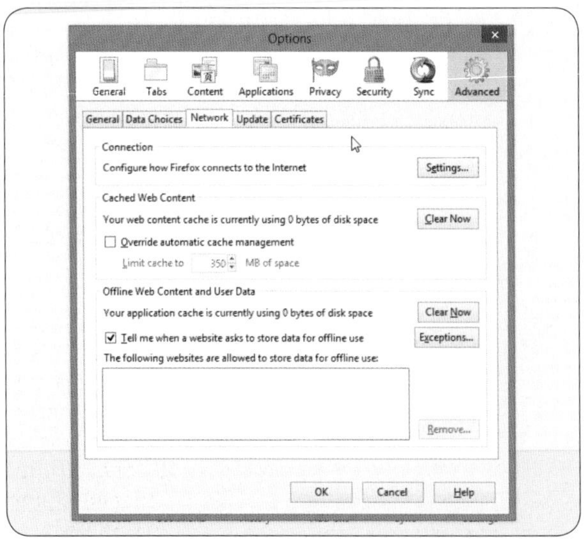

find the lines in the file that begin "#SocksPort". There should be two: one at line 18 and one at line 19. Remove the hash symbol from the front of the second line, and edit the IP address so it reads:

```
SocksPort ip-address:9100
# Bind to this address:port
too.
```

Swap ip-address for the static IP you chose for your Pi. Next, scroll down to the lines that begin "#SocksPolicy" and remove the hash symbol from the start of both before editing them to look like this:

```
SocksPolicy accept network-
address/24
SocksPolicy reject *
```

Replace network-address with the address of your network. For most home networks, this is simply the same as the static IP you've chosen for the Pi, with the last number set to 0. You may also need to adjust the number after the slash. This controls the size of the network and, while some home networks use a /16 (equivalent in range to 192.168.0.0-192.168.255.255), most use the smaller /24 (equivalent to 192.168.0.0-192.168.0.255.)

The remainder of the file can be left alone for now, although it's good

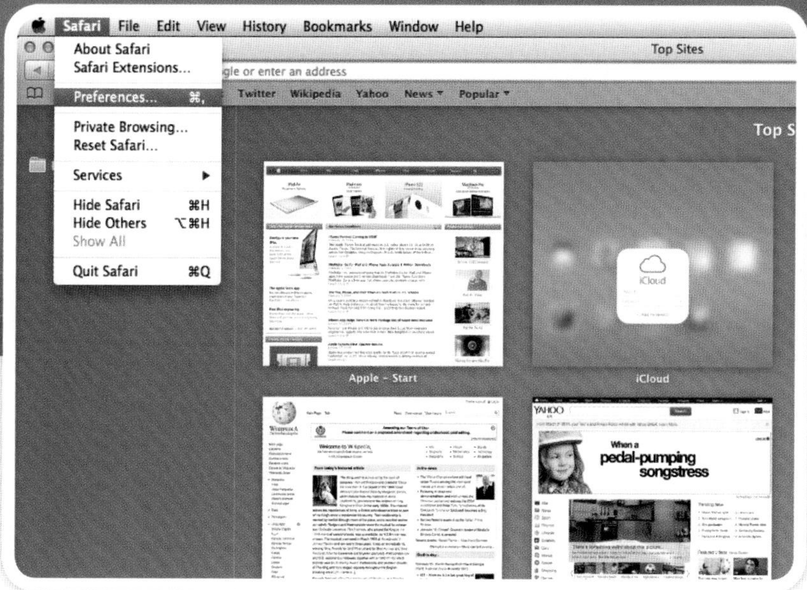

Safari shares the proxy settings of the underlying operating system.

practice to scroll down to the lines labelled "'ExitPolicy" and uncomment the last line, marked as "no exits allowed". This tells TOR that the Pi isn't to be used as an exit node, where traffic from the TOR network is decrypted and sent onto the internet. This only comes into effect when TOR is configured as a relay, which it isn't by default. With exit nodes being targeted for surveillance and being held liable for any criminal activity that passes through from the TOR network, however, it's better to be safe than sorry.

When you've completed the edits, save the new file with Ctrl+O before exiting Nano with Ctrl+X. Before TOR can use the new settings, it needs to be reloaded with this command:

```
sudo service tor restart
```

ENABLING AUTOMATIC CONFIGURATION

At this point, TOR is fully operational and can be used by any system on the network. To do so requires that the system – or an internet browser on the system – have its proxy settings altered to send traffic through the Pi. Not all devices support this: many mobile devices, in particular those running selected versions of Apple's iOS mobile operating system, refuse to allow manual configuration of proxy settings in favour of using an automated configuration system typically found in corporate networks.

Thankfully, it's very easy to implement the same automated configuration system directly on your Pi, bringing TOR support to devices on which it wouldn't normally be available. To do so, you'll need to create a Proxy Auto-Configuration (PAC) file that can be read by client devices. Create this file using Nano with the following command:

```
sudo nano /var/www/tor.pac
```

This folder, "/var/www", is used by the Lighttpd web server you installed earlier in this project to find files it can serve to clients. In this case, we're using it to serve a PAC file that will tell clients how they can access the TOR service through the Pi. Fill the blank file with the following contents, making sure to put a tab at the start of the "return" line:

```
Function
FindProxyForURL(url, host)
{
    Return "SOCKS ip-
    address:9100";
}
```

As before, change ip-address to match the static IP you gave to the Raspberry Pi. This file format is standard, and will be accepted by any web browser or network device that has an option to automatically configure a proxy server, including all iOS devices.

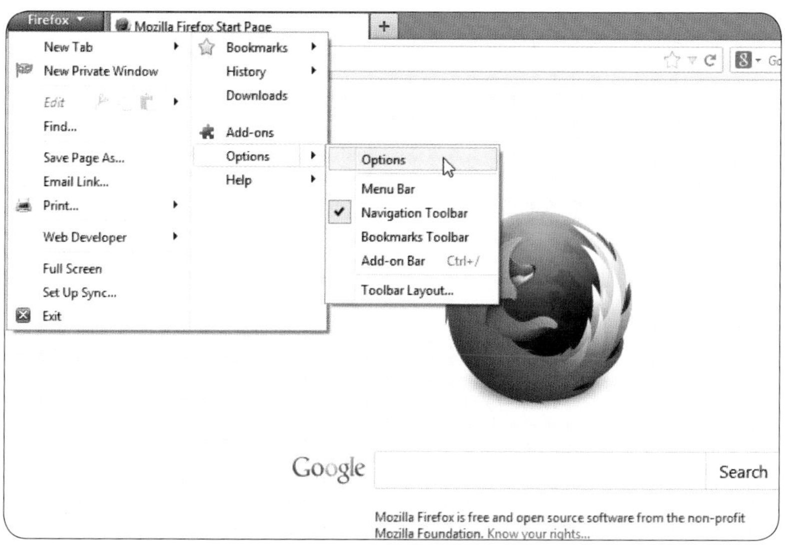

Firefox will use whatever proxy settings are configured for the host OS.

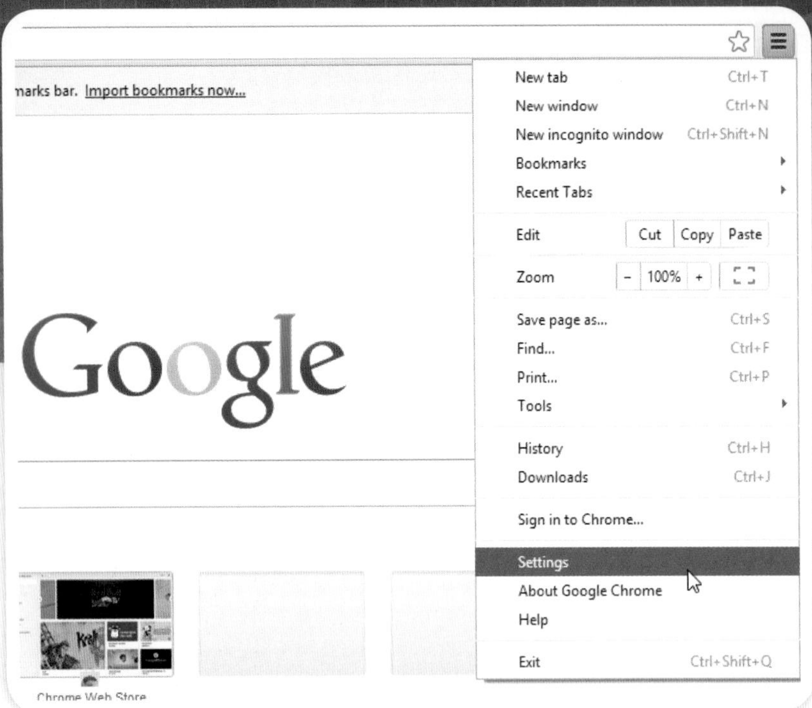

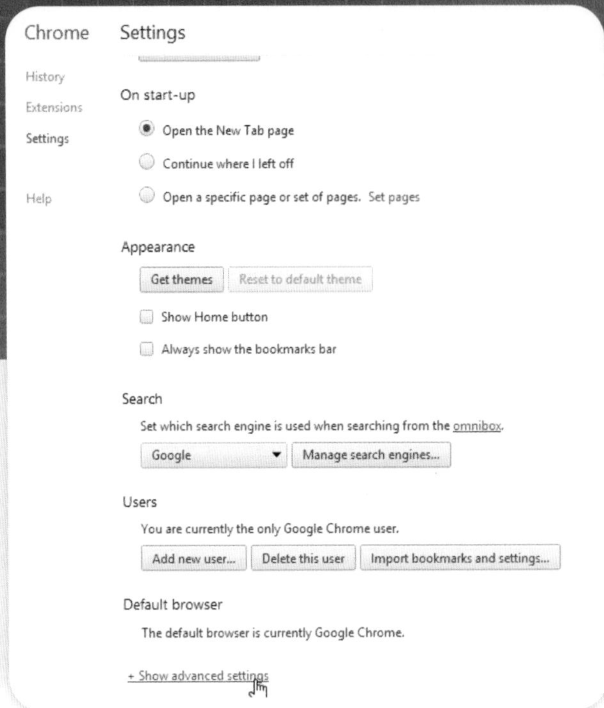

Chrome uses the same proxy settings as the host OS.

CONFIGURING CLIENTS

The Pi is now running TOR as a proxy service, and providing an auto-configuration file for clients that request it. The clients must still be told that the facility is there, however. How you configure your client device will vary, but in general you can look for a "Network Connection" dialog or "Proxy Server" settings page that will accept either the URL of the auto-configuration file or the IP address and port of the proxy server itself. If set in a system control panel, all applications on the client will default to using the TOR proxy. If set within a web browser, typically only the browser itself will use TOR, with all other traffic – such as games or Voice-over-IP (VoIP) packages – ignoring the proxy and using a direct connection.

MICROSOFT WINDOWS/ INTERNET EXPLORER

Microsoft's Internet Explorer doesn't use its own dedicated proxy settings, but rather those of the Windows operating system. To access these, click the cog icon at the top-right of the Internet Explorer window and choose Internet Options. Click on the Connections tab, followed by the LAN Settings button.

In the window that appears, tick the box labelled "Use an Automatic Configuration Script" and enter the following in the Address box:

```
ip-address/tor.pac
```

replacing ip-address with the static IP address you assigned to the Raspberry Pi. Click the OK button to save the changes, and again on the Internet Options window to return to Internet Explorer. Remember, that the change you've made will affect all software installed on the system, unless it uses its own proxy settings.

APPLE SAFARI/OS X

Like Internet Explorer, Apple's Safari browser doesn't have dedicated proxy settings, but instead shares those of the underlying operating system. To access these, click the Safari menu and choose Preferences. Click on the Advanced tab in the window that appears, then click the Change Settings button next to Proxies to load the proxy settings screen.

Tick the box next to Automatic Proxy Configuration to enable it, then write the following address in the URL box:

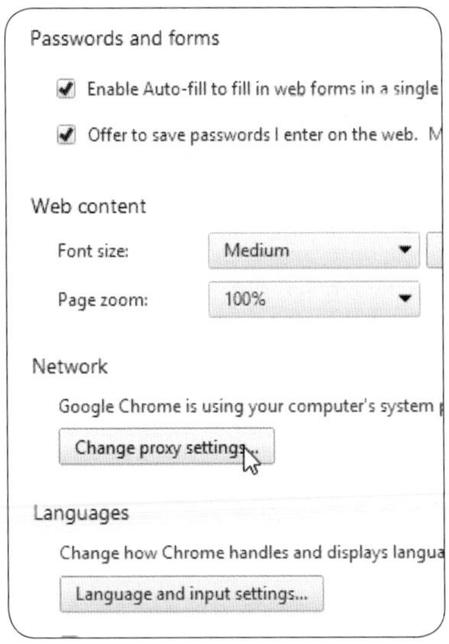

Quickly access the system proxy settings in Google Chrome.

```
ip-address/tor.pac
```

replacing ip-address with the static IP address you assigned to the Raspberry Pi. Click OK to save the setting, then close the Advanced window with the cross at the top-left. Remember, that the change you have made will affect all software installed on the system, unless it uses its own proxy settings.

MOZILLA FIREFOX

Firefox, regardless of the operating system on which it's running,

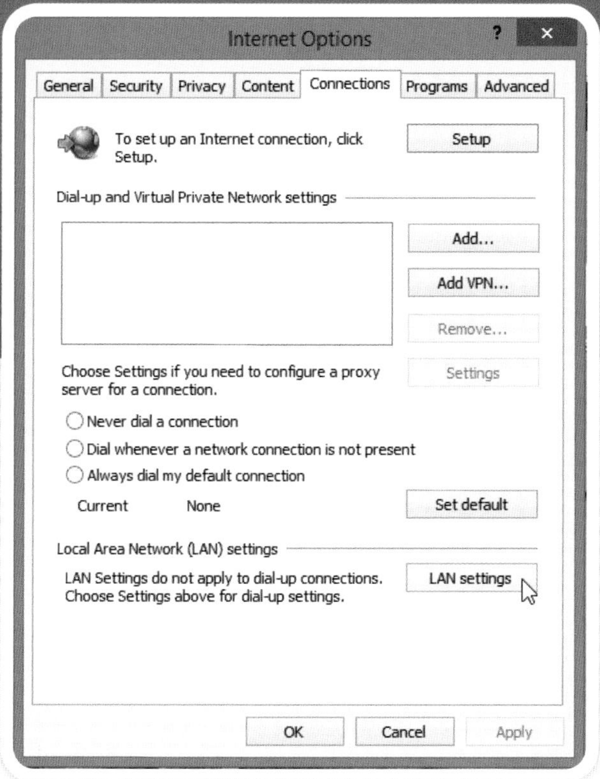

To access Internet Explorer's proxy settings, click the Connections tab.

Tick "Use an Automatic Configuration Script.

maintains its own proxy settings. To control these, enter the Preferences or Options menu – available in Options on Windows, Edit on Linux and the Firefox menu on OS X – and click on the Advanced icon. Click the Network tab, then the Settings button under Connection.

By default, Firefox will use whatever proxy settings are configured for the host operating system. To override them, click the Automatic Proxy Configuration URL radio button and enter the following into the box underneath:

```
ip-address/tor.pac
```

replacing ip-address with the static IP address you assigned to the Raspberry Pi. Click OK to save the

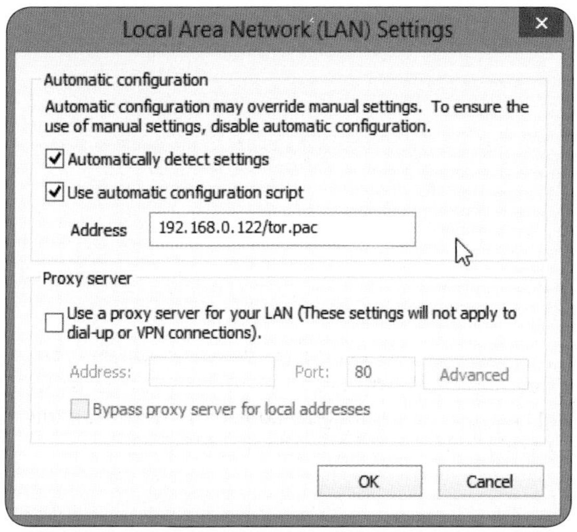

setting, then OK again to return to Firefox. This change only affects Firefox itself; any other software on your system – such as games or Voice-over-IP (VoIP) packages – will ignore the proxy and connect directly to the internet.

GOOGLE CHROME

Google Chrome uses the same proxy settings as your host operating system, like Internet Explorer. To quickly access the system proxy settings, click the three-row settings icon at the top-right of the Chrome window and choose Settings. Scroll to the bottom, and click Show Advanced Settings. Scroll down to Network, then click the Change Proxy Settings button. From there, Windows users can follow the instructions from the guide for Internet Explorer to make the necessary changes. OS X users should follow the instructions from the Safari guide.

If you use other browsers or operating systems, consult their help files for proxy configuration; most are accessible in very similar ways to those outlined above.

TESTING TOR

Your Pi is now running as a TOR proxy, and your client devices are configured. To test that the traffic is definitely being transmitted over TOR, load your browser and send it to **check.torproject.org**. This is a special page run by the TOR Project, which tests to see if your traffic is coming from a known TOR exit node. If successful, it should print a message confirming that you're using TOR and showing an IP address that isn't yours, usually one from a completely different country.

You can now browse as normal, in the knowledge that your traffic is being routed via the TOR network. Remember, however, that all TOR traffic can be observed by exit nodes, and by any network between the exit node and the site you're trying to visit. Make sure that the sites you're using have HTTPS or padlock symbols in the address bar before entering any personal information, and for improved privacy consider reading the TOR documentation at **www.torproject.org**.

To test the traffic is definitely being transmitted over TOR, load your browser and send it to check.torproject.org

RUNNING A WORDPRESS BLOG

Using little more than WordPress and Lighttpd web server software, we show you how to turn your Pi into a low-cost WordPress server

The word "server" conjures up images of towering racks of humming machines with incessantly blinking lights, kept cool only by the industrial-strength air conditioning running in the background. Even home servers, which are becoming increasingly popular for storing media files and backups, are typically sizeable affairs with relatively powerful processors. The Pi, then, isn't an obvious choice to take over the role of one such server, but its low power draw and silent operation make it a great choice for the hobbyist to use as a platform for experimentation.

WordPress, created by Automattic, is the world's most popular blogging platform and content management system. Operated entirely through a web browser, it allows the user to create anything from a simple weblog to large and complex websites. Some of the biggest websites in the world are powered by WordPress. Despite its flexibility, WordPress is surprisingly lightweight; combined with the excellent Lighttpd web server software, it's perfectly possible to turn your Pi into a low-cost WordPress server.

SETTING A STATIC IP ADDRESS

Using any system as a server is a lot more convenient if you know where on your network the system can be found. To do this, you'll need to configure your Raspberry Pi with a static IP address. For details on how this can be done, either through your router or directly on the Pi itself, see the chapter on Build a Privacy-Boosting Router.

INSTALLING THE SERVER SOFTWARE

WordPress requires a software stack beneath it in order to operate: a web server, to actually provide the pages to the visitor; a scripting engine, to generate interactive content like the page at which you write your posts; and a database engine, to actually store the content. To install these on your Pi, enter the following commands at the terminal:

```
sudo apt-get update
sudo apt-get upgrade
sudo apt-get install
lighttpd php5-cgi php5-mysql
php5-gd mysql-server mysql-
client
```

The first two commands, as is usual for starting a Raspberry Pi project, load the latest list of available software packages and ensure that any installed software is as up to date as possible. The third command installs the packages that you'll be using to provide WordPress with its supporting software stack: the Lighttpd web server; the PHP scripting engine plus libraries for handing database connections and image files; and the MySQL database engine plus its client. Don't worry if you've already installed Lighttpd in an earlier project; the package manager Apt is clever enough to know this and skip any packages that are already installed.

As the installation processor runs, you'll be prompted for a password. This is the password used to protect the MySQL "root" user, which has permissions to create, view and edit databases. Choose a long, secure

WHAT YOU'LL NEED

As a software project, you'll need little more than a Raspberry Pi with an active internet connection to complete the steps outlined. Acting as a web server requires a considerable amount of memory, however, which can mean a Raspberry Pi Model A – even when fitted with a USB network adapter – can struggle to keep up once the traffic rises above a handful of simultaneous visitors.

With clever use of plugins like WP Super Cache, which stores static versions of your blog's pages to save on memory and processor usage, it's certainly possible to use a Model A with its limited 256MB of RAM as a WordPress server, so long as your visitors are reasonably patient.

In either case, it's a good idea to boost the amount of memory available to the system by reducing the amount reserved for the graphics processor. For instructions on how to do this, see the chapter on using NOOBS earlier in this MagBook.

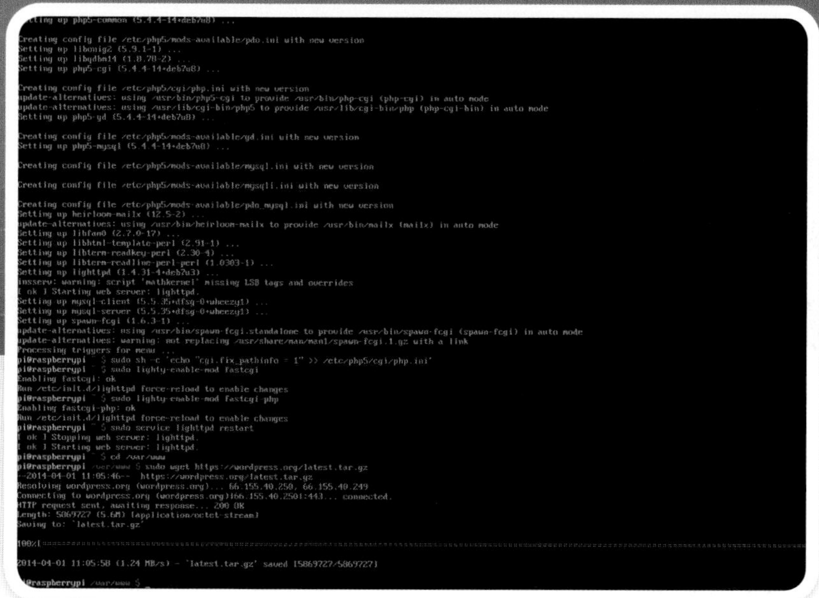

The WordPress installation could take some time.

password – one that is different from your user account on your Pi or on any other system, for preference – to ensure that nobody can gain access to the database engine without your consent.

The installation process for these packages takes some time to complete, as they're complex. Be patient, and the installation should be complete within five minutes.

CONFIGURING THE SERVER SOFTWARE

Before WordPress can use the software stack you've installed, certain settings need to be tweaked. Type the following commands at the terminal:

```
sudo sh -c 'echo "cgi.fix_
pathinfo = 1" >> /etc/php5/
cgi/php.ini'
sudo lighty-enable-mod
fastcgi
sudo lighty-enable-mod
fastcgi-php
```

These allow Lighttpd to link to the PHP scripting engine, which WordPress uses to generate dynamic content. Without this enabled, Lighttpd can only serve static pages, which is of no use to an interactive piece of software like WordPress.

When configured, Lighttpd needs to be restarted in order to make use of the new settings. Type the following at the terminal to reload Lighttpd:

```
sudo service lighttpd
restart
```

When Lighttpd has restarted, you can test to make sure that PHP is working correctly. To do so, you'll need to create a file that calls the built-in PHP Info service. Type the following command to create the file:

```
sudo sh -c 'echo "<?php
phpinfo(); ?>" > /var/www/
phptest.php'
```

In a web browser – either on the Pi or another computer connected to the same network – visit the test page at **ip-address/phptest.php**, where ip-address is the static IP address you assigned to the Pi. When the PHP status page has loaded, confirming that PHP is installed and active within Lighttpd, you should delete the test file. Leaving it in place, while it won't cause any immediate harm, can allow someone who guesses the name of the file to find out details that can aid in attacking your server. Type this command to delete the test file:

```
sudo rm /var/www/phptest.php
```

INSTALLING WORDPRESS

There are two ways to install the WordPress software itself: through the package manager, Apt, and as a

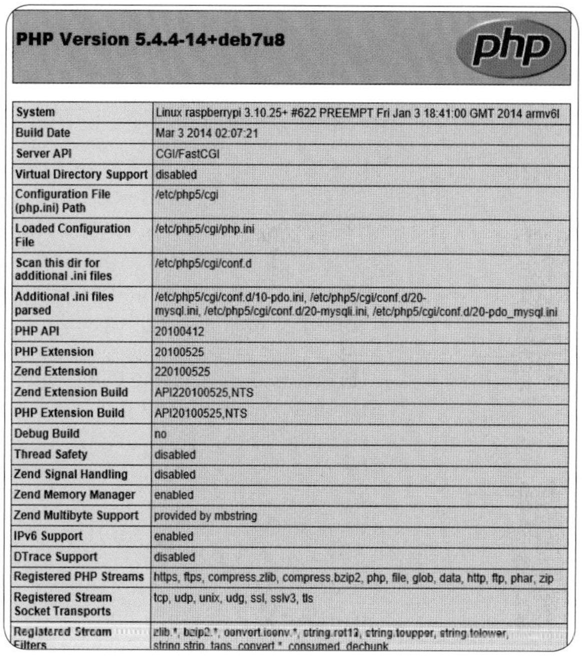

PHP Version 5.4.4-14+deb7u8

System	Linux raspberrypi 3.10.25+ #622 PREEMPT Fri Jan 3 18:41:00 GMT 2014 armv6l
Build Date	Mar 3 2014 02:07:21
Server API	CGI/FastCGI
Virtual Directory Support	disabled
Configuration File (php.ini) Path	/etc/php5/cgi
Loaded Configuration File	/etc/php5/cgi/php.ini
Scan this dir for additional .ini files	/etc/php5/cgi/conf.d
Additional .ini files parsed	/etc/php5/cgi/conf.d/10-pdo.ini, /etc/php5/cgi/conf.d/20-mysql.ini, /etc/php5/cgi/conf.d/20-mysqli.ini, /etc/php5/cgi/conf.d/20-pdo_mysql.ini
PHP API	20100412
PHP Extension	20100525
Zend Extension	220100525
Zend Extension Build	API220100525,NTS
PHP Extension Build	API20100525,NTS
Debug Build	no
Thread Safety	disabled
Zend Signal Handling	disabled
Zend Memory Manager	enabled
Zend Multibyte Support	provided by mbstring
IPv6 Support	enabled
DTrace Support	disabled
Registered PHP Streams	https, ftps, compress.zlib, compress.bzip2, php, file, glob, data, http, ftp, phar, zip
Registered Stream Socket Transports	tcp, udp, unix, udg, ssl, sslv3, tls
Registered Stream Filters	zlib.*, bzip2.*, convert.iconv.*, string.rot13, string.toupper, string.tolower, string.strip_tags, convert.*, consumed, dechunk

Test a file to make sure PHP is working correctly.

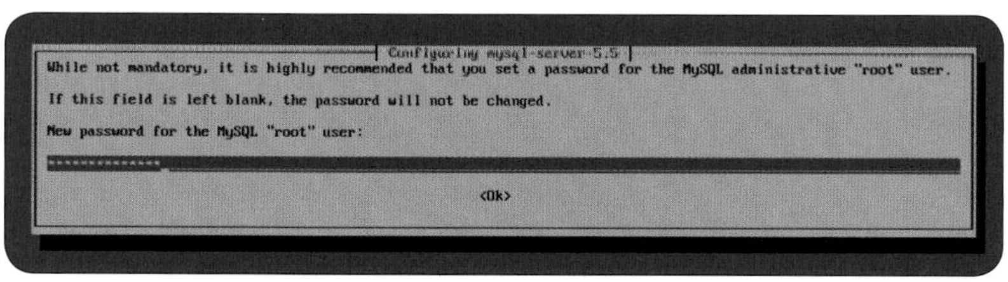

Configuring mysql-server-5.5
While not mandatory, it is highly recommended that you set a password for the MySQL administrative "root" user.
If this field is left blank, the password will not be changed.
New password for the MySQL "root" user:
<Ok>

Set up a password to protect the MySQL "root" user.

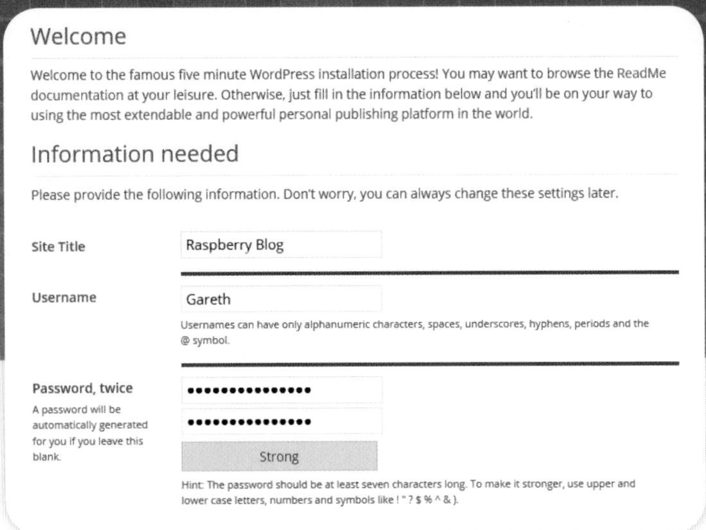

Welcome
Welcome to the famous five minute WordPress installation process! You may want to browse the ReadMe documentation at your leisure. Otherwise, just fill in the information below and you'll be on your way to using the most extendable and powerful personal publishing platform in the world.
Information needed
Please provide the following information. Don't worry, you can always change these settings later.
Site Title
Raspberry Blog
Username
Gareth
Usernames can have only alphanumeric characters, spaces, underscores, hyphens, periods and the @ symbol.
Password, twice
A password will be automatically generated for you if you leave this blank.
Strong
Hint: The password should be at least seven characters long. To make it stronger, use upper and lower case letters, numbers and symbols like ! " ? $ % ^ &).

WordPress
Success!
WordPress has been installed. Were you expecting more steps? Sorry to disappoint.
Username
Gareth
Password
Your chosen password.
Log In

There are two ways to install WordPress.

direct download from Automattic. Usually, software is best installed through the package manager, as it takes control of any other software on which a package may depend. Unfortunately, the version of WordPress offered with Raspbian is considerably out of date and lacking several security patches found in the latest version. As a result, installing manually is the way to go.

You'll first need to download the WordPress archive into the folder used by your web server to store hosted files, which on the Pi is /var/www. Type the following commands at the terminal:

```
cd /var/www
sudo wget https://wordpress.
org/latest.tar.gz
```

This will change into the web server's hosting directory, then download the latest version of WordPress from the official site. This link will always provide the very latest stable version, so don't worry if you're coming back to this project in a year or two's time; you don't need to change this command. The download is provided as an archive – specifically, a gzip-compressed Tar archive – which needs to be extracted with the following command:

```
sudo tar xvfz latest.tar.gz
```

This may take a short while, as there are a lot of files that need to be decompressed and installed in the web server's hosting directory. When the list of files has stopped scrolling and you've got your terminal back, use the following commands to set the file permissions correctly and delete the no longer required WordPress archive you downloaded:

```
sudo chown -R www-data
wordpress
sudo rm latest.tar.gz
```

CREATING THE DATABASE

WordPress stores almost everything, from the user accounts of its authors and guests to the content of posts themselves, in a database rather than as individual files. It's this use of a database that makes WordPress so flexible, but it does add an extra step to the configuration process compared with creating an old-fashioned static website.

To create a database for WordPress to store its files in, you'll need the password you set for the MySQL "root" user earlier. With that in mind, type the following to load the MySQL client software:

```
mysql -u root -p
```

You'll be prompted for the password; type it and press Enter to authenticate with the database and load the SQL prompt. This prompt is interactive, and is very specific about the syntax of its commands. When typing the following, make sure that you include the semicolon at the end of each line save for EXIT, or MySQL won't understand what you mean:

```
CREATE DATABASE pipress;
GRANT ALL PRIVILEGES
ON pipress.* to
'pipress'@'localhost'
IDENTIFIED BY 'password';
FLUSH PRIVILEGES;
```

Log into WordPress with your username and password.

HELLO WORLD!
APRIL 1, 2014
1 COMMENT
Welcome to WordPress. This is your first post. Edit or delete it, then start blogging!

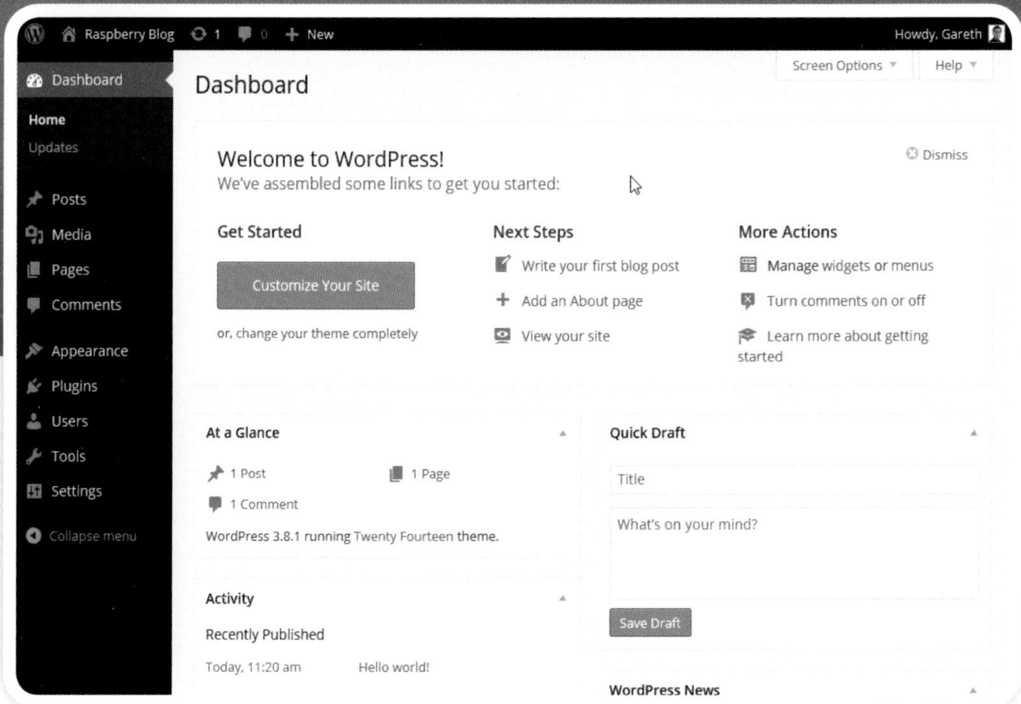


```
EXIT
```

These commands create a new database called "pipress" and a user with the same name, which has permission to read from and write to that database. You can, if you choose, increase the security of your site by choosing a different username and database name. If you do so, remember to swap out the names for your own when setting up WordPress. You should also change "password" to a long and secure password, separate to your user account or the password you chose for the "root" user. You won't need to remember this password once you've set up WordPress, so you can make it complex.

CONFIGURING WORDPRESS

The remainder of the WordPress installation process takes place within a web browser. Although it's possible to do this directly on the Pi, you'll find the installation goes faster if you connect to the Pi using a web browser on a separate system. This allows the Pi to concentrate on serving the website, rather than needing to spend time displaying it as well. To kick off the configuration process, visit the following URL in your web browser:

The first screen you're presented with is the Dashboard.

If prompted to create a WordPress configuration file, click the button.

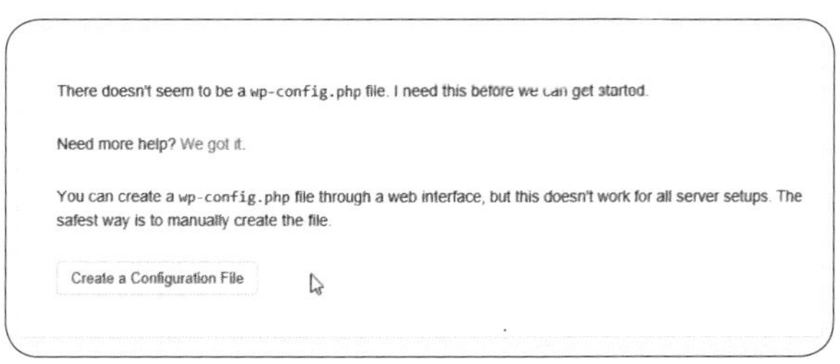

http://ip-address/wordpress/wp-admin/install.php

You'll be asked to supply the database name, username, password, host and table prefix of your MySQL WordPress installation. The name, username and password are all as you set when you created the database using MySQL. The database host should be "localhost", and you should change the table prefix – characters WordPress places at the start of any database tables it creates, to allow for more than one site on a single host – to something other than 'wp_' for security reasons. When you've filled in all the fields, press the Submit button.

There doesn't seem to be a wp-config.php file. I need this before we can get started.
Need more help? We got it.
You can create a wp-config.php file through a web interface, but this doesn't work for all server setups. The safest way is to manually create the file.
Create a Configuration File

With the database settings stored, WordPress loads its final configuration screen. Here, you'll be asked for the title of your site – which should be something descriptive of its contents – along with the username you'd like to use to administer WordPress. By default, this is "admin"; you should change it, as it's common for attackers to attempt to guess the password of default accounts. Pick a nickname or handle, or even just your first name, to improve the security of the site.

You'll also be asked for a password; this is one you'll actually have to remember, as it's the password with which you'll log into WordPress itself. Enter it twice, and pay attention to the strength indicator. If it says the password is weak, consider throwing in a few symbols like exclamation marks or percentage signs to improve security. Finally, enter your email address and choose whether or not you'd like search engines to be able to index the contents of your blog, should you choose to make it publicly accessible. Click the Install WordPress button, and the process is complete.

USING WORDPRESS

Logging into WordPress with the username and password you chose earlier, the first screen you're presented with is the Dashboard. This allows quick access to all the major features of WordPress, including managing photos and videos, pages, posts, and altering the appearance of your site. Before getting stuck in, however, you should run an update. Although the version of WordPress itself is the very latest available, some of the plugins that come bundled – such as Akimset, a plugin designed to reduce comment spam – are slightly outdated. Either click on Updates along the left-hand side, or click the

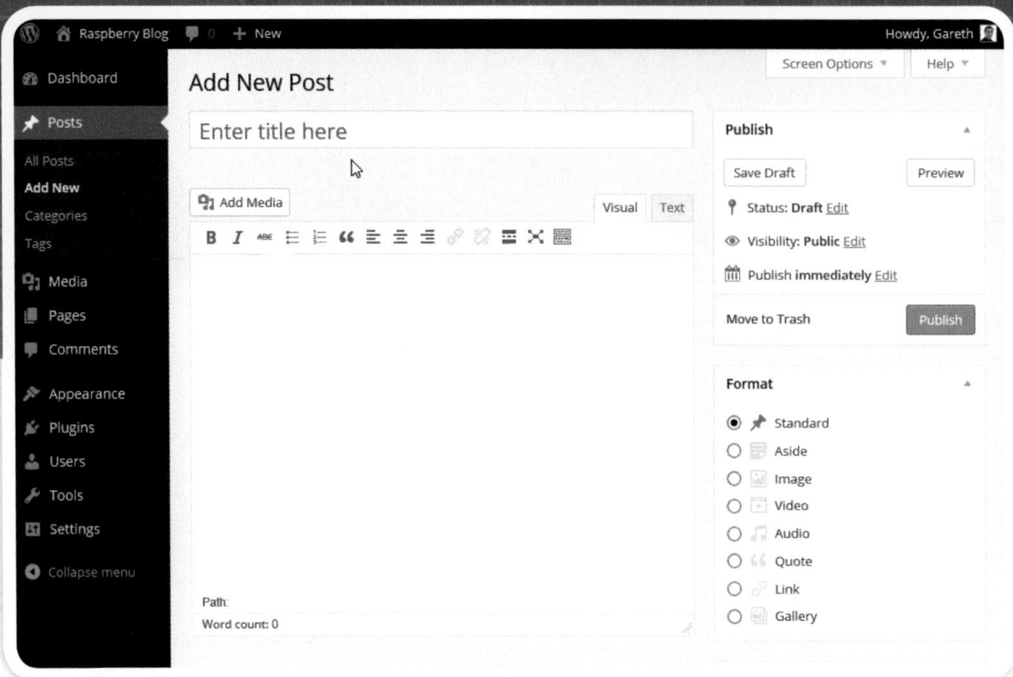

Here you can write a post and upload any supporting files.

If you want people to be able to access your website publicly, you'll need to forward a port from your router to the Pi

circular arrow icon across the top to view available updates.

WordPress handles its own security updates automatically, but updates for plugins and themes – add-ons that change the appearance or basic functionality of the site – need to be updated manually. To do so, scroll through the list of available updates – plugins and themes are found in separate sections – and tick the boxes next to each, or tick the box at the top or bottom of the list to select all available updates. When selected, click on Update Plugins or Update Themes to download and install the latest versions of each.

Once the update process is completed, you can begin using your site. Click the Posts option – or the plus icon at the top of the page – to begin writing a new post. Here, you can write the post and upload any supporting files such as photographs or screenshots you want to include. You don't need to resize the images before uploading. The PHP GD library you installed earlier is used by WordPress to automatically create a variety of different-sized thumbnail versions of any image you upload. Note that there is a file size limit, however: files larger than 2MB can't be uploaded by default and, while it's possible to change this restriction, doing so on a Pi is ill-advised due to its limited memory capacity.

The Appearance section, available from the left-hand menu, provides a range of settings for adjusting how your site appears. Themes can be downloaded and installed directly from the Appearance menu, and Widgets – boxes containing anything from a list of your tweets to a quick-find calendar of entries – add to the ease of navigation.

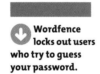

Wordfence locks out users who try to guess your password.

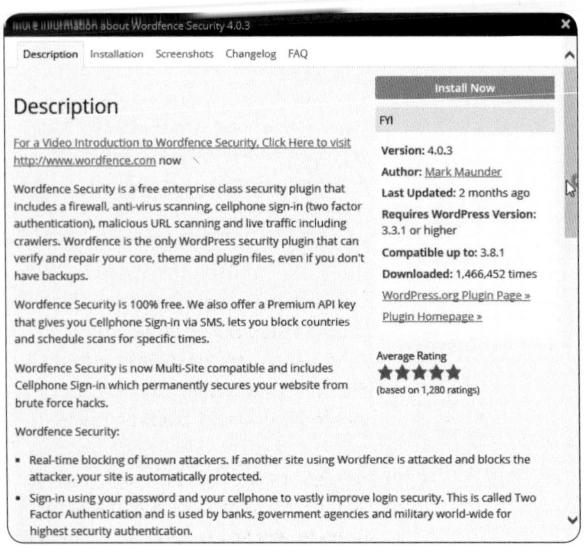

GOING LIVE

If you want people to be able to access your website publicly, you'll need to forward a port from your router to the Pi. Before you do, a warning: WordPress, as the most popular content management system in the world, is under constant attack. If your installation uses insecure passwords, it will almost certainly be hijacked to serve spam. The easiest way to avoid this is to ensure that your password is a secure mixture of letters, numbers and symbols, or a long yet memorable phrase. Another handy tool is the Wordfence plugin, available by searching in the Plugins menu, which can automatically lock out users who try to guess your password and can even be upgraded to support two-factor authentication via SMS for a subscription fee.

You may also want to consider installing a caching plugin. By default, WordPress doesn't store any of its pages directly on the server; instead, pages are generated dynamically for each visitor, based on content stored in the database. This is extremely flexible, but means that more than a handful of simultaneous users can overwhelm the Pi's limited resources. A caching plugin allows WordPress to save static versions of its pages, which are provided to users in place

3

TURN AN OLD TV INTO A SMART TV

Adding a Raspberry Pi to an existing TV set will give you all the capabilities of your average Smart TV at a fraction of the cost. Find out how

Give your TV a new lease of life and turn it into a Smart TV.

The Smart TV, with its built-in access to services like iPlayer and YouTube, is a tempting proposition for many, but replacing an entire TV just to gain extra features isn't a great idea. Thankfully, the technology that goes into turning a TV into a Smart TV is almost identical to the technology on which the Pi was based. Its processor, in fact, was originally developed for multimedia set-top boxes.

WHAT YOU'LL NEED

The majority of the features of a Smart TV, whether Pi-based or not, require internet access. As a result, users of Raspberry Pi Model As will need to add a USB network adapter to get the most out of this project. You'll also need a USB storage device for adding BBC iPlayer support.

You may need some additional cables: a standard HDMI cable (from 99p, ebay.co.uk) will connect the Pi to an HDTV for both audio and video, but using the Pi with an older CRT set will require a composite video cable and a 3.5mm-to-RCA audio cable (from 99p each, ebay.co.uk). You may also need an adapter that takes RCA connections and converts them to SCART if your TV doesn't have dedicated inputs (from 50p, ebay.co.uk).

Lastly, a case (from £2.50, ebay.co.uk) is a sound investment for a Pi that's going to spend its time sat in your living room. Without it, the Pi does look a little industrial for most tastes.

Adding a Pi to an existing TV set gives it all the capabilities of your average Smart TV at a fraction of the cost, and with none of the environmental concerns of disposing of a perfectly good TV set. Better still, it can even be used to get a new lease of life from older CRT-based TV sets – great for adding to a bedroom or kitchen.

CONNECTING THE PI

The Pi includes video and audio connectivity suitable for most TV sets. If you own a modern Full HD or HD Ready TV, or an AV receiver with HDMI inputs, you can simply connect a single HDMI cable to the Pi. This carries a digital video signal at resolutions as high as 1,920 × 1,080 – also known as 1080p or Full HD – as well as digital audio. The Pi can't, however, use the Ethernet functionality of some HDMI systems; you'll still need a dedicated network cable, or a USB wireless adapter.

If you have an older TV, you can still use all the features of the Pi – just at a lower resolution. You'll need to see if your TV has round RCA connectors on its rear that look like the one on the top edge of the Pi. These will be coloured yellow for video, and white and red for audio on stereo sets, or just a single white or red connector for monaural sets. If you don't have RCA connectors on your TV, but you do have a rectangular SCART connection, you can buy a low-cost adapter that will accept the RCA cables from the Pi.

In either case, older TV sets need a separate cable for audio. While this is carried alongside video on HDMI, the composite video lead carries only images. The Pi's analogue audio output is a 3.5mm jack, as used on the majority of portable audio devices. To

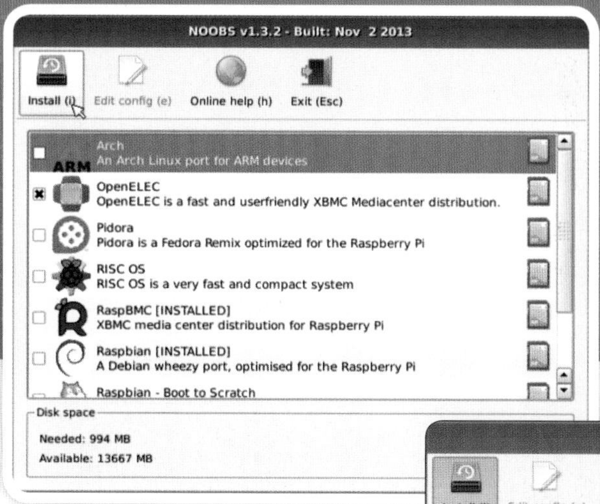

The most popular Smart TV software for the Pi is OpenElec.

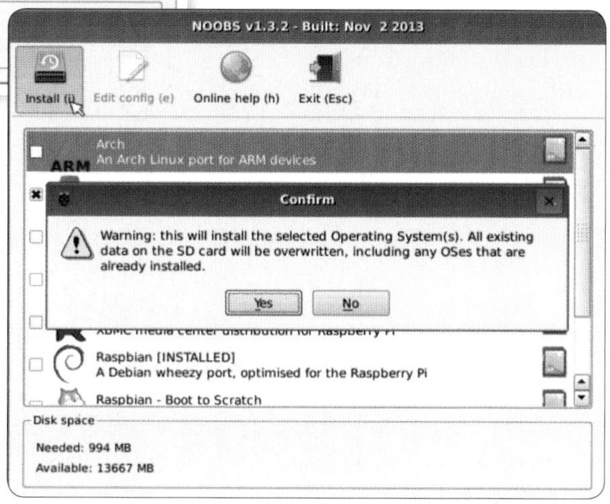

NOOBS wipes anything already stored on the SD card.

connect this to a TV, SCART adapter or AV receiver, you'll need an extra cable: a 3.5mm to RCA adapter. This has a single 3.5mm connector at one end, which plugs into the Pi's audio output next to the composite video connector, and a pair of RCA connectors at the other.

When the Pi is connected to the TV, you'll also need to ensure it's connected to a network and power source. If you have a recent TV, it's possible that it has a USB socket on its rear or side. Don't be tempted to use this to power the Pi, as it's unlikely to provide enough current and will cause glitches or simply fail to work. Instead, use a dedicated power supply for the Pi.

INSTALLING OPENELEC

The most popular Smart TV software for the Pi is a specialised Linux distribution called OpenElec. Also available on other platforms, and preinstalled on home theatre hardware, OpenElec is designed specifically for playing back video and audio files, either from local storage or across a network. It uses Xbmc as its front end, which started life as an unofficial media-centric add-on for Microsoft's original Xbox console, but has since grown into an impressive piece of cross-platform software.

The easiest way to install OpenElec is to do so using NOOBS. If you haven't already installed NOOBS on an SD card, flick back to the chapter on using NOOBS and do so. If you have, you can connect the Pi to power and hold down the Shift key to enter NOOBS' recovery mode.

Installing a new operating system, or reinstalling an existing operating system, via NOOBS wipes anything that's already stored on the SD card. This is true even if you're choosing to install an operating system already present. Anything stored within that operating system, such as files you've saved or non-standard programs you've installed, will be lost. Before continuing, make sure you've taken a copy of anything you want to keep from your SD card or use a fresh SD card instead.

In the NOOBS screen, tick the box next to OpenElec to select it for installation. Confirm that you're happy for the SD card to be overwritten, and wait a few minutes for the software to install. When you see the message that OpenElec has installed successfully, click OK to reboot the Pi and load OpenElec.

When OpenElec loads into its homescreen, wait a minute or two and a setup wizard will appear. Choose your language on the first screen, and click Next. You'll be asked to give the OpenElec installation a name. If you're only planning on installing one Smart TV on your home network, you can leave the name as OpenElec; otherwise, give each Pi its own unique name and click Next again.

The next screen of the wizard will confirm that OpenElec can access your network. If you see an error here, check that the network cable is properly connected to the Pi and to the router or switch, and check it for damage along its length. When OpenElec confirms the network is ready, click Next.

Finally, OpenElec will give you two choices for remote administration services: SSH and Samba. The latter, enabled by default, allows you to browse files held on your Pi over the network. The former, disabled by default, allows you to load a terminal and perform custom maintenance or install your own software. If you choose to enable SSH, remember to

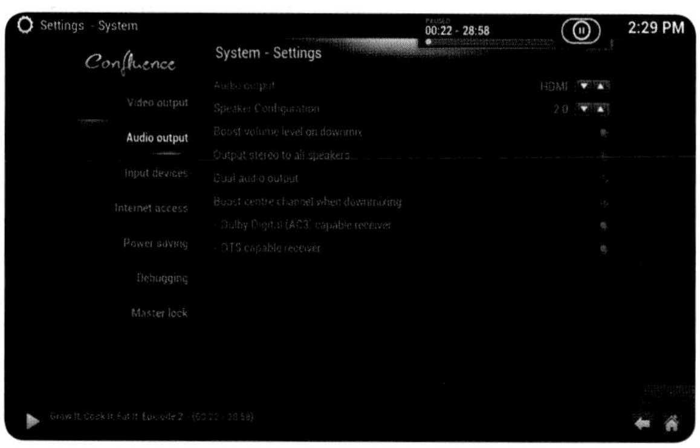

For most users, the defaults here should suffice.

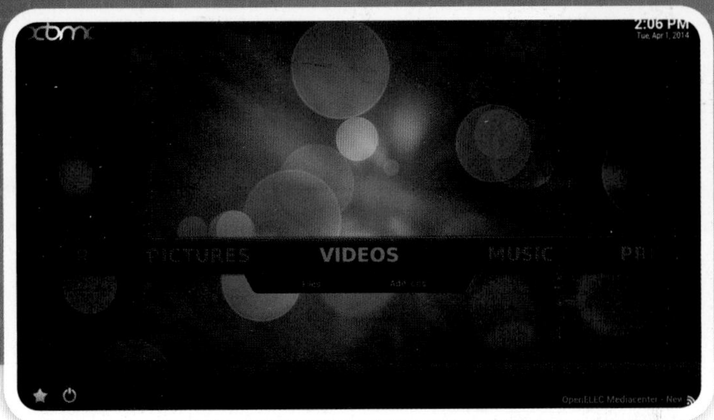

change the password – using the "passed" command – from the default of "openelec" to remain secure. Click Next twice to close the wizard.

CONFIGURING OPENELEC

OpenElec is a user-friendly yet powerful package, and it needs a little bit of tweaking once installed. Your first port of call should be the System menu, accessible by moving your mouse to the right of the menu bar or by pressing the right arrow key on the keyboard until it appears. Click System, then click Settings to bring up the main configuration menu.

In the Video Output section of this menu, which opens by default, you can choose the resolution at which OpenElec should run. This is frequently set to 1,920 × 1,080i by default, an interlaced mode that updates only half the screen at a time. When things move quickly, this is visible as the picture breaking up into visible bars running across the screen. Clicking the down arrow next to the resolution once will set OpenElec to 1,920 × 1,080p, a progressive mode that offers improved picture clarity. If you're using the Pi's composite output, however, you'll be restricted in which modes you can choose; leaving the resolution menu alone is well advised here.

The Audio Output menu is your next port of call. For most users, the defaults here should suffice. If you're using the Pi's 3.5mm audio connector, however, you'll want to click the down arrow next to HDMI on the Audio Output section or the Pi will default to sending all audio via the HDMI cable. Additional settings, including configuring the keyboard and mouse, setting a proxy for OpenElec's internet connectivity, or allowing the Pi to go into a power-saving mode when not it use, can be explored in the menu at the left-hand side. When you're finished, click the Home icon at the bottom-right of the screen or press the Escape key on the keyboard to return to the main screen.

The main user interface of OpenElec, Xbmc, is controlled via the central bar. Here, you can choose the type of media you want to view: videos, pictures, music and so on. At the moment, however, you haven't got anything to watch. You could, if you wanted, connect an external hard drive or a USB flash drive with media on it and play that. Alternatively, you can explore the network features of OpenElec.

To connect OpenElec to a network media source, such as a Universal Plug and Play (UPnP) server running on a NAS box, smartphone or tablet, click on the type of media – such as Music – and then Files. You'll be given the option to Add Source; click this, then click Browse. OpenElec supports numerous different network protocols, including Windows SMB and Unix NFS. For UPnP, just click the UPnP Devices option followed by OK.

You'll be given a list of active UPnP devices on your network. Choose one from the list and click OK to load it into the path box on the previous screen. Click OK again, and it will become a permanent choice for loading media. Just click on the name of the server to browse its files and stream music, videos or pictures.

For non-local sources, click the Video option in the menu bar, then the Get More option. This will load a list of all the video-related add-on software that can be downloaded and installed in OpenElec. Browse

OpenElec supports numerous network protocols.

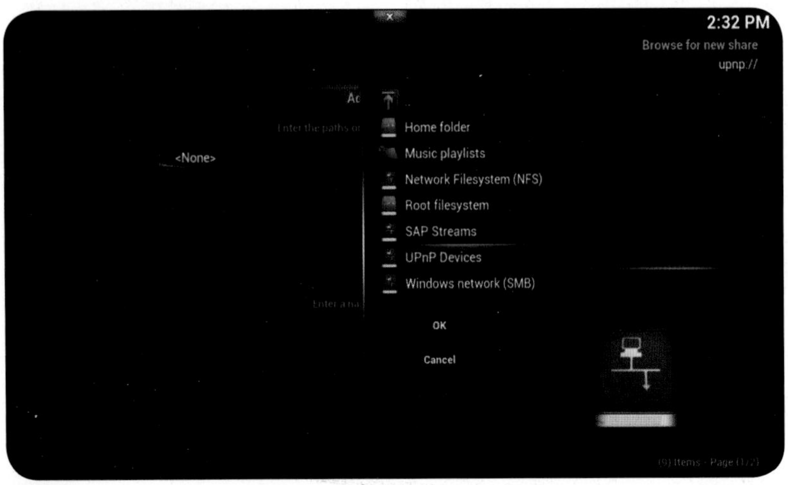

You'll get a list of active UPnP devices on your network.

For iPlayer support, download it manually.

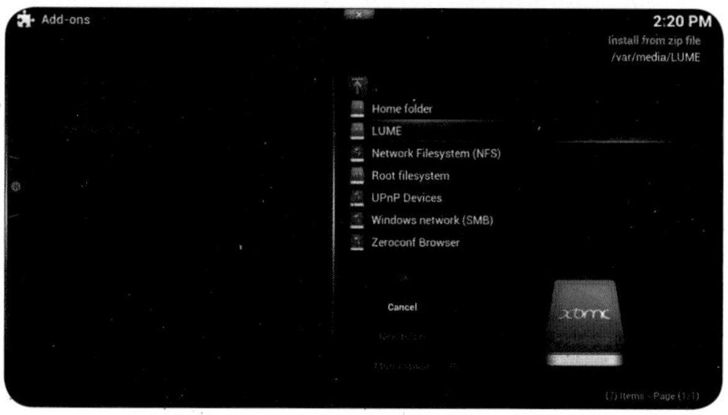

Find the newest version of the iPlayer plugin.

the list, and click on any entries that take your fancy. Near the bottom, as an example, is YouTube. Clicking this and choosing Install will allow you to stream YouTube videos from the Add-Ons menu. Similar add-ons are available from the Music and Pictures menus, too.

INSTALLING IPLAYER

Some add-ons don't appear in the main list, however, and need to be found separately. One such add-on is for the BBC's iPlayer catch-up TV service. To install iPlayer support, you need to download it manually. Load a web browser on your PC, and visit the following site: **code.google.com/p/xbmc-iplayerv2/downloads/list**

Find the newest version of the iPlayer plugin – version 2.5.4 at the time of writing – and click on the filename. Click on the name of the file on the next screen, and choose Save when prompted to download the file. When the download has completed, click Open Folder and insert your USB storage device into the PC.

The iPlayer plugin is a ZIP archive, but you don't want to extract it; instead, drag the whole file across to the storage device. When the copy has finished, eject the drive and insert it into one of the Pi's USB ports. If you're using both ports for a keyboard and mouse, disconnect the keyboard temporarily to make room.

Go into any Add-Ons menu on the Pi, and click the ".." symbol at the top of the list. Keep doing so until you get to a screen that includes the option to Install from ZIP File. Click this, then find your USB storage device in the list on the right-hand side of the screen. Click the drive, and click the iPlayer ZIP file you downloaded. Click the OK button to install the add-on from the drive. When a message appears in the bottom-right of the screen telling you the add-on has been installed, you can click the Home icon and remove the USB storage device.

If you go back into the Videos menu and choose Add-Ons, you should find an option for iPlayer. Click this, and you'll be able to choose from the various categories and channels on offer, or search for a programme you've missed. Click on an episode of any listed program, and it will begin streaming over the internet.

For more information on using OpenElec, including how to use non-media add-on programs like the built-in web browser or the weather forecast facility, visit the official site at **wiki.openelec.tv**

MINECRAFT: PI EDITION

Minecraft: Pi Edition is a cut-down version of the game for the Pi with a hidden feature: an API that players can access to alter the game world

Mojang's Minecraft, a game in which the player is given the task of building whatever he or she wants from blocks of varying materials, is little short of a cultural phenomenon. From its origins as a virtually unknown indie game to its present status as one of the world's best-selling titles – nearly 15 million copies at the time of writing – Minecraft has been ported from the PC to smartphones, tablets, consoles and even inspired a LEGO kit. It was inevitable, really, that it would come to the Pi.

WHAT YOU'LL NEED

Minecraft: Pi Edition is designed to work on any Raspberry Pi, and once the files are downloaded – which you can do on a desktop PC, transferring them via USB storage – it doesn't require an internet connection. As a result, it's well-suited to use on a low-cost Model A, although the extra memory available to Model B users can help performance, especially if you're writing complex programs that interact with the API.

Gameplay is controlled via keyboard and mouse, so if you're running Minecraft: Pi Edition on a Model A you'll need either a USB hub or a combination keyboard and pointing device that takes up a single USB port.

Minecraft: Pi Edition was developed by Aron Nieminen and Daniel Frisk. A cut-down version of the game designed specifically for the Pi, based on the work already carried out on the mobile release, the Pi release works perfectly as an introduction to the game. Players can explore randomly generated worlds, digging and using construction mode to build their own creations.

There's a hidden feature of Minecraft: Pi Edition, however: an application programming interface (API) that can be accessed using Python, the programming language of choice for the Raspberry Pi Foundation. Using the API, players can alter the game world in a variety of ways: they can teleport the player miles into the air, or deep underground, they can receive in-game alerts when an email comes in or a certain amount of play time has elapsed; they can even create interactive sculptures such as working clocks or automatic bridges. Some intrepid coders have even linked Minecraft: Pi Edition to the real world, creating a physical door lock that only releases when a certain pattern of blocks is placed in the game.

As well as being an amusing diversion in its own right, Minecraft: Pi Edition is a great way to get kids learning the art of programming, without them even realising.

INSTALLING MINECRAFT

Minecraft: Pi Edition isn't supplied with any of the operating systems available on the Pi as standard software, and nor is it available through the Apt package manager of Raspbian. To install it, you'll need to download the archive manually. Load the graphical user interface on your Pi, if it isn't already loaded, with the following terminal command:

```
startx
```

When the GUI has loaded, double-click the Midori icon on the desktop to load a web browser. Visit **pi.minecraft.net**, and find the word "download" in blue; this is the link to download the software archive. Click it and, when Midori prompts for what it should do with the file, choose Open.

The archive will open in a separate window, with a single folder visible: "mcpi". Click the Extract icon at the top of the window, or choose Extract from the Actions menu, and type this path into the Extract To box:

```
/home/pi/
```

Click Extract, and the contents of the archive will be placed in a folder within the user Pi's home directory called "mcpi". You can then click the cross at the top-right of the archive and browser windows to close them; you wont need them, or an internet connection, from this point on.

RUNNING MINECRAFT

Installing Minecraft: Pi Edition doesn't create a shortcut on the desktop or in the Applications menu. To run it, you need to browse to the directory where it was extracted. Click on the software menu at the bottom-left of the screen, and scroll to Accessories. Click on File Manager to browse the files stored on the Pi's

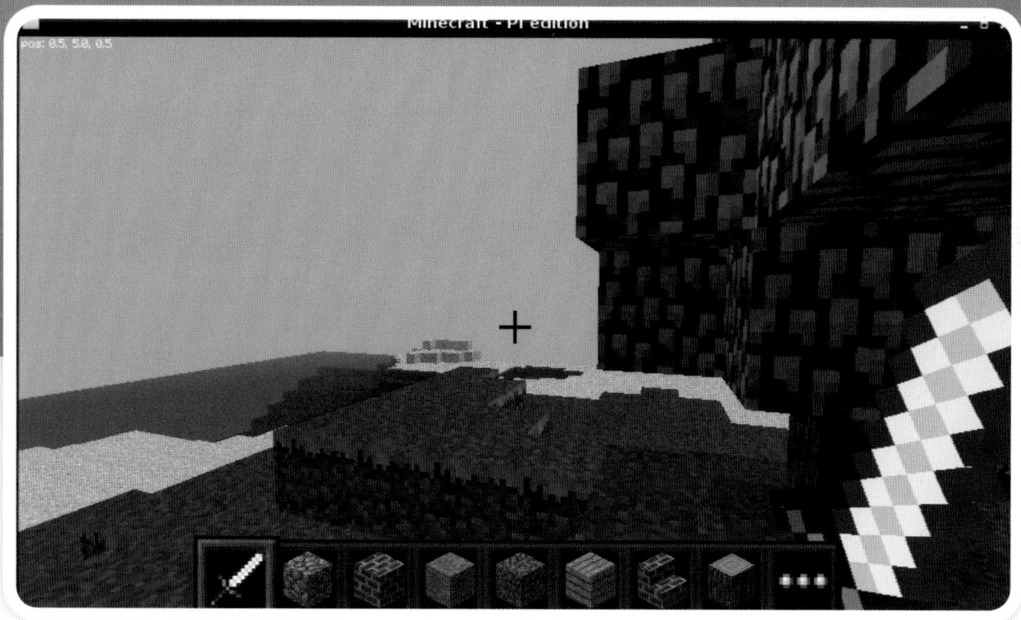

You have an unlimited supply of all the block types.

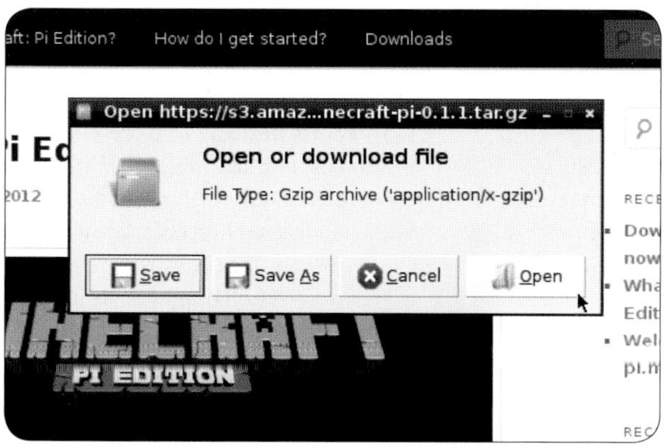

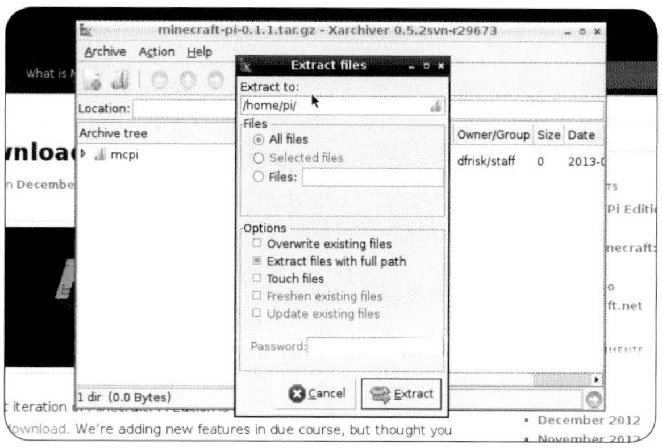

To install, you need to download the archive manually.

SD card, then double-click on the "mcpi" directory. Find the file called "minecraft-pi" in this folder and double-click it. In the pop-up dialog, choose Execute to run the game.

Minecraft loads on the Pi in a window at the centre of the screen. Although it's possible to maximise the window in order to run full-screen, it's not advised. Doing so makes the mouse difficult to control, due to bugs in the low-level way Minecraft: Pi Edition accesses the Pi's hardware. To begin exploring the world of Minecraft, click Start Game. This will take you to the world selection screen. At the moment, it's blank, as this is the first time you've run the game. Click Create New to start a new world.

Each world in Minecraft: Pi Edition is generated at random; the world you generate now is statistically unlikely to have the same layout as a world you generate tomorrow. When you next run the game, you'll be able to choose your existing world, create a brand-new world, or delete an existing one. Minecraft worlds retain whatever you create in them; if you build a house in Minecraft: Pi Edition and delete that world, you'll lose the house, too.

The world generation process takes a while on the Pi due to its relatively slow processor compared to the platforms for which Minecraft was originally written. Don't worry if the progress bar on the world generation screen appears to pause; you'll soon be placed into your unique world.

PLAYING MINECRAFT

Minecraft is controlled using the keyboard and mouse, in a way that will be familiar to players of first-person shooters. The player character can be moved using the W, A, S and D keys, while the viewpoint is shifted using the mouse. One peculiarity of the Minecraft controls is the ability to fly: a single press of Space will jump, as in any other game, but a double-tap will begin flight. While flying, pressing Space will increase your altitude, and pressing Shift will decrease your altitude.

In Minecraft: Pi Edition, the need to mine is removed; you have an unlimited supply of all the block types available in the game. This makes it a great way to experiment with building structures, free from the constraints of what in the main game is known as "Survival Mode". The blocks available are displayed along the bottom of the window; the

To begin exploring the world of Minecraft, click Start Game.

block you have currently active can be altered using the mouse wheel or keys 1 to 8. Pressing the E key will bring up a list of all the blocks available in the game; you can then swap these for the ones currently in your inventory.

Although Minecraft is far from a simulation, different blocks have different effects. A block of wood placed near a hot block of lava will set the wood on fire, for example. Using these interactions, it's possible to build complex interactive creations. The main fun of Minecraft is in experimentation, however, so you'll have to learn about all the ways the blocks can be combined yourself!

You can destroy blocks – including those that make up trees – by centring them in your view and pressing the left mouse button. This works even if you aren't holding one of the "tool" objects, like the iron sword. You can also hold the mouse button and swipe the mouse to delete a swathe of blocks. New blocks are placed with the right mouse button in a similar manner. The Escape key takes you back to the menu, and allows you to return to the main menu, where you can quit altogether by clicking the X at the top-right or pressing Alt+F4.

HACKING MINECRAFT

There's plenty to keep you amused in the main game of Minecraft, but the true flexibility of the Pi Edition comes from its API. A unique feature of the Pi release, the API was designed to make it easy to control the game world from external programs, encouraging kids to learn coding through play.

The API can be accessed from a variety of languages, but the most common is Python. This is a popular language for beginners, and the language chosen by the Raspberry Pi Foundation to support its educational aims. To begin writing a Minecraft-linked program, you'll first have to access the software development kit (SDK). It's best to create a copy outside the main Minecraft directory to do this. That way, any changes you make in the name of experimentation won't harm the main game. Double-click the LXTerminal icon on the desktop and type the following commands:

Each world in Minecraft is generated at random.

```
mkdir ~/minecraftcode
cp -r ~/mcpi/api/python/mcpi
~/minecraftcode/minecraft
```

The first command makes a new directory called "minecraft code" in your home folder, where you can store your projects. The second creates a copy of the SDK in a way that makes it accessible to your software. Next, you need to create a blank project file for your code. You can do this in any text editor, but it's easiest to use the IDLE Python integrated development environment. This includes features like syntax highlighting and the ability to directly run your code, which are missing from most text editors. To load it, double-click the IDLE icon on the desktop. Make sure it's IDLE and not IDLE 3; the latter uses a subtly different version of the Python language, which is, as yet, incompatible with the Minecraft SDK.

In the Python Shell window that appears, click the File menu and choose New Window. Before you begin any work, click the File menu and again, and choose Save As. Browse to your "minecraftcode" directory and save the file as "testing.py". Make sure you save the file in "minecraftcode" and not the "minecraft" sub-directory, or your program won't work.

The IDLE IDE works much like a normal text editor, except that it understands how Python programs should appear. As a result, it colours in sections according to their use, shows which brackets are matched, and even automatically indents certain lines – a key part of Python syntax. To start your program, you need to type the following line:

```
#!/usr/bin/env python
```

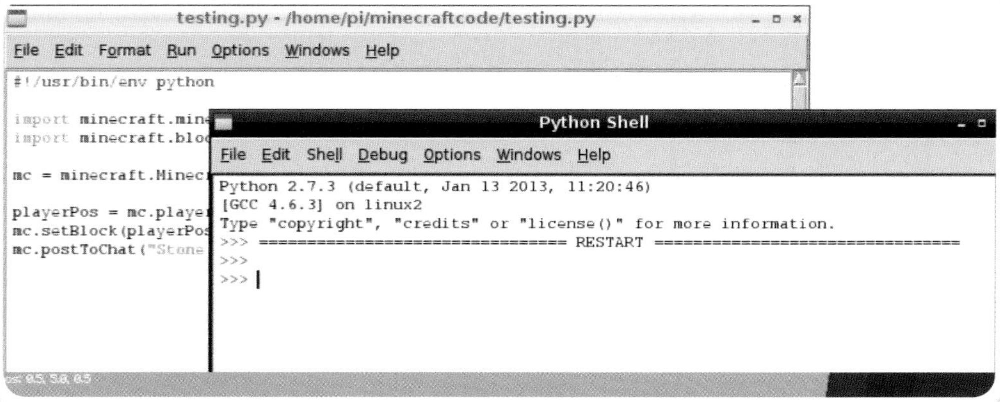

This is known as the "shebang line" – so named for the hash and exclamation mark, or "bang", at the start – and lets the Pi know that the program you're writing should be run through the Python interpreter. This line isn't strictly necessary for writing code in IDLE, but if you later want to distribute your creation as a standalone file it will make life easier. Next, import two of the main functions from the Minecraft API:

```
import minecraft.minecraft
as minecraft
import minecraft.block as
block
```

These two instructions tell Python to load functions from libraries included with the Minecraft SDK. These libraries control how Python should communicate with Minecraft, and how to control the in-game environment through the creation and deletion of blocks. Libraries are code fragments that perform common tasks, and are frequently used in programming. There's no point writing something like a way of tracking elapsed time from scratch every time you need it.

Next, you'll need to set up the connection to Minecraft in a way that minimises typing. Enter this line:

```
mc = minecraft.Minecraft.
create()
```

This takes the instructions for controlling Minecraft from Python – the awkward statement to the right of the equals symbol – and converts it to the simple "mc". Every time you need your program to do something in Minecraft, you can just start your command with "mc" instead of having to type out the whole thing.

Using Python to control Minecraft is very powerful.

As an example of what the Minecraft API allows you to do from Python, type in this simple program:

```
player.Pos = mc.player.
getTilePos()
mc.setBlock(playerPos.x+1,
playerPos.y+1, playerPos.z,
block.STONE)
mc.postToChat("Stone block
created.")
```

The first instruction gets the player's current position, accurate to the nearest block. The second creates a new stone block, at the position specified in the brackets. The positioning is relative to the player. The block will be placed on the player's level as specified by the Z coordinate, but shifted one block along the X and Y coordinates. Creating a stone block at the exact same location as the player wouldn't be good for his or her health, after all.

The final line uses the in-game chat functionality, originally designed for multiplayer gaming, to post a message confirming that the block has been created. It's a convenient way of checking that the program is working correctly. Because the block might not be created in the direction the player is facing, it provides immediate feedback that the Python program can communicate with Minecraft correctly.

Save the file from the File menu, and load Minecraft. Enter into a world, then press Alt+Tab to change your focus back to the IDLE window. You may need to drag the Minecraft window out of the way by clicking and holding on the title bar at the top to see what you're doing. Because of the way Minecraft uses the Pi's graphics hardware, it will always appear on top of any other windows.

In IDLE, click the Run menu and choose Run Module or press F5. A Python Shell window will appear, which will show you any error messages caused by missing libraries or mistyped commands, and after a few seconds you should see the message "Stone block created" printed in the Minecraft window. If you click on the title bar of the Minecraft window to return its focus, then click within Minecraft itself, you'll regain control of the game. Look around, and you'll see your stone block.

Using Python to control Minecraft is extremely powerful, with flexibility that puts it beyond the scope of this short project. The best way to learn is to experiment, and to investigate code that others have written. Try the following sites and tutorials to learn more:

www.themagpi.com/issue/issue-11/article/minecraft-pi-edition/

www.stuffaboutcode.com/2013/04/minecraft-pi-edition-api-tutorial.html

mcpipy.wordpress.com

RETRO GAMING EMULATION

Paired with a classic joystick, it's easy to transform your Raspberry Pi into a retro gaming system using emulation. We show you how

While the games of today are multimillion-pound affairs created by teams of hundreds, and with graphics designed to mimic the real world as closely as possible, that wasn't always the case. In the early days of computing, games couldn't rely on special effects and orchestral scores to impress. Instead, they used simple yet effective gameplay techniques to lure users in, often with great success.

It should be no surprise, then, that vintage gaming is a popular hobby. Whether it's driven by nostalgia or curiosity, people spend thousands filling entire rooms with the computers, consoles and peripherals of yesteryear.

There is an alternative, however: emulation. The machines of the past – particularly those that were around in the 1970s and 1980s – were so simple compared to modern computers that even the humble Raspberry Pi dwarfs their capabilities. As a result, it becomes possible to turn a Pi into wide range of classic gaming machines – functionally, if not aesthetically – without having to dedicate storage space to the hobby.

INSTALLING RETROPIE

The easiest way to start playing vintage games on the Raspberry Pi is to install RetroPie, a bundle of emulators and supporting software coded specifically for the Pi's hardware. As with any Raspberry Pi project, the first step is always to make sure that you're running the most recent versions of all software packages by typing the following commands at the terminal:

```
sudo apt-get update
sudo apt-get upgrade
```

When the upgrade process is complete, you'll need to install some supporting software followed by the script that actually downloads and installs RetroPie itself using the following commands:

```
sudo apt-get install dialog
git clone git://github.com/
petrockblog/RetroPie-Setup.
git
```

The second command uses a tool called Git, which is designed for collaborative programming and version control. It lets users store multiple versions of source code files in a central repository, and download any version at any given time, allowing mistakes to be quickly reverted. It's a very powerful utility, but here it's used simply to download the latest RetroPie setup script created by PetRockBlog.com. The installation process can then be kicked off with the following two commands:

```
cd RetroPie-Setup
sudo bash retropie-setup.sh
```

The script will present you with a menu, of which the top two choices are of interest at present. The first

WHAT YOU'LL NEED

The main attraction of emulation is that you don't need any of the original hardware in order to do it – simply a computer sufficiently powerful enough to translate the instructions expected of the classic code into those used by modern machines. As a result, any Raspberry Pi – Model A or Model B – with a keyboard and mouse is more than enough to get started, although installing the software itself will require an active internet connection, and you'll need a large SD card – 8GB or more – to store all the files.

The experience does become more enjoyable when paired with some classic control systems, however. A USB adapter (from £20, ebay.co.uk) that converts the nine-pin plug of most joysticks from the eight-bit era – including those used by Commodore and Atari – into a connection suitable for the Raspberry Pi is a sound investment.

Alternatively, most PC USB joysticks and gamepads will be detected by the Pi and work just fine for gaming. Avoid those with rumble or force feedback features, as these require more power and typically work only when connected to a Windows system. The same applies to any joysticks that boast programmability, which again largely rely on Windows-only drivers to operate.

A shareware version of Doom is available to test emulation.

option downloads and installs precompiled binaries of all the software used to make RetroPie. The second downloads the source code for the software and compiles it on the Pi itself. The advantage to the second approach is that you're always guaranteed to receive the latest versions of all software, which may include performance improvements and better stability, but installation will take upwards of 20 hours to complete. The more common first option downloads precompiled binaries, which may not represent the latest version of each package, but that does take a lot less time to install.

Choose one of the first two options with the cursor keys and confirm with Enter. When you've made your choice, regardless of which option you pick, be prepared for a wait. RetroPie is a comprehensive collection of all the most popular emulators for the Raspberry Pi. This makes it supremely flexible: using just one tool, you can have your Pi emulate everything from a Commodore VIC-20 to a 1990s arcade cabinet. Sadly, it also means that there's a considerable amount of data to download and install. It's not uncommon for the binary installation process to take upwards of an hour on even a fast SD card and overclocked Pi.

When the installation has completed, a message will appear onscreen telling you where you can find the installation logs. You only need to look at these in the event that something has gone wrong. Press Enter to confirm the message, then after a few moments you'll be returned to the main installation menu. Scroll down to the Perform Reboot option with the cursor keys, and press Enter to restart the Pi and complete the installation.

OBTAINING ROM FILES

The emulation scene has always had an air of illegitimacy about it. So-called ROMs, named after the read-only memory chips used to store the games on cartridge-based consoles, are often found being traded on underground sites with little regard to copyright. Unlike film and music piracy, however, there's a generally held belief that there's nothing morally wrong with sharing, copying and downloading ROM files for systems and games that are long out of production, frequently from companies that no longer exist.

The law, however, is clear: copying commercial software is a crime, with no exceptions for so-called "abandonware". This leaves the emulation enthusiast in a bit of a sticky situation when it comes to finding things to actually emulate. Some believe that owning an original copy of the software in question – a cartridge for a Nintendo Entertainment System, for example, or a board from an arcade

Most PC USB joysticks and gamepads will be detected by the Pi.

A shareware version of Duke Nukem 3D is included with RetroPie.

The easiest way to play vintage games on the Pi is to install RetroPie.

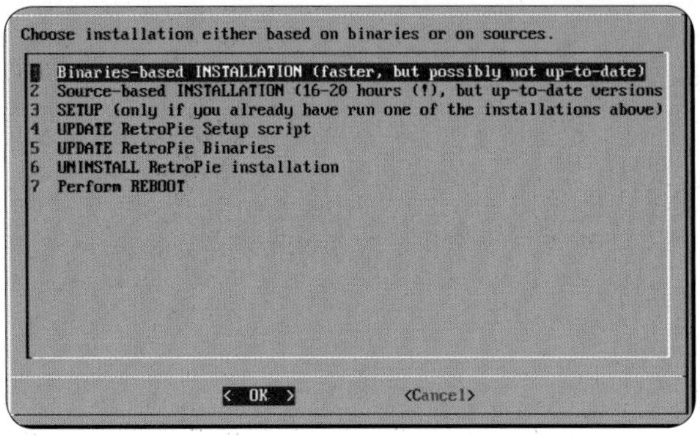

Choose installation either based on binaries or on sources.
1 Binaries-based INSTALLATION (faster, but possibly not up-to-date)
2 Source-based INSTALLATION (16-20 hours (!), but up-to-date versions)
3 SETUP (only if you already have run one of the installations above)
4 UPDATE RetroPie Setup script
5 UPDATE RetroPie Binaries
6 UNINSTALL RetroPie installation
7 Perform REBOOT
< OK >
<Cancel>

The more common first option takes less time to install.

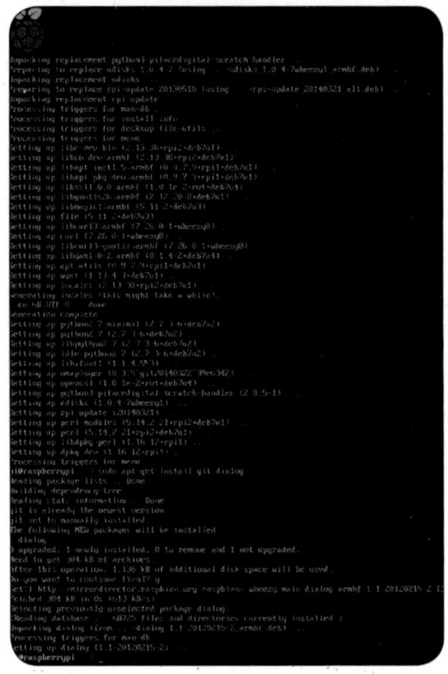

cabinet – is grounds enough to be able to download ROM files for personal use. Others believe that as long as the company behind the software isn't attempting to still profit from its sale, the seemingly abandoned software is now fair game – a perilous assumption, given the current trend for classic titles to be dusted off, given touchscreen-friendly controls and re-released on tablets and smartphones.

There are perfectly legitimate ways to use the emulation capabilities of your Pi that don't come with an

Even today, coders are creating games for systems the mainstream market had long since abandoned

implied threat of legal action from a company that may have quietly bought the rights to software you thought was abandoned: the homebrew scene. Even today, coders are creating games for systems the mainstream market had long since abandoned, like the Sinclair ZX81 with its tiny 1KB of memory – less than a 500,000th the RAM available to a Raspberry Pi Model B Revision 2 board. Better still, manufacturers of classic systems have sometimes given their permission for the software that drove their computers and consoles to be distributed publicly so long as no attempt is made to profit from that distribution.

One such platform is the Sinclair ZX Spectrum, a low-cost colour computer built for the home market by Sinclair Computers in 1982. The follow-up to the well-received Sinclair ZX81, the Spectrum introduced sound, colour graphics and a choice of 16KB or 48KB of RAM. It proved a popular choice in the UK, but lost out internationally to the more powerful – but significantly more expensive – Commodore 64.

When Amstrad bought the rights to the Sinclair ZX Spectrum, it obtained all copyrights on the ROM-based operating system that drove the machine. Following the demise of the Spectrum and the growth of emulation, the company was contacted to confirm whether or not it was happy for emulator writers to include ROM images for the Spectrum for public use. "Amstrad are happy for emulator writers to include images of our copyrighted code as long as the copyright messages are not altered," Amstrad's Cliff Lawson explained in a public message to the comp.sys.sinclair newsgroup in 1999, "and we appreciate it if the program/manual includes a note to the effect that 'Amstrad have kindly given their permission for the redistribution of their copyrighted material but retain that copyright'."

Since that release, the Spectrum copyright has changed hands once again and now resides with satellite broadcaster Sky. Thus far, the company has shown no interest in rescinding the rights for the ROM files to be distributed with emulation software, so long as no charge is

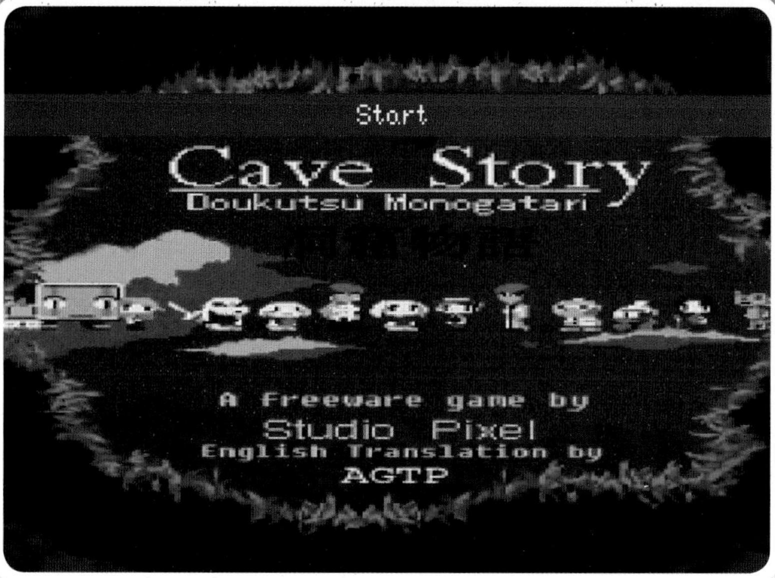

RetroPie also includes a freeware version of Cave Story.

levied for said software. While the copyright status of other systems of a similar vintage may be vague, Spectrum fans can rejoice in knowing they can emulate their system with a clear conscience.

RetroPie comes with the system ROMs required for each of the systems it can emulate preinstalled. In the case of the Spectrum and selected other systems, this is with the permission of the original copyright holder; in other cases, it is not. It also comes with a small selection of free and shareware games to test the emulation with, including an Apple][emulator, the shareware versions of Doom and Duke Nukem 3D, and the freeware version of Cave Story.

If you want to install your own games, the ROM, disk or tape images are kept in a subfolder called "roms". List the contents of the folder at the terminal with this command:

```
ls ~/RetroPie/roms/
```

This will provide an overview of the machines that RetroPie is capable of emulating. Games for each system should be placed into their respective directories. If you already own the original cassettes, disks or cartridges for a given game, it's general considered acceptable – morally, if not strictly speaking legally – to download a ROM from the web; these are readily accessible to most search engines. There also exists a thriving community of homebrew coders who create modern games for vintage systems. Their titles are typically available to download free of charge, and are a great way to play some classic games without falling foul of copyright law.

To get started, try downloading the free platformer Dogmole Tuppowski for the ZX Spectrum 128K using the following commands:

```
cd ~/RetroPie/roms/
zxspectrum
wget http://www.mojontwins.
com/colegas/jarlaxe--
dogmole-
tuppowski-the-new-
adventures.
zip
unzip jarlaxe--dogmole-
tuppowski-the-new-
adventures.
zip
rm jarlaxe--dogmole-
tuppowski-the-new-
adventures.
zip
```

FIXING SPECTRUM EMULATION

Sadly, while RetroPie is by far the easiest way to set up the Pi for emulation duties, it's far from perfect. The Spectrum emulation, in particular, is rather broken, but

```
= = = = = = = = = = = = = = = = = = = = =
Updating APT-GET database
= = = = = = = = = = = = = = = = = = = = =

Hit http://raspberrypi.collabora.com wheezy Release.gpg
Hit http://archive.raspberrypi.org wheezy Release.gpg
Hit http://mirrordirector.raspbian.org wheezy Release.gpg
Hit http://raspberrypi.collabora.com wheezy Release
Hit http://mirrordirector.raspbian.org wheezy Release
Hit http://archive.raspberrypi.org wheezy Release
Hit http://raspberrypi.collabora.com wheezy/rpi armhf Packages
Hit http://repository.wolfram.com stable Release.gpg
Hit http://mirrordirector.raspbian.org wheezy/main armhf Packages
Hit http://mirrordirector.raspbian.org wheezy/contrib armhf Packages
Hit http://mirrordirector.raspbian.org wheezy/non-free armhf Packages
Hit http://archive.raspberrypi.org wheezy/main armhf Packages
Hit http://mirrordirector.raspbian.org wheezy/rpi armhf Packages
Hit http://repository.wolfram.com stable Release
Ign http://raspberrypi.collabora.com wheezy/rpi Translation-en_GB
Ign http://raspberrypi.collabora.com wheezy/rpi Translation-en
Ign http://archive.raspberrypi.org wheezy/main Translation-en_GB
Ign http://archive.raspberrypi.org wheezy/main Translation-en
Hit http://repository.wolfram.com stable/non-free armhf Packages
Ign http://mirrordirector.raspbian.org wheezy/contrib Translation-en_GB
Ign http://mirrordirector.raspbian.org wheezy/contrib Translation-en
Ign http://mirrordirector.raspbian.org wheezy/main Translation-en_GB
Ign http://mirrordirector.raspbian.org wheezy/main Translation-en
Ign http://mirrordirector.raspbian.org wheezy/non-free Translation-en_GB
Ign http://mirrordirector.raspbian.org wheezy/non-free Translation-en
Ign http://mirrordirector.raspbian.org wheezy/rpi Translation-en_GB
Ign http://mirrordirector.raspbian.org wheezy/rpi Translation-en
Ign http://repository.wolfram.com stable/non-free Translation-en_GB
Ign http://repository.wolfram.com stable/non-free Translation-en
Reading package lists..._
```

The binary installation process can take over an hour

it can be fixed with only a few short commands.

RetroPie ships with a version of the popular Fuse Spectrum emulator configured for use in the X Windows graphical environment. As the user interface used by RetroPie works only when the X Windows layer is not loaded, this causes a conflict. Thankfully, there's an alternative: a version of the same emulator that works fine without X Windows loaded. Install it with this command:

```
sudo apt-get install fuse-
emulator-sdl
```

Now you need to tell EmulationStation, the graphical front-end that ships with RetroPie, about the new emulator or it will attempt to use the original, glitchy emulator by default. Edit the EmulationStation configuration file

Free platformer Dogmole Tuppowski for the ZX Spectrum 128K.

with the following command:

```
nano ~/.emulationstation/
es_systems.cfg
```

Scroll down to the bottom of the file until you find the entry for the ZX Spectrum. Find the line that starts "COMMAND=" and delete everything on that line following the equals symbol. Then replace it so the line reads as below:

```
COMMAND=fuse-sdl %ROM%
```

Before you leave the file, go up to the line immediately above, which begins "EXTENSION=". This is a list of file extensions that EmulationStation will know are compatible with the Spectrum emulator, but it's incomplete. Go to the end of the line, and edit it to read as follows:

```
EXTENSION=.z80 .Z80 .tap
.TAP
```

This adds support for tape image format files, a very common format for the distribution of Spectrum software – the format, in fact, used by the Dogmole Tuppowski game you downloaded earlier. Save the file with Ctrl+O, then exit Nano with Ctrl+X.

RUNNING THE EMULATOR

Rather than forcing you to run each emulator individually, RetroPie comes with a graphical front-end called EmulationStation. This is designed in such a way that it can be operated without a keyboard or mouse, which is good news if you're looking to use a joypad, joystick or adapter cable for your gaming. Load the front-end with the following command:

```
emulationstation
```

After few seconds, a configuration screen will appear. This allows you to set up the control method – keyboard, joypad, joystick or anything else you can connect to the Pi – for use in the menu system. Start by pressing any button or key on your chosen control device. If you have more than one connected, for multiplayer games, use the controller for the first player. You'll then be prompted to press a series of buttons in turn, configuring the directions and the control buttons. Follow the onscreen instructions to complete the process.

If you're using an Atari-style joystick through an adapter, you may run into difficulties partway through the process: following the setting of up, down, left, right and accept, you'll have run out of buttons. To solve this, temporarily insert a keyboard and set some of its keys for the remaining controls. These are rarely used, and it shouldn't cause a problem in everyday usage.

When you've completed the configuration, the main

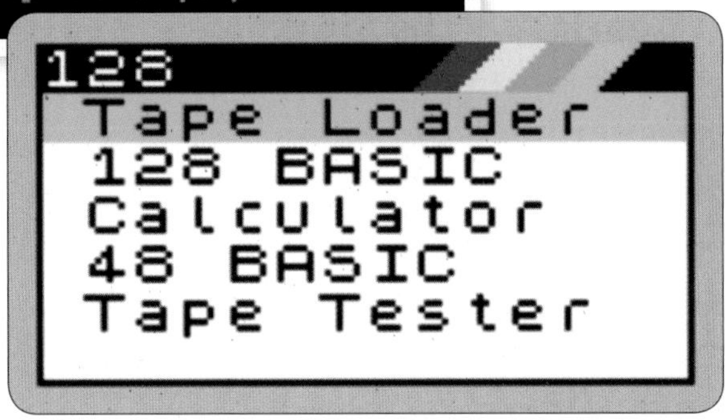

The emulator can load and run the game automatically.

Resize the emulator to take up the entire screen.

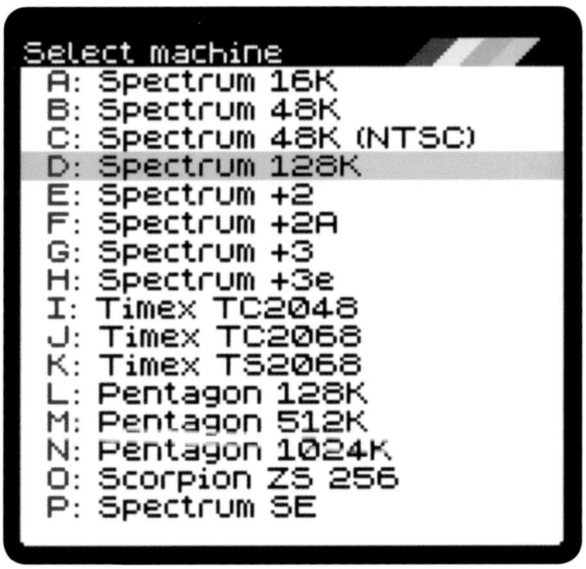

Select machine
A: Spectrum 16K
B: Spectrum 48K
C: Spectrum 48K (NTSC)
D: Spectrum 128K
E: Spectrum +2
F: Spectrum +2A
G: Spectrum +3
H: Spectrum +3e
I: Timex TC2048
J: Timex TC2068
K: Timex TS2068
L: Pentagon 128K
M: Pentagon 512K
N: Pentagon 1024K
O: Scorpion ZS 256
P: Spectrum SE

Reset the emulator to run as a ZX Spectrum 128K.

EmulationStation screen will appear. This provides access to all emulators that have games available, sorted alphabetically. Initially, you'll be presented with an Apple][emulator. Press whatever button or key you assigned to the Right direction in EmulationStation, and you'll move onto the next emulator, a freeware copy of the game Cave Story. Press Right again, and you'll find a copy of id Software's Doom; right again and you can find 3D Realms' Duke Nukem 3D. Keep scrolling, and eventually you'll reach the screen for the ZX Spectrum emulator.

Emulators that don't have any games installed in their "roms" directory won't be visible in this menu. Because you downloaded and installed a game earlier, the ZX Spectrum option will appear. At the moment, there will only be a single game available; you can launch this game by pressing the Accept button you configured earlier.

If you're playing Dogmole Tuppowski, you'll find that the emulator boots into a black screen. This is because the version you downloaded is an enhanced edition designed for the ZX Spectrum 128K, while the emulator defaults to acting as a ZX Spectrum 48K. To fix this, bring up the Fuse menu with the F1 key on the keyboard; scroll to Machine with the cursor keys and press Enter. In the menu that appears, scroll to Select and press Enter; find the entry for Spectrum 128K in the list, and confirm with Enter. The emulator will then reset.

When the emulator restarts, it doesn't try to automatically load the game. To do so, press the Enter key while the option Tape Loader is highlighted. The game will load and run automatically and, compared to the speed at which a traditional Spectrum game used to load from tape, near instantaneously. It will do so, however, in a small box at the centre of the screen. To fix that, press F1 again and scroll to the Options menu. There you'll find the Full Screen option; press Enter on this and the emulator will be resized to take up the entire screen.

To quit the emulator, press the F1 key again and scroll to Exit. To quit EmulationStation altogether, press Alt+F4, and you'll be returned to the terminal.

ZX Spectrum
Dogmole Tuppowski - The New Adventures (128k by Jarlaxe)

INTERNET RADIO RECEIVER

Coupled with an onboard display, the Raspberry Pi makes a great choice for an internet radio receiver. Follow our guide to start streaming radio

The radio, a remarkable invention, was all but supplanted as the centre of home entertainment by the television, and as a source of up-to-the-minute news by the internet. Its biggest drawback, aside from sometimes questionable audio quality, is its limited range. Even today, with the rise of digital radio, channels are typically national rather than international in their reach.

Internet radio is a different beast. Streaming over a global network rather than the airwaves, a single station can reach almost anywhere on Earth if only the receiver has a device capable of decoding and playing the audio stream. A device, in fact, like the Pi.

The pi is a great choice for an internet radio receiver. It's small, unobtrusive and silent in operation, while its analogue audio output means it can be connected to powered speakers or an existing hi-fi setup to extend its capabilities. Coupled with an onboard display, you won't even need a TV or monitor to control the playback.

INSTALLING THE SOFTWARE

The software that drives the PiFace Control & Display is available through the Apt package management system in Raspbian. Log into the Pi, and type the following commands at the terminal to download and install the required software:

```
sudo apt-get update
sudo apt-get upgrade
sudo apt-get install python-
pifacecad python3-pifacecad
mplayer
```

This installs versions of the PiFace software for both Python 2 and Python 3, allowing you to make use of it regardless of which version of the language you prefer. Note, however, that the internet radio utility that comes with the PiFace works only with Python 3 and won't run at all under Python 2. This isn't a distinction you need to worry about if you just want to stream some music; both versions of Python are installed by default in Raspbian. The command-line music player Mplayer is also installed via the last command.

Before you can begin using its software, the PiFace requires a configuration change on the Pi: the enabling of the Serial Peripheral Interface, or SPI, feature of the general-purpose input-output (GPIO) header. To load the Raspberry Pi Software Configuration Tool, type the following at the terminal:

```
sudo raspi-config
```

At the menu, use the cursor keys to scroll to the Advanced Options choice and press Enter to confirm. At the next screen, scroll to the option labelled "A5 SPI" and press Enter again. A window will appear confirming the current status of SPI. Usually, this will be disabled and you can press Enter to toggle the setting to Yes. If the setting is already enabled, be sure to move the cursor

WHAT YOU'LL NEED

Streaming internet radio stations requires, naturally, an internet connection. Audio-only streams are typically low bandwidth and don't require particularly fast connections, so a Pi connected wirelessly should perform just as well as one connected to a wired network. As this project uses an add-on board for its input and display, the usual limitations surrounding a Raspberry Pi Model A and its single USB port don't apply here. It's perfectly possible to complete this project using a Model A with a wireless network adapter connected over USB (from £5.50, amazon.co.uk).

You'll also need some way of listening to the radio. You can connect a pair of headphones directly to the Pi's 3.5mm analogue audio output, but the result will be quiet. You're better off investing in a pair of powered, amplified speakers (from £3, ebay.co.uk), or using a 3.5mm-to-RCA adapter (from 99p, ebay.co.uk) to connect your Pi to an existing but internet-lacking stereo system or amplifier.

Finally, you'll need the PiFace Control & Display (£25.20, code SC13206 from cpc.farnell.com), an add-on board that provides the Pi with a small LCD screen and a series of buttons to enable interaction without a TV, monitor or connection from another computer.

The PiFace is dominated by a two-line LCD panel.

off the No option before pressing Enter. Confirm the change again with Enter, then exit the menus by pressing the Tab key until Finish is highlighted and pressing Enter.

If the Raspberry Pi Software Configuration Tool prompts you to reboot – it may not, depending on any other changes you've made – choose No and press Enter. As you're about to install the board itself, you should instead manually shut down the Pi with the following command before removing the micro-USB power and any other connected cables:

```
sudo halt
```

The shutdown process will take a short while to complete; check the Pi's status LEDs to see if it's finished before pulling the power. When the Pi has shut down, all LEDs except "PWR" should be switched off.

INSTALLING THE PIFACE

Although it's possible to stream internet radio on the Pi without any additional hardware, it's not convenient. You need to have it connected to a TV or monitor at all times to see what you're doing, and you need a keyboard and mouse to perform even simple tasks like pausing the stream or skipping to a different station.

The PiFace Control & Display board, designed by a team led by honorary research fellow Dr Andrew Robinson specifically for use with the Pi, is an alternative to traditional control methods. The front of the board is dominated by a LCD panel offering two lines of up to 16 characters, while the edges feature five buttons and a three-way joystick. The board also includes an onboard infrared receiver designed to work with your existing remote controls with a little extra configuration.

The PiFace is designed to install on top of the Raspberry Pi as a piggy-back board, connecting to the GPIO header at the top-left of the board. Its lower board includes a supporting strut designed to sit on top of the Ethernet port to provide rigidity once installed. Although the board works perfectly well with the Ethernet-less Model A, it can wobble a little when held via that corner.

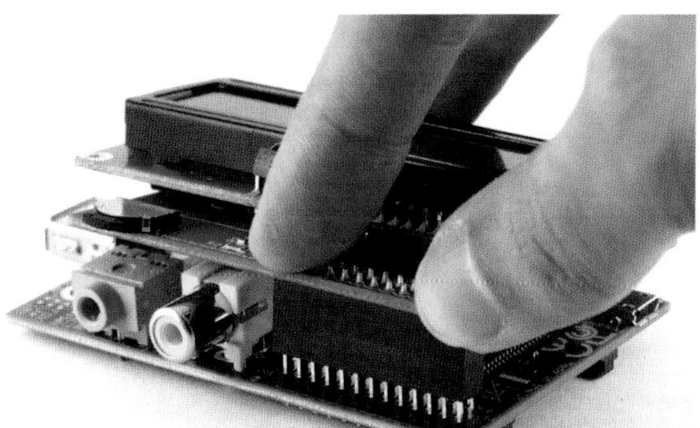

The PiFace installs on top of the Pi as a piggy-back board.

Whenever you're installing hardware onto the Pi's GPIO header, ensure you've shut down the Pi safely – using the "sudo halt" command at the terminal – and removed the micro-USB power connector. Plugging devices into the GPIO header while the Pi is powered on is ill-advised. The pins connect directly to various components of the Broadcom BCM2835 processor, and have no protection against shorts or spikes.

The Pi should be positioned face-up on a flat surface with the HDMI connector facing you. Take the PiFace, with the five buttons facing you and the joystick and infrared receiver furthest away, and carefully position the black connector on its underside over the Pi's GPIO header. Make sure it's aligned correctly and press it down gently but firmly with your fingers to either edge of the board on the top of the connector. It should slide into place easily; if it feels like you're having to apply excess pressure, remove the PiFace and check the Pi for bent pins before trying again.

The PiFace takes its power directly from the Pi, and needs no power adapter of its own. This can, however, put a strain on lower-specification power adapters. If after installing the PiFace you find that the Pi begins to respond erratically to the keyboard – especially by skipping letters or

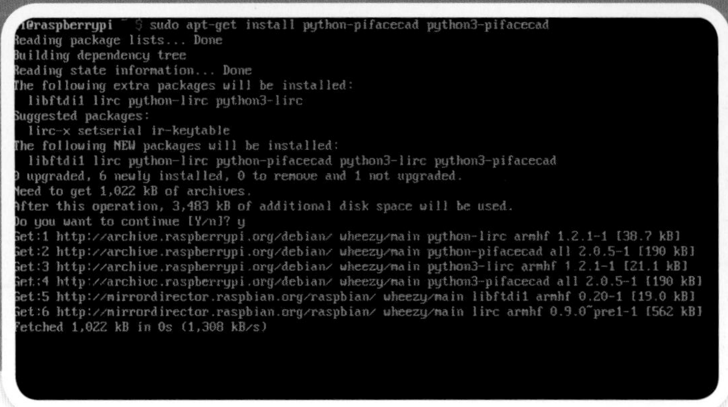

i@raspberrypi ~ $ sudo apt-get install python-pifacecad python3-pifacecad
Reading package lists... Done
Building dependency tree
Reading state information... Done
The following extra packages will be installed:
libftdi1 lirc python-lirc python3-lirc
Suggested packages:
lirc-x setserial ir-keytable
The following NEW packages will be installed:
libftdi1 lirc python-lirc python-pifacecad python3-lirc python3-pifacecad
0 upgraded, 6 newly installed, 0 to remove and 1 not upgraded.
Need to get 1,022 kB of archives.
After this operation, 3,483 kB of additional disk space will be used.
Do you want to continue [Y/n]? y
Get:1 http://archive.raspberrypi.org/debian/ wheezy/main python-lirc armhf 1.2.1-1 [38.7 kB]
Get:2 http://archive.raspberrypi.org/debian/ wheezy/main python-pifacecad all 2.0.5-1 [190 kB]
Get:3 http://archive.raspberrypi.org/debian/ wheezy/main python3-lirc armhf 1.2.1-1 [21.1 kB]
Get:4 http://archive.raspberrypi.org/debian/ wheezy/main python3-pifacecad all 2.0.5-1 [190 kB]
Get:5 http://mirrordirector.raspbian.org/raspbian/ wheezy/main libftdi1 armhf 0.20-1 [19.0 kB]
Get:6 http://mirrordirector.raspbian.org/raspbian/ wheezy/main lirc armhf 0.9.0~pre1-1 [562 kB]
Fetched 1,022 kB in 0s (1,308 kB/s)

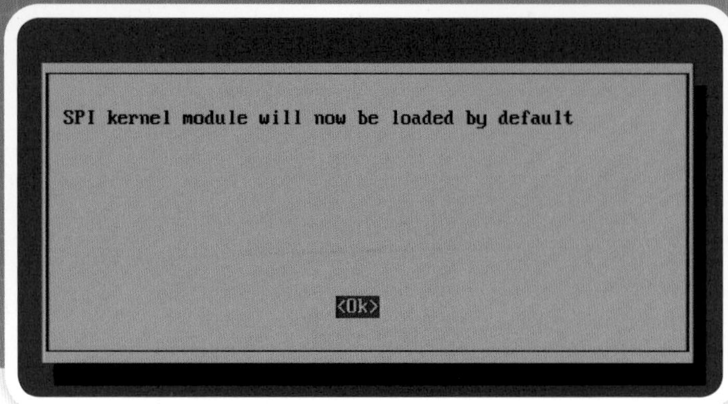

The SPI feature of the GPIO header needs enabling.

repeating them as though you've held down the key – this is a sign that the power supply can't cope. Try replacing it with one rated to a higher amperage, removing any overclock you have set on the Pi, or both.

With the PiFace firmly installed, and its seating double-checked to ensure it hasn't missed any pins, you can reinsert the micro-USB cable and allow the Pi to boot back up again.

TESTING THE PIFACE

When the Pi has loaded up, you may notice that the PiFace has remained switched off; this is normal. The PiFace's display is controlled entirely from the Pi's GPIO header via software. Until it receives an instruction from the software, it won't do anything at all.

Before you start configuring the Pi to stream internet radio, it's worth testing that the PiFace is properly installed and working. The canonical way of doing this is by using the system status script supplied with the software. Log into the Pi, and type this command at the terminal:

```
python3 /usr/share/doc/
python3-pifacecad/examples/
sysinfo.py
```

After a few seconds, the display on the PiFace should light up and display a message regarding the Pi's IP address. A few more seconds later, and the screen will refresh to show the Pi's currently assigned IP address – a handy way of finding it on the network if you haven't assigned a static IP – and two statistics: the temperature of the Pi's BCM2835 processor, as reported by its internal sensor, and the percentage of the Pi's memory that's currently in use.

You may notice that while this is running, your terminal remains in use. The Python script to drive the PiFace, as called using the above command, always runs in the foreground, meaning it ties up your terminal. To quit the script, now you've proven the PiFace is working as expected, press Ctrl+C. Later, you'll learn a trick for running scripts like this in the background, so you don't lose your terminal and can multitask.

CONFIGURING THE RADIO SCRIPT

Handily, the creators of the PiFace Control & Display have included an example Python script designed for streaming internet radio, which works out of the box and can be configured to stream almost any standards-compliant station. This script is compressed, along with some other example scripts, and must be uncompressed before use. Type the following commands at the terminal:

```
cd /usr/share/doc/python3-
pifacecad/examples
ls
```

The first command takes you to the directory where the PiFace example scripts are kept. The second lists the contents of that directory, showing you all the scripts provided as standard with the PiFace. As well as the system status script you've already used and the radio script you're looking for, there will be a game of hangman, a tool for looking up train times, one for displaying Twitter messages, and a script for generating weather forecasts. They can all be extracted and used for experimentation by following the same instructions as for the radio script.

The majority of scripts are compressed to save space, using a tool called gzip. Before they can be easily used, the scripts must be uncompressed back into their plain-text formats. To uncompress just the radio script, type the following command at the terminal:

```
sudo gunzip radio.py.gz
```

Alternatively, if you'd prefer to extract all the compressed scripts at the same time, type:

```
sudo gunzip *gz
```

If you type "ls" again now, you'll see that the ".gz" extension has disappeared from all the files in the directory. This shows that they're uncompressed and ready for use.

It's possible to just run the radio script now and start streaming, but it's worth spending some time customising it to your tastes first. Run the following command to edit the file in Nano:

```
sudo nano radio.py
```

Before you start configuring the Pi to stream internet radio, it's worth testing that the PiFace is properly installed

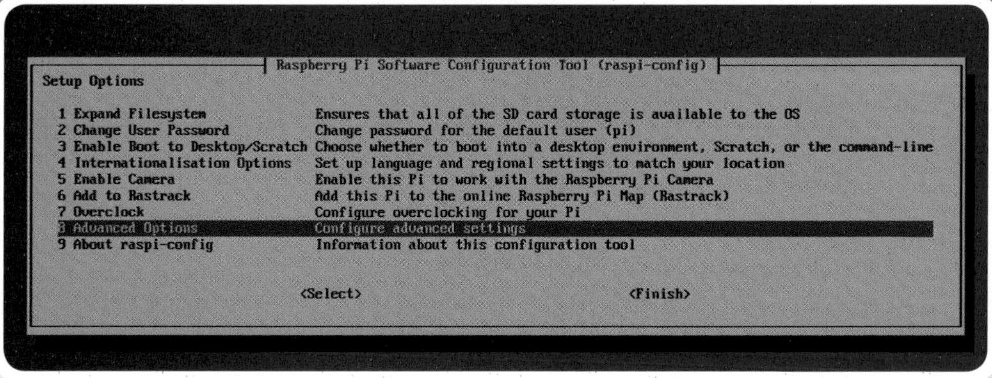

Raspberry Pi Software Configuration Tool (raspi-config)
Setup Options
1 Expand Filesystem Ensures that all of the SD card storage is available to the OS
2 Change User Password Change password for the default user (pi)
3 Enable Boot to Desktop/Scratch Choose whether to boot into a desktop environment, Scratch, or the command-line
4 Internationalisation Options Set up language and regional settings to match your location
5 Enable Camera Enable this Pi to work with the Raspberry Pi Camera
6 Add to Rastrack Add this Pi to the online Raspberry Pi Map (Rastrack)
7 Overclock Configure overclocking for your Pi
8 Advanced Options Configure advanced settings
9 About raspi-config Information about this configuration tool
<Select>
<Finish>

Load the Raspberry Pi Software Configuration Tool.

The Python code for streaming internet radio stations isn't well documented, but is thankfully very simple in its layout. Partway down the file, there's a list of radio stations that the script can access. These are specified in the following format:

```
    {'name': "Friendly Station Name",
     'source': 'URL of stream playlist or file',
     'info': 'URL of information stream' or None},
```

Note that each station is enclosed in braces, and has spaces at the beginning. Python's syntax relies heavily on indentation to know which lines belong to which part of the program. To add your own choice of radio station to the list, you can simply copy these lines, making sure to place them before the "]" symbol that sits at the bottom of the list. Ensure you include the spaces, four on the first line and five on the remaining two, or the script won't be able to understand your formatting.

As an example, to add the station Champion Radio UK to the list, you'd write an entry as below:

```
    {'name': "Champion Radio UK",
     'source': 'http://uk2.internet-radio.com:31216/listen.pls',
     'info': None},
```

You can create as many custom entries as you like, and delete or edit the existing entries until the list is more to your taste. Compatible radio stations are easily found on a web search. Try **www.internet-radio.com** for a wide selection. Stations are played in the order in which they are listed; try putting your favourite stations closer to the top of the list, or sorting alphabetically. When creating a new entry, bear in mind that not all stations have an information URL as with the example above.

When you've completed the list, and double-checked it includes the right indentation, commas at the end and matching braces, save the file with Ctrl+O and exit Nano with Ctrl+X.

STREAMING RADIO

To start the radio streaming script, simply type the following command at the terminal:

```
python3 radio.py
```

The PiFace display will clear, and after a few seconds display the name of the first radio station in the list, then status information about the stream will appear on the terminal. At the same time, you should be able to hear the station's stream coming out of your speakers. If you can't hear the stream, the Pi is most likely trying to output it via the HDMI connection instead of the 3.5mm connection. Exit the radio script with XXXXX, then type this command at the terminal:

```
amixer cset numid=3 1
```

This tells the Pi to send all audio through the analogue output. Replacing the number 1 at the end of the command with 0 returns to the default of attempting to automatically detect the appropriate output, and using 2 forces the audio to output via the HDMI connector. Restart the script with the following command:

```
python3 radio.py
```

The radio script makes use of the buttons on the PiFace to control playback. The joystick at the top-right of the board can be moved left and right to skip between stations. Pressing the joystick inwards while at the centre position toggles between play and pause. To exit streaming altogether, press the right-most button at the bottom of the PiFace; this quits the script.

Having to plug in a display and keyboard to start up the script makes the PiFace a little redundant, however. To have the script automatically load in the background every time the Pi boots, load the "rc.local" file in Nano with the following command:

```
sudo nano /etc/rc.local
```

Add the following line above "exit 0", then save the file with Ctrl+O and exit with Ctrl+W.

```
nohup python3 /usr/share/doc/python3-pifacecad/examples/radio.py &
```

This will run the script in the background every time the Pi restarts. Test it by rebooting the Pi with the following command:

```
sudo reboot
```

CHAPTER FOUR

PLUG-IN HARDWARE

The Pi is a powerful piece of computing equipment on its own, but its true potential is only exposed when you start connecting it to more hardware. Since its launch, an entire cottage industry of manufacturers designing and building ingenious add-ons to expand and enhance the capabilities of the Pi has sprung up, with some great results.

In keeping with the Pi's low-cost ethic, these add-ons are rarely expensive for what they provide. Even with several in your collection, the chances that you'll have spent more than achieving the same goals using traditional computers is unlikely.

Whether it's adding a tablet-like touchscreen display, increasing the Pi's computing power to mine the Bitcoin cryptocurrency, expanding the potential for electronics projects by adding an Arduino, or creating an internet-connected smart security system, low-cost add-ons make the Pi come alive and open up the potential for far more impressive and expansive projects.

4

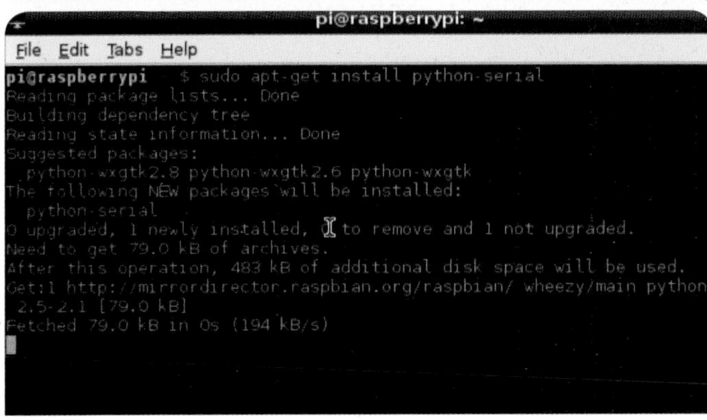
pi@raspberrypi: ~
File Edit Tabs Help
pi@raspberrypi $ sudo apt-get install python-serial
Reading package lists... Done
Building dependency tree
Reading state information... Done
Suggested packages:
python-wxgtk2.8 python-wxgtk2.6 python-wxgtk
The following NEW packages will be installed:
python-serial
0 upgraded, 1 newly installed, 0 to remove and 1 not upgraded.
Need to get 79.0 kB of archives.
After this operation, 483 kB of additional disk space will be used.
Get:1 http://mirrordirector.raspbian.org/raspbian/ wheezy/main python-
2.5-2.1 [79.0 kB]
Fetched 79.0 kB in 0s (194 kB/s)

BUILDING A DIGITAL PHOTO FRAME

The Raspberry Pi's powerful graphics- and video-handling capabilities make it a great choice for creating your own low-cost digital photo frame

The Raspberry Pi was designed around existing components originally built for low-power embedded platforms. Its processor, in particular, offers powerful graphics- and video-handling capabilities along with a rather more sedate general-purpose central processor, hinting at its origin as a chip for set-top boxes and other video-centric applications.

While this can make the Pi a little slow for general-purpose use compared to a traditional PC, it means it has considerable flexibility for creating your own embedded multimedia devices, such as a low-cost yet extremely versatile digital photo frame, while pulling double duties as a platform for experimentation, gaming or programming.

BUILDING THE PITFT

The PiTFT colour display board is supplied partially assembled, but requires a small amount of soldering in order to finish it off. Find a light place to work with good ventilation, to protect yourself from solder fumes, and put some newspaper or magazine sheets down to protect the surface from errant drops of solder. Take the PiTFT out of the packaging, and separate it into its three components: the board and screen module; a black plastic female header, with pins on either side; and a black male header, with pins on the underside and holes on the top. It's this latter header you'll need, so you can put the male header to one side for now.

Place your soldering iron into its stand and connect it to a mains socket, then wet the cleaning sponge; it should be damp, but not sodden. Allow the iron to come up to temperature, then wipe it on the sponge to clean the tip. It can help to apply a small amount of solder to the tip before you start, a process known as tinning: melt a small amount of solder onto the tip of the iron, then wipe it clean on the sponge. A thin layer of solder will remain on the tip, and help transfer heat to the components when soldering.

Take the female header and insert it on the Pi's general-purpose input-output (GPIO) header on the top-left of the board, so that its pins stick up. Next, take the PiTFT display board itself and hold it so that the Adafruit logo is on your right. Lower the board over the pins of the female header so that they stick up through the holes on the top-left of the board. If you're installing the PiTFT on a Model A, you may need to put something solid like a blob of Blu-Tak under the right-hand side of the board to support it during the soldering process.

The pins of the header need to be soldered onto the board one at a time. This is a lot easier if you move the display module out of the way. Either flip it horizontally from the left edge, or turn the board upside-down and pull the two small tabs at either side

WHAT YOU'LL NEED

Using a Pi as a digital photo frame doesn't require an active internet connection, unless you'd like to be able to transfer photographs over the network. Coupled with the fact that the photo frame will be switched on permanently, this makes it a great candidate for a Raspberry Pi Model A project. The Model A's lack of Ethernet connection is no barrier to its use in the project, while its lower power draw will help make the final creation more energy efficient. Model A owners will, however, need an active internet connection during the building process, to install the required software.

Aside from the Pi itself, you'll also need a display. For this project, we've picked the Adafruit PiTFT (£34.68, skpang.co.uk), an add-on board that features a compact 2.8in colour display designed to sit on top of the Pi as a piggy-back board. Although relatively low resolution – 320 × 240 – it offers a crisp and clear picture, while taking up very little room.

You'll also need a soldering iron (£9.50, oomlout.co.uk), as the PiTFT is supplied in kit form. The soldering is a good starter project, but require cares, and the supervision of an adult if you're looking to build this project with children.

You'll also need some pictures to display. These can be copied onto the Raspberry Pi's SD card, in a subdirectory of /home/pi, or stored on a USB storage device connected to the Pi.

The Adafruit PiTFT features a compact 8in display.

of the connector to free the ribbon cable and remove the display entirely.

The technique for good soldering is to push the tip of the iron so that it's in contact with both the pin and the copper encircling the hole on the circuit board. Hold the iron's tip there for a few seconds, then push some solder against the pin and copper – not against the iron – so that it melts. If the solder doesn't melt easily, pull it back and wait a couple more seconds, especially if you're using a low wattage iron or one with a small tip.

When the solder has melted, it will form a conical pool around the bottom of the pin. Remove the solder, then remove the iron. When the solder has hardened, it should be in complete contact with the pin and circuit board with no gaps. Use only a small amount of solder. Too much and you risk connecting multiple pins together, creating a short circuit that can damage the Pi and the PiTFT board.

Repeat this for each pin, remembering to clean your iron on the sponge regularly during the process. When all pins are soldered, and you've checked for shorts or bad connections, give the iron a final clean with a small amount of solder to repeat the tinning process before unplugging it and allowing it to cool. This will protect the tip during storage, prolonging its life. Alternatively, you can repeat the process to add the male connector to the left-hand side of the PiTFT. This allows you to access the GPIO pins not used by the display, for more complicated projects. You don't need to do this for the photo frame project.

You should now be able to replace the screen back on the PiTFT board. Before you do, peel the protective cover from the two strips of adhesive tape on the rear before positioning the display carefully on the centre of the board and gently pushing it into place. Leave the PiTFT board to one side, and connect the Pi

INSTALLING THE SOFTWARE

The PiTFT requires several packages to be installed, all of which have been tweaked and customised by Adafruit to run the display. Ordinarily, this is a lengthy process as the files required aren't found in the Apt software distribution system. Full instructions for the process can be found at **learn.adafruit.com**, but an easier way is to use an automated installation script. Type the following at the terminal to download the script:

```
wget http://tinyurl.com/
pitftinstall
```

This script automates the following tasks: downloading the various Adafruit-customised software packages required for PiTFT support; installing the drivers in the /etc/modules directory; setting up the display configuration; creating calibration settings for the PiTFT's touchscreen functionality; and configuring the Pi to use the PiTFT as its default frame buffer, meaning that upon reboot the terminal will appear on the PiTFT instead of an external

WARNING

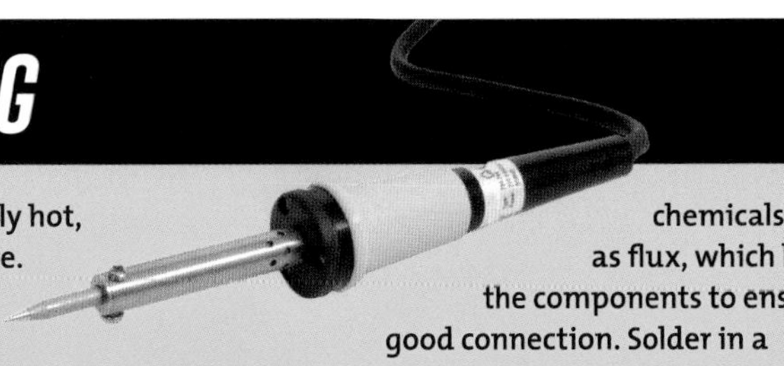

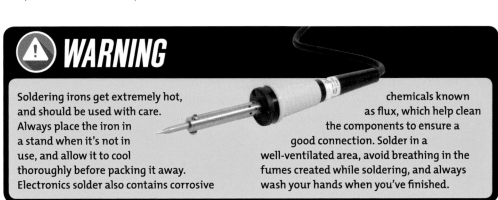

Soldering irons get extremely hot, and should be used with care. Always place the iron in a stand when it's not in use, and allow it to cool thoroughly before packing it away. Electronics solder also contains corrosive chemicals known as flux, which help clean the components to ensure a good connection. Solder in a well-ventilated area, avoid breathing in the fumes created while soldering, and always wash your hands when you've finished.

monitor. It also sets the terminal typeface to a size appropriate for the small, low-resolution screen, ensuring that text is as easy to read as possible. Note that this will affect the console on all devices, so don't be surprised if things look different when you've finished. Run the script with the following command:

```
sudo bash pitftinstall
```

There's no need to manually update and upgrade the system before running the script; this is done automatically the first time it runs. The installation process will take a few minutes to complete, after which the Pi will shut down. When the shutdown process has fully completed – as indicated by all status lights at the top-right of the board going out except for "PWR" – remove the micro-USB power cable and carefully install the PiTFT board onto the Pi's GPIO header. Remember whenever you're disconnecting hardware from the GPIO header, always ensure the Pi is switched off and the USB power cable is disconnected.

Make sure you use only a small amount of solder.

Double-check that the PiTFT is securely seated, and that you haven't missed a column of pins. It should press down with a gentle push, and any excess force indicates it's misaligned and may bend some pins. When you're sure it's properly connected, plug in the micro-USB power cable and let the Pi boot up. Initially, nothing will appear on the PiTFT screen; after a few seconds, you'll see the familiar text-based terminal appear. You can then log in using a USB keyboard, as normal, to continue the process of building your digital photo frame.

If you find the font on the screen too large, you can switch to a more compact and easily readable typeface. Type the following command at the terminal to bring up a menu:

```
sudo dpkg-reconfigure
,console-setup
```

At the first screen, press Enter to confirm the default choice of UTF-8. Confirm the second dialog with Enter again; choose the default of "Guess optimal character set" with Enter again on the third screen. The message that appears on the next screen is too large to view on the PiTFT. Press Tab to move to the OK button, and Enter to confirm. Use the cursor keys to scroll through the list that appears, and choose "Terminus" with Enter; choose "6×12" as the size on the next screen. This will take a minute to take effect; when it does, the terminal should be much more readable.

Remember, whenever you're disconnecting hardware from the GPIO header, always ensure the Pi is switched off

MAKING THE FRAME

Now you've got a terminal visible on the PiTFT, you should have an idea of just how useful it can be. When configured as a default frame buffer – as the installation script does – anything that would normally appear on an external monitor will instead appear on the PiTFT. This includes the graphical user interface. If you type "startx" at the terminal, the graphical user interface will load and can be interacted with by tapping on the screen. At 320 × 240, however, it may be too small to be of use as a general-purpose interface.

To use the PiTFT as a digital photo frame, it's easier to install software that works at the terminal than to try using software in the graphical user interface that was designed for far higher-resolution displays. Thankfully, there's a piece of software designed specifically for viewing images on framebuffer devices: the Linux FrameBuffer Imageviewer, or "fbi." To install it, type the following at the terminal:

```
sudo apt-get install fbi
```

If you haven't already, copy some photographs across to your Pi. For this

Double-check that the PiTFT is securely seated.

example, we've created a directory called "photos" and filled it with some holiday snapshots. Change to the directory containing the photos – it can be an external storage device connected via USB, if you like – and run fbi with the following command:

```
fbi -a -t 10 --noverbose *
```

This tells fbi to automatically rescale images for the low-resolution 320 × 240 screen of the PiTFT, to change to a new photo every ten seconds, and to skip displaying the filename and other information at the bottom of the screen, which takes up valuable room on the 2.8in PiTFT. The slideshow will continue forever, looping through the images in the directory, until you quit with the Escape key; this will return you to the console.

Having to manually run the above command every time you plug in the Pi is inconvenient, however. A better solution is to have fbi run automatically when the Pi is started, without needing the user to log in. To do this, edit the rc.local file with the following command:

```
sudo nano /etc/rc.local
```

This file contains instructions on what the Pi should run when it first boots. Scroll towards the bottom of the file, and insert the following just above the line that reads "exit 0":

```
fbi -a -t 10 --noverbose /
home/pi/photos/*
```

Don't worry if the beginning of the line scrolls off the screen and is replaced with a dollar sign. This is Nano's way of showing you that the line is longer than it appears. This command tells the Pi that when it boots, it should run fbi using the secondary framebuffer – the one associated with the PiTFT, rather than the HDMI or composite video output – and show the photographs in the "photos" directory under the user Pi's home directory. If your photos are stored elsewhere, change the directory in the command. You can also alter the "10" to a higher value if you'd like a longer delay between the pictures. Reboot the Pi with the following command:

```
sudo reboot
```

When it next starts up, the Pi will begin displaying the slideshow automatically. This works even if there's nothing plugged into the Pi except power and the PiTFT. Note that this doesn't stop you from using the Pi for something else at the same time. If the Pi is connected to a network, you can still make a connection to it via SSH and run commands without it interfering with its photo frame duties. ●

If you find the font too large, switch to a more compact one.

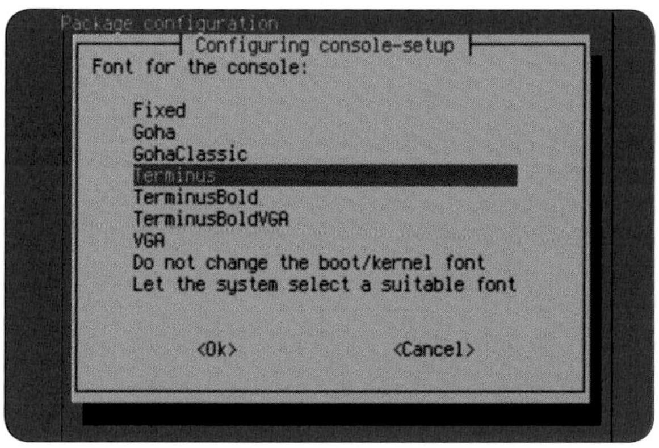

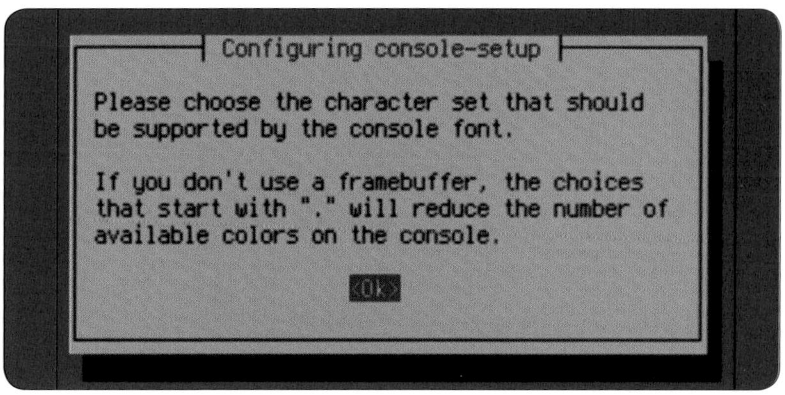

MINING BITCOIN CRYPTOCURRENCY

Bitcoin mining may seem bizarre at first. We explain the basics, and show you how your Raspberry Pi connected to an ASIC can be put to work

Insert the ASIC into the USB hub with care.

The Bitcoin cryptocurrency is the centre of the financial world's attention. Despite the fact that it doesn't exist in the physical realm, being little more than a string of numbers in a computer's memory, its decentralisation and ability for people to conjure the "coins" out of thin air has caused an explosion of interest. Where a single Bitcoin would once have cost less than a penny, each is now worth around £500.

When Bitcoin was first introduced, the process of "mining" the coins – generating them by putting your computer to work validating others' transactions, a key element of the currency's decentralisation – took powerful processors. Later, enthusiasts moved onto ever more powerful graphics cards to perform the calculations. Now, the secret to success at Bitcoin mining is application-specific integrated circuits (ASICs) – chips that do nothing but mine Bitcoin, and do it in such a low-power envelope that they can be controlled from a Raspberry Pi.

Although the currency is gaining mainstream acceptance – numerous retailers around the world have begun to accept Bitcoin for everything from cinema tickets to furniture – it's worth remembering that it's a volatile market. Recent high-profile crashes of Bitcoin exchanges, where the currency can be exchanged for real-world money and vice-versa, have harmed its value from a one-time high.

WHAT YOU'LL NEED

Mining Bitcoins is a connected endeavour, with your system accepting work packets from a central server, while the ASIC hardware connects to the host system over USB. As a result, a Model A might seem a poor choice, but with the use of a USB hub you can connect a wired or wireless networking adapter to get the device online.

You'll also need a Bitcoin-mining ASIC. These range in price from around £15 to more than £20,000, depending on the hardware's performance. A good device for experimenting with Bitcoin mining is the Bitmain Antminer U2 (from £25, ebay.co.uk).

ASIC hardware such as the Antminer is powered via USB, and each ASIC draws more power than the Pi can provide. As a result, it's vital that you use a powered USB hub (from £5, amazon.co.uk). This can also be used to power the Pi, meaning only a single electricity socket is required to run the whole system.

THE BASICS OF MINING

Bitcoin mining seems bizarre at first glance: by doing little more than leaving your computer switched on, you can generate currency that can be spent like money. The secret of how this works lies at the heart of the Bitcoin: transaction validation.

Because there are no physical pieces of money being transferred, Bitcoin is vulnerable to attack by clients who simply lie about how much money they have, or where they're transferring money from or to. The network is secured using a cryptographic hashing technique known as SHA. Only when several clients have agreed that a transaction matches the expected hash is it entered into the ledger as genuine.

When mining Bitcoins, your hardware is performing these hashing calculations over and over again, every few seconds. In exchange for its efforts, each system has a

With everything connected, it's time to begin the boot process.

Insert the hub's USB cable into one of the Pi's USB ports.

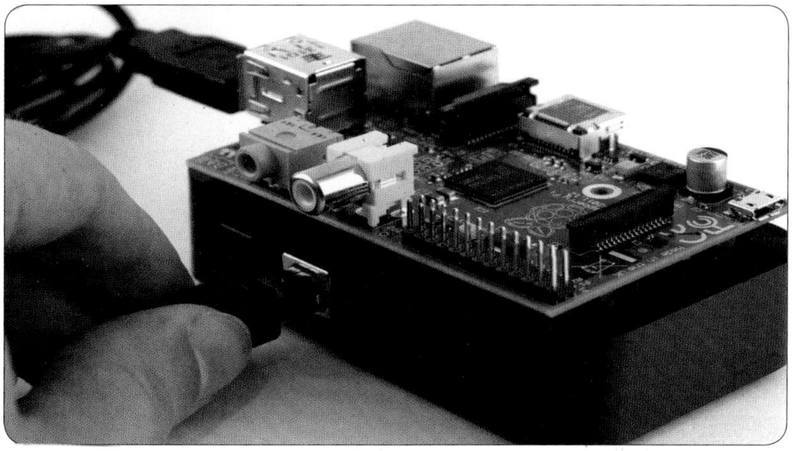

The Pi can draw its power from the hub as well.

small chance of earning a parcel of Bitcoins to spend. As the network has grown, however, the complexity of the hashing operation has grown, too, and now the chances of earning those Bitcoins alone are significantly worse than winning the Lottery several times in a row.

The solution, aside from a move to ultra-fast ASICs that can perform the hashing calculations far faster than any other general-purpose device, is mining pools. Like Lottery pools, these are groups of people who band their hashing power together: when a payout is made, it's shared between members of the group.

The technical details of how Bitcoin truly operates are long and involved, but an understanding that your hashing efforts are monetarily rewarded, pool contributions are a positive, and the millions of hashes you generate that don't result in a direct payout go towards keeping the network secure from fraud will stand you in good stead for this project.

INSTALLING THE SOFTWARE

One of the most powerful Bitcoin mining packages is cgminer, created by Con Kolivas. It's an open-source program, which makes it easy to port to new processor architectures, like the ARM architecture used by the Pi's Broadcom BCM2835 processor. It does, however, mean that to get the latest version and all its features, you need to download the source and compile it. Thankfully, this is a straightforward process on the Pi.

Open the terminal and begin by updating your system and installing the packages on which cgminer depends, using the following commands:

```
sudo apt-get update
sudo apt-get upgrade
sudo apt-get install libusb-
1.0-0-dev libcurl4-openssl-
dev libncurses5-dev libudev-
dev autoconf automake
libtool
```

The first two commands, as usual, download the latest package information and ensure that the Pi's software is up to date. This is an especially important step when compiling software from source, as outdated packages can cause the compilation process to fail. The

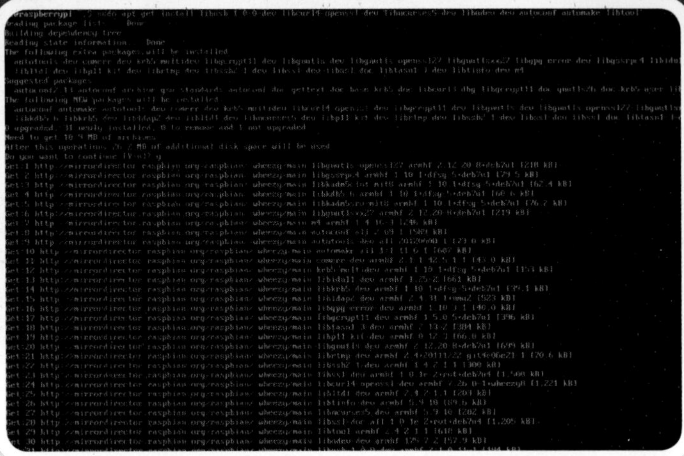

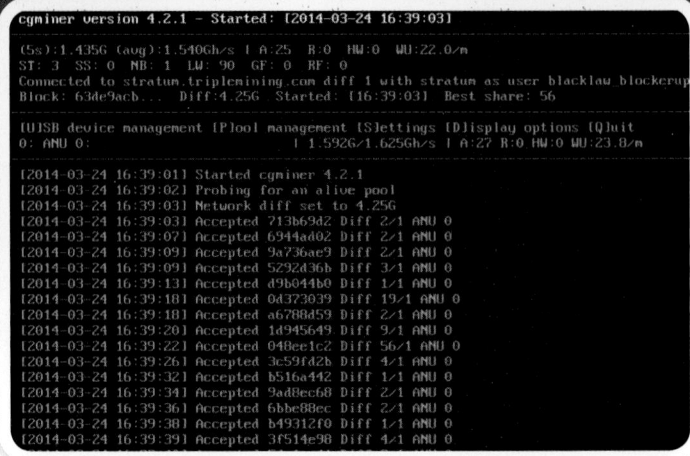

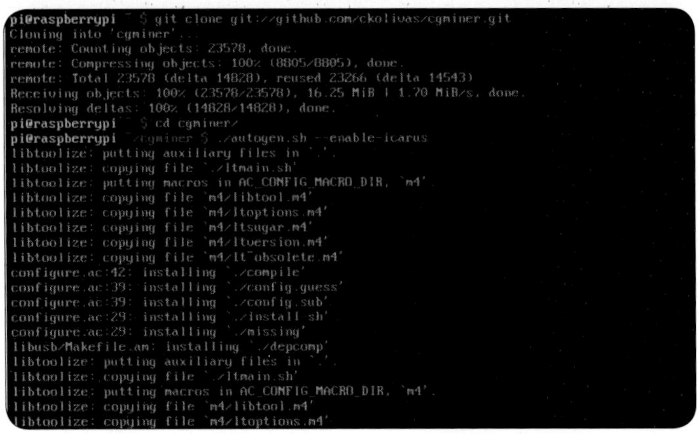

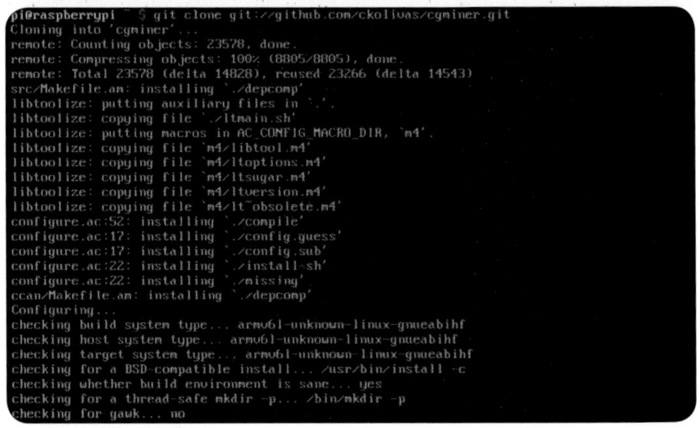

last command downloads various development libraries, which were used to build cgminer, along with some tools to aid in the compilation process.

To download the source code for cgminer, type the following command at the terminal:

```
git clone git://github.com/
ckolivas/cgminer.git
```

This uses the Git tool, designed to make collaborative programming easier by keeping track of different versions of files, to download the source code for cgminer. This shouldn't take long; cgminer is a relatively simple program compared to something like a web browser or an office suite.

Joining a pool doesn't tie you to that pool forever; you can leave at any time, or have multiple accounts

The process of compilation can take a few minutes.

Before compiling – the process of translating the source code into binary files that can be executed by the Broadcom BCM2835 processor – you need to configure cgminer for your system. Type the following commands at the terminal:

```
cd cgminer
./autogen.sh --enable-icarus
```

This tells cgminer that you're going to be using a particular type of USB-connected Bitcoin ASIC, which communicates using what's known as the Icarus standard. This is common for stick-type USB ASICs, including the Antminer and Block Erupter. If you have a different type of ASIC, in particular ones that have their own external housing or come with multiple ASICs on a single circuit board, you may need to use a different instruction here. Consult the documentation for your ASIC for the right enable command.

When the configuration has finished, begin the compilation process with the following command:

```
sudo make
```

The process of compilation can take a few minutes, during which time status messages will scroll up the screen. When the process has completed, you need to copy a particular file into the Pi's system directory in order for the ASIC to be recognised when it's plugged in. Type the following commands to copy the file, and to restart the service that looks for USB-connected hardware:

```
sudo cp 01-cgminer.rules /
etc/udev/rules.d/
sudo service udev restart
```

4

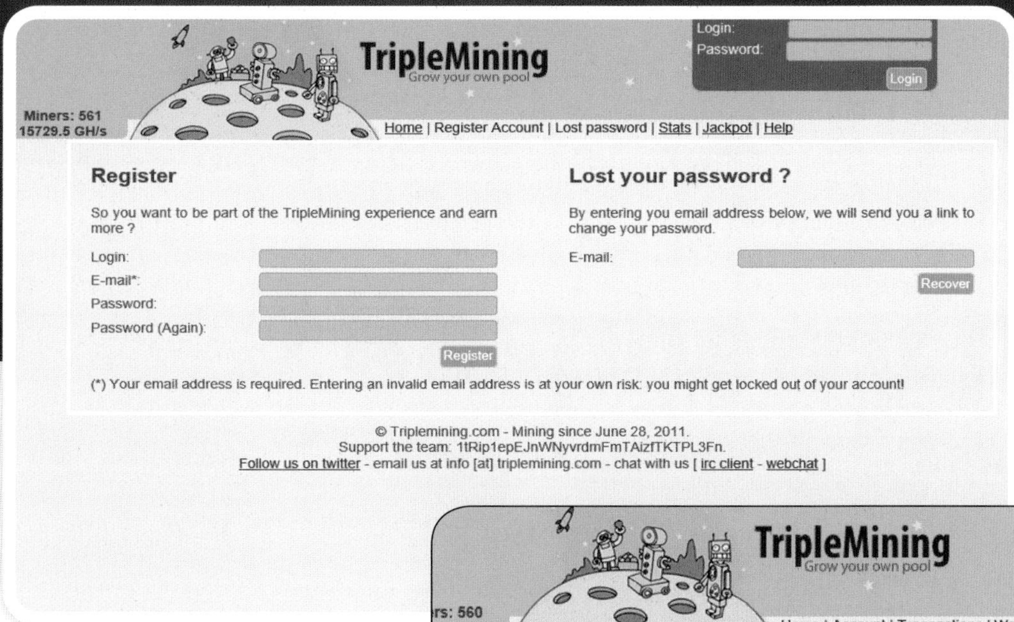

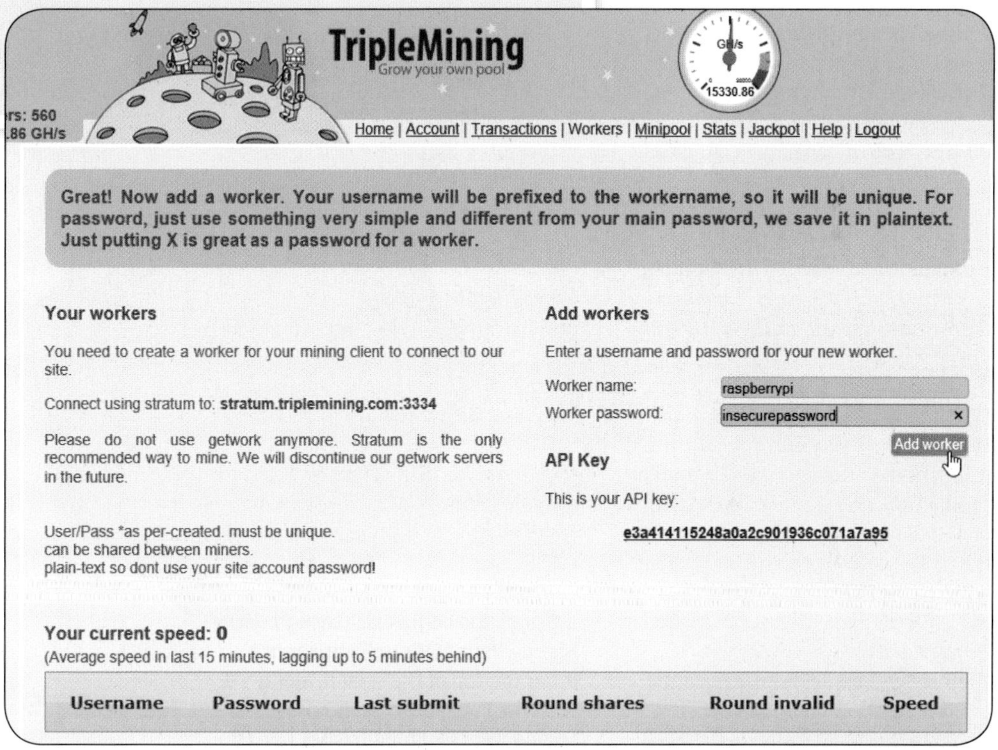

Finally, install cgminer into Raspbian with this command:

```
sudo make installing
```

JOINING A POOL

To mine Bitcoins, you'll need an account with a mining pool. There are many different pools, all of which offer different advantages and disadvantages. A larger pool might have more chance of finding new blocks and earning a payout, but charge a higher fee and split the profit among more members. A smaller pool means a long time between payouts, but will typically charge a smaller fee accordingly.

Joining a pool doesn't tie you to that pool forever; you can leave at any time, or have multiple accounts with multiple pools. Pools will store your earned Bitcoins, unless you transfer them to your own wallet. Your chosen pool will have instructions on how to set up your own Bitcoin wallet and transfer your balance across, although many have minimum payout levels below which you can't make a transfer.

To try the mining process out, set up an account with TripleMining. Load a web browser on your PC, visit **www.triplemining.com**, and click on Register Account. Choose a username, enter your email address and pick a long, secure password before clicking the Register button. You'll be prompted to create a worker; click the Workers option along the top of the page to do so. Enter a name for the worker and a password on the right. This will be stored by cgminer in plain text, so make sure it's different to the password for your main account. Click the Add Worker button to confirm.

Set up an account with TripleMining to try out mining.

There are three pieces of information you need from this screen, and they're the same for any pool: the username for your worker, its password, and the URL of the pool itself. For TripleMining, these are the worker name prefixed with your username and an underscore, the password you set for the worker, and stratum.triplemining.com:3334. Make a note of these before continuing.

INSTALLING THE HARDWARE

Bitcoin ASIC hardware draws close to the maximum permissible from a USB port; far more than the ports of the Raspberry Pi, which don't meet the USB standard, can handle. As a result, you'll need to power the ASIC – or, if you're using more than one,

TWEETING SECURITY SYSTEM

Discover how you can turn your Pi into a low-cost security system that posts images to Twitter. All you'll need is the Pi Camera Module and a case

The release of the Raspberry Pi Camera Module in 2013 opened up new possibilities for the low-cost computer. Based on the same technology that goes into a modern smartphone, the module connects to the previously unused Camera Serial Interface (CSI) port near the right-hand side of the board, and offers Full HD video capture and five megapixel still captures. A variant, the NoIR Camera Module, even offers night vision when coupled with infrared LEDs.

The Pi's network connectivity and low power, combined with the vision capabilities of the Camera Module, make it a highly flexible addition to a home security system. For significantly less than the cost of a commercial camera system, it can be configured to capture and record images and even to send you an alert if unexpected movement is detected.

WHAT YOU'LL NEED

Having the Pi capture images or video requires no network connectivity, but a security system that just sits there and watches you get burgled isn't much use. A better idea is to have the Pi send out an alert when movement is detected, something that will require the use of a Model B or a Model A with an optional USB wireless adapter.

You'll also need the Raspberry Pi Camera Module itself (£20.60, cpc.farnell.co.uk) or its NoIR variant. If using the latter, you'll also need some form of infrared light source; without it, the NoIR camera is no better at seeing in the dark than the regular version.

Finally, you'll need a case that includes a mount for the Raspberry Pi Camera Module (from £4.99, ebay.co.uk). Look for cases that can be wall mounted to increase the flexibility of the final camera system, and whether the angle of the camera can be adjusted once it's inserted into the case.

INSTALLING THE SOFTWARE

Although the code you'll be using to analyse and capture images is written in Python, it relies on a few utilities that aren't available on the Pi by default. As with any Raspberry Pi project, start the process by updating the installed software with the following terminal commands:

```
sudo apt-get update
sudo apt-get upgrade
```

When the process has finished, install the Python Package Index (PyPI) and the Python imaging library by typing the following command at the terminal:

```
sudo apt-get install python-
imaging-tk python-pip
```

The first package is an imaging library, which will take care of analysing the images captured by the camera to determine if movement has occurred. Pip is a package manager for the Python Package Index, and works in much the same way as Apt. Rather than installing general-purpose software, it installs libraries designed for use with the Python programming language. It's one of these libraries, Twython, that you'll use to tie your doorbell script into Twitter. You can install it, along with other libraries on which it depends, by typing the following command when Pip has installed:

```
sudo pip install twython
```

BECOMING A TWITTER DEVELOPER

In order to use Twython, you need to have a Twitter developer account, which is freely available to anyone with a general Twitter account. If you're not already on Twitter, sign up at **twitter.com**; otherwise, visit **dev.twitter.com** in your PC's web browser, and sign in with your normal Twitter username and password.

The Pi security camera will post images it captures to your public Twitter feed. If you'd rather keep the images private, sign up for a new Twitter account and make it non-public before following it with your normal user account. That way, only you will be able to see the images.

Twitter will then ask you if you want to authorise the Twitter developer site to use your account. Re-enter your username and password, and click the Authorise App button. When the page reloads, click on your avatar at the top-right of the screen and click My Applications in the dropdown box.

Everything that connects to Twitter using its application programming interface (API) is known as an application, and it requires special keys to gain access to your account. Begin by giving

Editing the rc.local file in Nano.

your application a name; this has to be unique, so try your name and "Doorbell". Fill in a description, and link to your website; leave Callback URL blank. Scroll to the bottom, click the tickbox to agree to the terms and conditions, and save the changes.

Initially, your application will be created with read-only permissions. Scroll down to Application Settings and click on Modify App Permissions Choose Read and Write, then click Update Settings. Click the API Keys tab, then click Create My Access Token at the bottom of the page. The token takes a while to generate, so keep refreshing the page until it appears in the Your Access Token section.

This provides everything your application needs to access Twitter. Make a note of the API Key, API Secret, Access Token and Access Token Secrets. You'll need to fill these in when you create your doorbell program. Keep them private, as with those keys anybody can access your Twitter account and send messages as though they were you, even if they don't know your password.

CUSTOMISING THE SCRIPT

Computer imaging – the process of analysing images for movement or depth, as an example – is a complex subject and the code to drive even a simple security camera can be obtuse. Thankfully, a team of volunteers from the Raspberry Pi community have written a Python program that's designed specifically to detect motion and capture images, which has been further modified for this project with the inclusion of Twitter connectivity for remote alerts.

To download the script, rather than having to type it all in by hand, type these commands at the terminal:

```
curl https://raw.
githubusercontent.com/
ghalfacree/bash-scripts/
master/picamera-securitypy >
picamera-security.py
chmod +x picamera-security.
py
```

The first downloads the script itself, and the second makes it executable. This means it can be run at the terminal like any other program, without the need to call Python first. Using the API keys and secrets you noted down from the Twitter developers site, you need to put your own details in the script. Open the file for editing with the following command:

```
nano picamera-security.py
```

Near the top, you'll find the following lines, which should be replaced with the settings you noted. Remember to keep these keys and secrets private. Anyone with access to these keys will be able to read your Twitter messages and post on your behalf, so if you share the source code to the program take your keys out first:

```
api_token =
'InsertTokenHere'
api_secret =
'InsertSecretHere'
access_token =
'InsertOAuthTokenHere'
access_token_secret =
'InsertOAuthSecretHere'
```

Further down the script, you'll find details on how to customise the sensitivity of the motion detection. For now, you can leave these at their default setting. If you find that the camera is taking pictures when there's no obvious movement, especially if the camera is outside, you can use the instructions within the script to alter the sensitivity or ignore entire areas of the image – rustling trees or moving traffic, for example.

For now, just save the file with Ctrl+O and exit Nano with Ctrl+X.

CONNECTING THE CAMERA

As with any peripherals, it's a good idea to switch the Pi off before you connect the camera. Before you shut it down, however, you'll need to load the Raspberry Pi Software

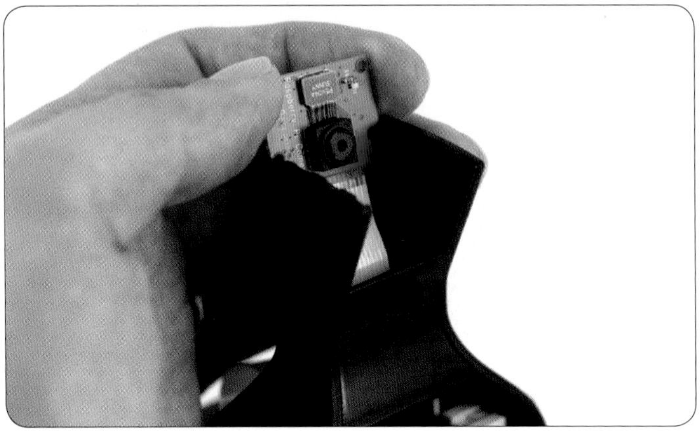

Configuration Tool in order to enable camera mode. Type the following at the terminal:

```
sudo raspi-config
```

In the menu that appears, use the cursor keys to scroll to "Enable Camera" and press Enter. Make sure that the Enable option is highlighted, and press Enter again. Press the Tab key twice to select Finish, and press Enter. When asked if you wish to reboot, select No with the cursor keys and press Enter to leave the Software Configuration Tool. Back at the terminal, type the following command to shut down the Pi:

```
sudo halt
```

When the Pi has powered off, disconnect the USB power lead and any other cables. Take your Camera Module, and find the bare end of the ribbon cable. You'll see protective plastic on one side, and bare silver connectors on the other. Orient the Pi so that the HDMI connector is at the bottom, the composite video and 3.5mm audio connectors at the top, and find the thin rectangular connector on the board at the right-hand side. This will be just to the left of the Ethernet connector on a Model B, or just behind the silk-screen markings where the Ethernet connector would normally be if you're using a Model A.

This is the Camera Serial Interface (CSI) connector, and looks identical to a similar connector on the left-hand side of the board; that's the Display Serial Interface (DSI) connector, which won't do the camera any good if you get them mixed up. The connector may be protected by a thin layer of plastic tape. If so, peel this off. Using your fingernails, lift the connector's grip up from the top and bottom edges. It should lift a few millimetres up from its current position.

Take the camera's ribbon cable and hold it so that the silver contacts

Install the Camera Module into the CSI connector. (top photos)

Enable camera mode in the Software Configuration Tool. (screenshot below)

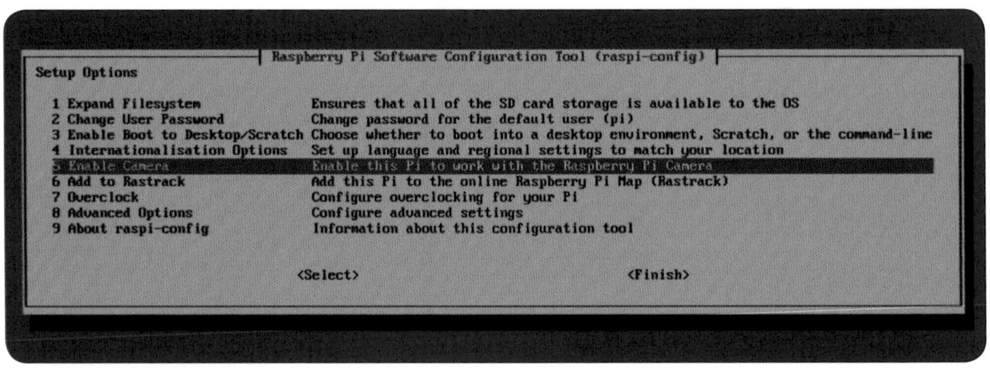

are facing to the left of the board and the protective plastic towards the right. Push it gently between the CSI connector and the grip you just lifted. When it won't push any further down, use your fingernails again to push the grip back downwards. When you've finished, the grip should be back in place and the ribbon cable should be firm enough to stay in place if you give it a gentle upwards tug. Don't pull too hard, or the grip will loosen and the cable will come free. If you're using a case, you should now position the camera so that it's pointing towards the part of the room you want to monitor.

With the camera securely connected, you can plug the Pi back in and allow it to boot.

With the camera connected, you can plug the Pi back in.

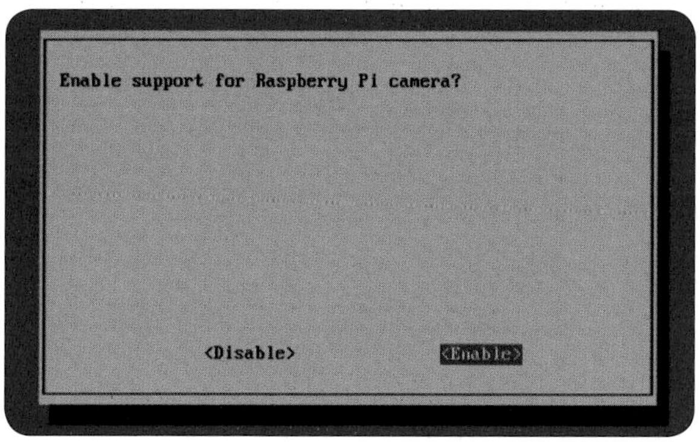

Make sure that the Enable option is highlighted.

RUNNING THE PROGRAM

Log back into the Pi and type the following command to run the motion-detecting script:

```
./picamera-security.py
```

After a few seconds, the Camera Module's status light will start blinking; this indicates that the camera is active. The script works by taking a low-resolution image and storing it; another low-resolution picture is taken, and the two are compared. If the two images are different, that's used as an indicator that something has moved; the script then captures a higher-quality image.

This image is then uploaded as a Tweet to the user account assigned to the API keys you inserted at the top of the script. So you're not overwhelmed with Tweets, if motion is detected the script will wait 60 seconds before resuming its search for motion. This prevents a deluge of messages if something is continuously moving.

When the Tweets appear in your timeline, you can manage them the same way as any other Tweet, including deleting them if you want. If you don't want the Tweets to be public, set up a new private account specifically for the camera. High-resolution images are also stored on the Pi's SD card for later retrieval.

Running the program manually can be a pain if you're planning on mounting the Pi and its Camera Module somewhere unobtrusive. To have the script load every time the Pi starts up, exit it with Ctrl+C and type the following to load the rc.local file in Nano:

```
sudo nano /etc/rc.local
```

Insert the following line into the file, just above the line that reads "exit 0":

```
/home/pi/picamera-security.
py &
```

The ampersand symbol at the end of the line tells Linux that it should run the command in the background. This allows the rc.local script to continue on and bring up the normal login screen, despite the Python program running continuously. Save the file with Ctrl+O and exit Nano with Ctrl+X. ●

SECURITY SYSTEM WALKTHROUGH

Follow our step-by step guide to setting up a developer account on Twitter, to allow your security camera to post images to your Twitter feed and to set up your application settings

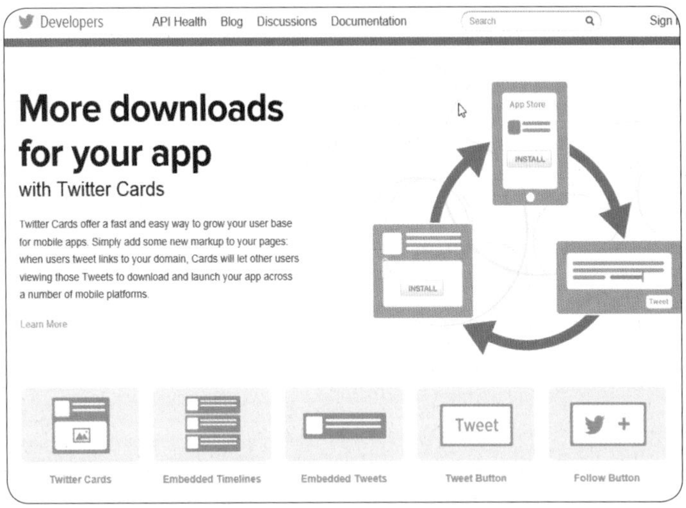

1 A Twitter developer account is freely available, and required to create your own applications that use the service to read or write messages.

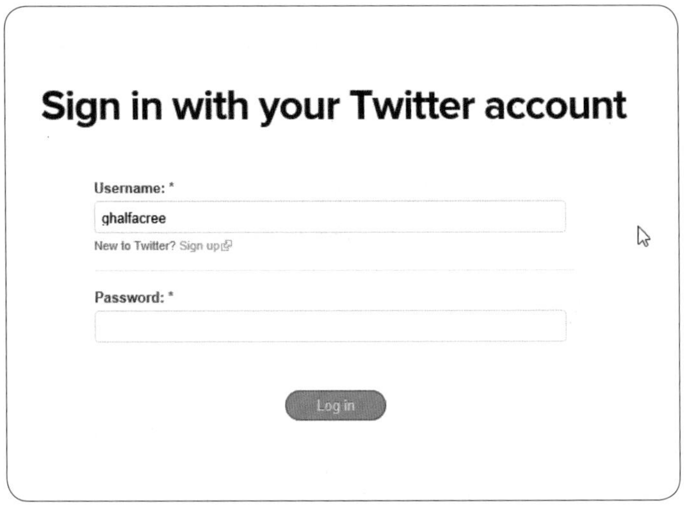

2 You'll need to sign in with your Twitter account details to continue; if you don't have an account, sign up for one at twitter.com

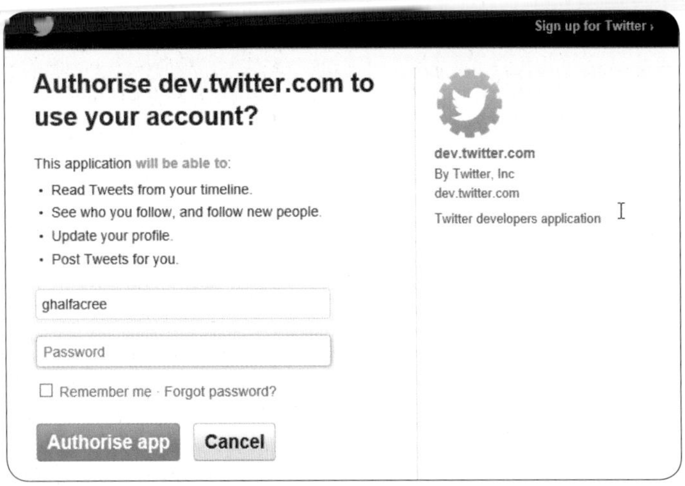

3 To authorise the development system to connect to your Twitter account, you'll need to re-enter your username and password.

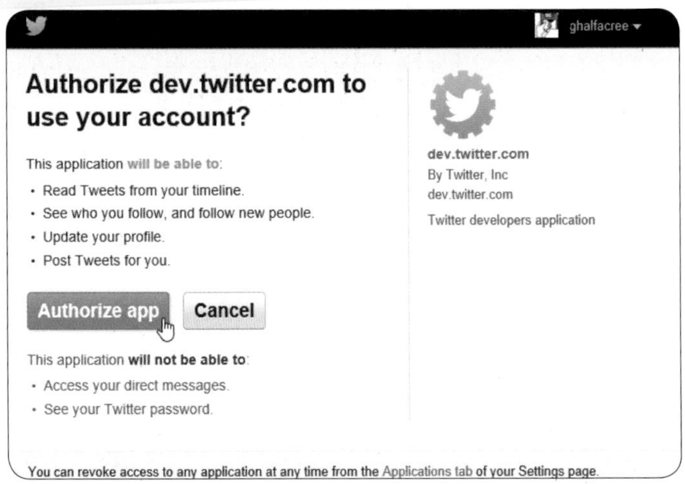

4 Click Authorise App to allow the Twitter Developer system to access you Twitter account; this will enable access to everything but Direct Messages.

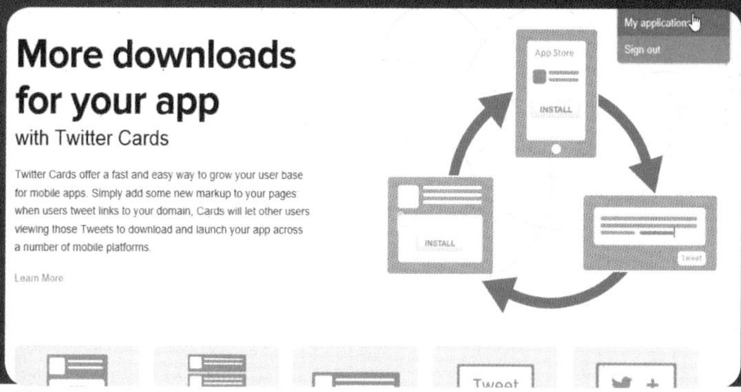

5 You can create or edit Twitter applications using the dropdown menu at the top-right of the page, accessible by clicking on your Twitter avatar.

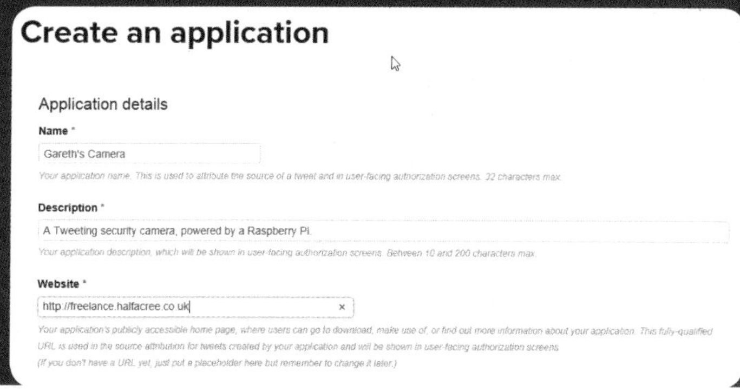

6 Choose a unique name for your app and describe what it does, and fill in your website address; you can leave the Callback URL box empty.

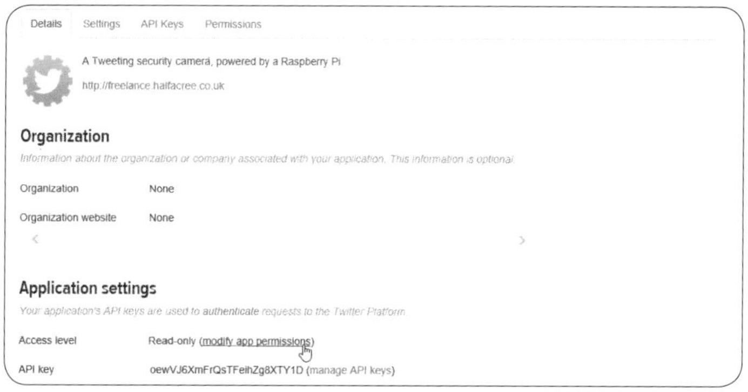

7 To allow your app to post, not just read, messages, click on Modify App Permissions in the Access Level section of Application Settings.

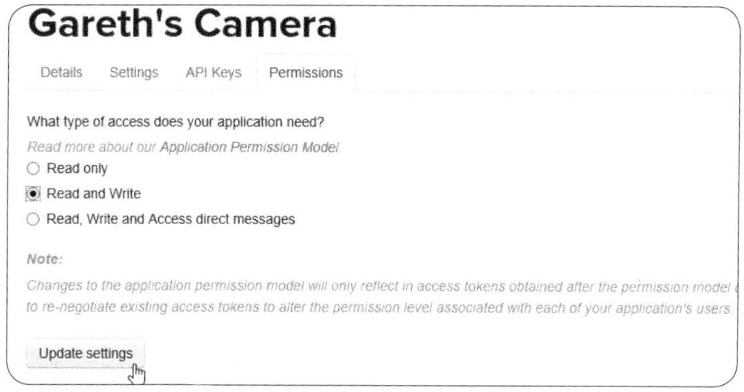

8 The security system only needs to post to Twitter; you can add the ability to access Direct Messages if you wish, but it's not required.

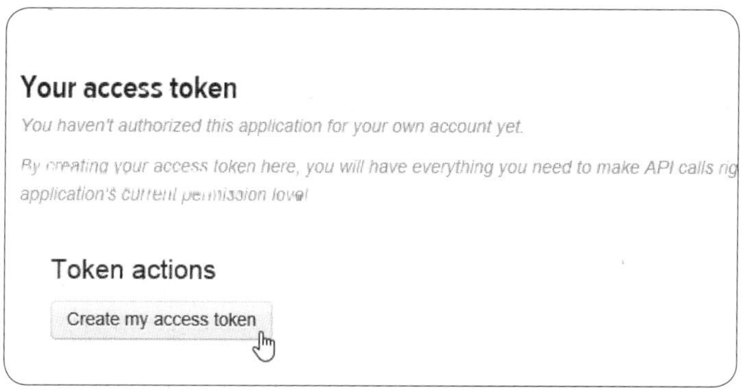

9 Click the Create My Access Token button to generate an authorisation token that will allow the Pi to post messages to your Twitter account.

10 Make a note of the API Key, API Secret, Access Token and Access Token Secret; these need to be added to the security camera script.

11 Rather than typing the security camera script out by hand, it can be downloaded from the internet using the command-line utility curl.

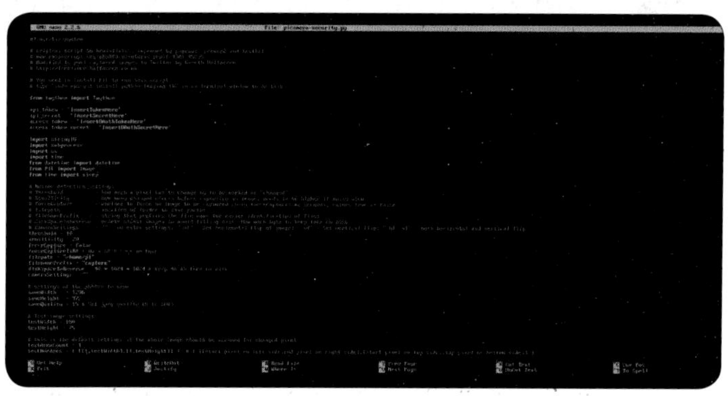

12 You need to edit the script and fill in the API Key, API Secret, Access Token and Access Token Secret details you generated for your Twitter app.

RUNNING THE PI WIRELESSLY

Thanks to its power-sipping processor, the Pi is well suited to running from battery power. First, you need the right battery and dongle to get started

The Raspberry Pi uses a processor instruction set architecture (ISA), ARM, more commonly associated with battery-powered smartphones and tablets. Many of its more esoteric features – the Camera Serial Interface (CSI) and Display Serial Interface (DSI) ports, as an example – are the result of this shared evolution.

Its use of a low-power ARM-based processor, just like in a smartphone, means that the Pi is well suited to running from battery power. Whether you want to build your own laptop or tablet, create a self-contained cordless environmental monitor, or even run it from the power of the sun, learning how to sever the cords and run the Pi as a wire-free unit is well worth the effort.

WIRELESS POWER

The Pi's power-sipping processor means that it can easily move from being powered by a mains-connected USB power adapter to a battery pack, running at full speed and with no discernible difference to its use so long as the battery holds a charge.

The capacity of a battery is typically measured in milliamp-hours, or mAh; larger batteries may use amp-hours, or Ah, which represent 1,000mAh. This measurement tells you how long the battery lasts at a certain power draw. A device that draws 100 milliamps (100mA) would run for around ten hours on a battery rated at 1,000mAh, reducing its stored charge by 100mA per hour. A device that draws 200mA would run the same battery dry in just five hours; a device that draws 50mA would last for ten.

To calculate the capacity of battery you'll need, you need to know how much power the Raspberry Pi draws during use. The official specifications for a Raspberry Pi Model A claim a peak power draw of 500mA, while the more powerful Model B draws up to 700mA. In general use, the power draw is likely to be considerably lower – down to as little as 110mA for the Model A – unless the Pi is working heavily, taxing both its central and graphics processors simultaneously, the entire time it's running.

You'll also need to allow for power drawn by any peripheral devices. A good rule of thumb is to allow at least 100mA for each device connected to the Pi's USB ports, and 10mA for each GPIO pin in use. This, coupled with the Pi's worst-case power draw figure, will give you a comfortable margin of error when shopping for a battery.

As an example, a Raspberry Pi Model A with no accessories except a USB wireless adapter would draw around 600mA at peak. To run the Pi for around 24 hours between battery charges, a battery of at least 14,400mAh capacity would be required. Assuming the Pi isn't running CPU- and GPU-heavy applications for the whole time, the battery would likely last considerably longer. But assuming worst-case

WHAT YOU'LL NEED

The Raspberry Pi Model A is the perfect choice for a wireless setup. Its single USB port can house a network adapter, and the removal of the chip that drives the Model B's Ethernet and extra USB port means the Model A draws less power than its more expensive stablemate, leading to longer life between battery charges. That's not to say it's not possible to run the Model B from batteries, but be aware that your runtime will suffer as a result of the device working to drive the now-redundant Ethernet port.

To run without a power cord, you'll need a battery of some description. The easiest option here is to use a USB powerpack, often sold as an emergency charger for smartphones and tablets. These are available in capacities of 20,000mAh or more, and can run a Pi for a considerable length of time between charges.

For network connectivity, you'll need a USB wireless dongle. Look for models that guarantee compatibility with the Raspberry Pi, such as the Wi-Pi (£8.39, cpc.farnell.com). Others may not have Linux driver software available, or may attempt to draw more power than the Pi's pseudo-USB ports can provide.

For portability, you may want to also invest in some reusable cable ties, sticky-back hook-and-loop tape and a case for the Pi. This will allow you to connect the battery pack to the Pi when it's in use but easily remove it for recharging.

figures for power draw means you're unlikely to be disappointed or surprised by a sudden outage partway through use.

If you're on a tight budget and want a more accurate estimate without the margin for error of the above, assume that the Pi draws around 75% of the above figure. This allows for times when the Pi is idle and not actively processing data, during which time it will be drawing considerably less power than the worst-case peak figures above. Using that rule of thumb, the same Pi would require only a 10,800mAh battery pack to run for the same 24-hour period.

For accurate results, the best option is to actually measure the power draw of your Pi and its accessories. To do this, you'll need a multimeter with a current, or ammeter, setting. This should be placed in-line with the power cable

For accurate results, the best option is to actually measure the power draw of your Pi and its accessories

A USB battery connects to the micro-USB port of the Pi.

going into the Pi. If you're connecting the Pi via USB, you'll need to sacrifice a micro-USB cable to do this. Cut the cable, and strip back the outer insulation and shield to expose the inner wires. Find the black and red wires; strip them and connect black to black. Now, connect the red wire from the USB A end of the cable to the red probe on your multimeter, and the red wire from the micro-USB end to the black probe.

With the multimeter wired in place and set to ammeter mode, carefully reconnect the USB cable to the Pi and the power adapter. As the Pi boots, the display of the multimeter will change to show you the actual power draw of your Pi. This reading will allow you to accurately estimate how long a battery will last when connected to the Pi, but remember to leave a margin for error. Manufacturers tend to overstate the capacities of their batteries, which will also decrease over time as they're charged and discharged.

If you're using the Raspberry Pi with nothing connected to the composite video or HDMI sockets, you can gain a little extra life from your battery by turning the display outputs off. At the terminal, type the following command:

```
sudo /opt/vc/bin/tvservice
--off
```

Note that this will immediately deactivate any video outputs currently running. Connect to the Pi over the network using SSH to continue configuring the system if required.

CHOOSING A BATTERY

When you know the capacity of the battery you need, you'll then need to choose the type of battery you buy. By far the easiest battery type to integrate into a Raspberry Pi project is the USB battery, typically sold as an emergency charger for smartphones and tablets. These batteries come in plastic or metal casings, which protect them from being crushed, and can be recharged simply by connecting them to the USB port of a PC or laptop, or to the mains via a USB power adapter.

Another major advantage of USB batteries is that they provide protection to the Pi by using the device's built-in voltage regulators. A USB battery connects to the micro-USB port of the Pi, just like a USB power adapter. This takes the 5V power and runs it through a voltage regulator, which converts it to the 3.3V on which the Pi's logic circuitry runs. If the power supplied through the micro-USB socket is slightly higher or lower than 5V due to faulty components or manufacturing tolerances, it won't permanently damage the Pi thanks to this regulator.

Connecting power to the Pi in other ways than the micro-USB socket

Ensure your USB wireless dongle supports the Raspberry Pi.

can bypass the 3.3V regulator. In some cases, this is a good thing. If you're feeding regulated 3.3V power from another source, the additional power drain of the Pi's voltage regulator is removed from the equation. In other cases, it can mean that any voltage spikes have a damaging effect on the Pi's circuitry.

When buying a USB battery, look at the measurements; buying one a similar size to the Raspberry Pi itself will make carrying the two devices around a lot easier and mean a neater appearance. The Pi's printed circuit board (PCB) measures around 85 x 56mm; try to match this in the footprint of your battery.

Try to buy a USB battery that has a regular USB A connector on it, the same as the USB ports you'd find on a desktop or laptop. Some USB batteries come with specialist cables with esoteric connectors, and if you lose these it can mean having to replace the entire battery. Buying a battery with standard USB ports means you can use any existing micro-USB cable, although many come bundled with short-length cables to keep things neat.

Finally, if you're considering using the Pi on battery power long term, buy two batteries. This way, you can be powering the Pi from one battery while the other recharges. When the battery has recharged, you can swap the batteries over. When swapping batteries, remember to shut down the Pi – the command "sudo halt" at the terminal – before unplugging the battery. Sudden power loss can corrupt the contents of the Pi's SD card, requiring the reinstallation of the operating system to repair.

WIRELESS NETWORKING

No current model of Raspberry Pi comes with integrated wireless networking hardware, although several of its rivals – such as the Olimex OlinuXino family, an open hardware design that offers improved connectivity and performance over the Pi – do include such a feature. All models can, however, have wireless network connectivity added through the use of a cheap USB wireless adapter, more commonly known as a dongle.

When buying a USB wireless dongle, make sure that its description mentions support for the Raspberry Pi. Not all dongles work with the Pi's underpowered USB ports, attempting to draw more power than the Pi can provide. Most can be made to work through the use of a powered USB hub, but that would need connecting to a mains power supply, negating the benefits of going wireless in the first place.

Most dongles that claim support

Buying a battery similar in size to the Pi looks neater.

for Linux will work fine on the Pi, but buying a specialised version such as the Wi-Pi means guaranteed support without the need to manually install drivers or firmware. The recommended Raspbian operating system includes these drivers as standard, so using the dongles is as easy as plug-and-play.

Remember to buy a dongle that matches the type of wireless network to which you're trying to connect. Most home networks today run on the 802.11n Wi-Fi standard, typically using frequencies in the 2.4GHz portion of the spectrum. Older networks may run 801.11g or 801.22b, again at 2.4GHz, which is compatible with any 802.11n 2.4GHz wireless dongle.

The newest networks may run 802.11n in the 5GHz portion of the spectrum. In many cases, this is provided alongside connectivity on the 2.4GHz spectrum. Where it's provided alone, you need to make sure that any wireless dongle you buy supports the 5GHz spectrum – many do not. Finally, some corporate networks use the 802.11a standard. These will require a specialist dongle, or one that specifically mentions support for 802.11a networks.

When you've purchased your dongle, connect it to the Pi's USB port – either port, in the case of the Model B – and boot up the system as normal to begin configuration.

CONFIGURING WIRELESS – GUI

If you're using your Pi with its graphical user interface, the easiest way to configure the wireless dongle and connect to your wireless network is to use the wpa_gui tool provided as standard in Raspbian. If you haven't loaded the GUI yet, do so with the following terminal command:

```
startx
```

When the GUI has loaded, look for the icon on the desktop labelled WiFi Config and double-click it to load the tool. In the window that appears, you'll find two dropdown lists labelled Adapter and Network. If you have a single USB dongle attached to your Pi, the Adapter box will already be filled in with its details. If you have more than one, you can choose which to configure by clicking on the dropdown arrow. If nothing is listed in Adapter, the dongle is likely not supported by the Raspberry Pi.

Before you can choose a network, you need to perform a network scan. Click the Scan button at the bottom-right of the window to initiate a scan. This will use the USB dongle to find all networks within range. Note that the results of a scan will be limited to those networks using frequencies and standards supported by the dongle. It's also possible to prevent the network name from being broadcast, a feature known as hidden SSID, which will also prevent a network from appearing in the list.

When the scan results are displayed, find the entry in the list corresponding to your network. It should be the network with the highest signal strength. Double-click on the network to bring up the network configuration window. If you're connecting to an unencrypted network, which is a very bad idea from a security standpoint, you can simply click the Add button to save the network into wpa_gui's memory.

If you're connected to an encrypted network, you'll need to supply details of the encryption type in use and its password or key. The type of encryption in use – the old Wired Equivalent Privacy (WEP) standard or the newer and more secure Wireless Protected Access (WPA) and WPA2 standards – should be automatically detected by wpa_gui and entered into the

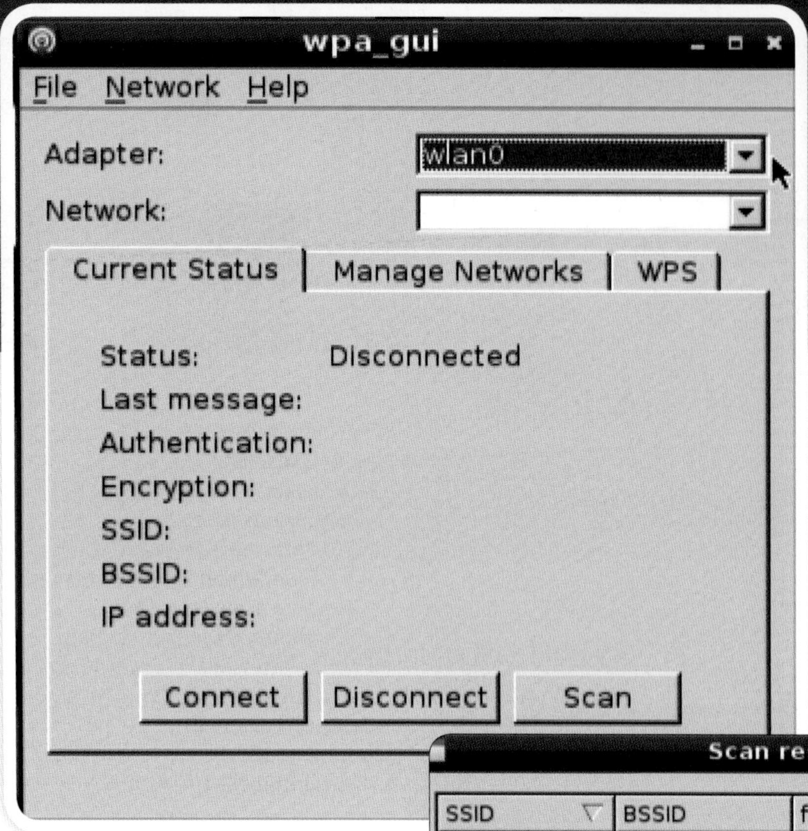

Connect to your wireless network using the wpa_gui tool.

Remember to buy a dongle that matches the type of wireless network to which you're trying to connect

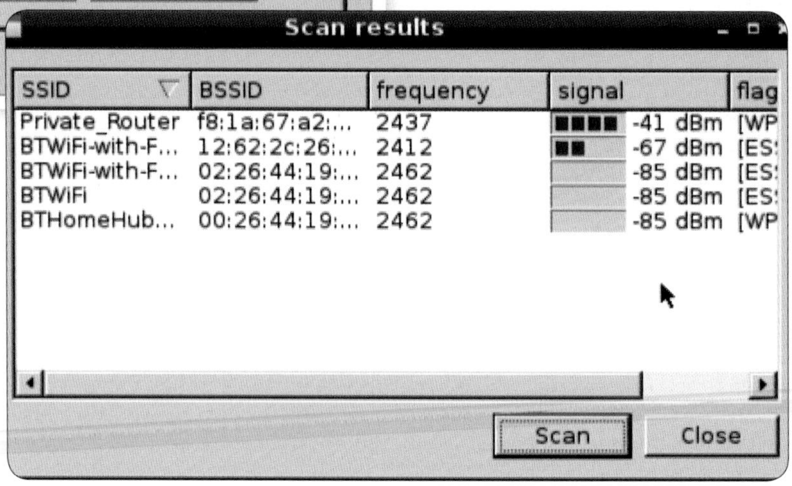

To choose a network, first perform a network scan.

relevant field. If this is listed incorrectly, you can change it manually.

With the encryption type set, you'll need to enter the password for the network. In the case of WEP networks, you'll need to enter at least one key to connect. For WPA and WPA2 networks, type in the key. Alternatively, if your router or wireless access point supports Wi-Fi Protected Setup (WPS), press the WPS button on the device and click the WPS tab within wpa_gui followed by the PBC button on the screen. This will automatically configure the network's encryption type and key. With the details filled in, click the Add button to save the network and close the window.

The name of your saved network will appear in the Network box in the main wpa_gui window, and the Pi will automatically try to connect. When connection is completed, the bottom of the window will fill in with an IP address on your local network. This means the connection has been successful. If you want to add more networks, repeat the Scan process and double-click on the entry for the network you wish to add. When you've filled in its encryption details, you can toggle between any number of networks by choosing their entries in the Network dropdown list.

If you want to disconnect from the network, click the Disconnect button. While disconnected, the USB dongle will enter a low-power mode. To reconnect, simply click Connect. While connected, you can close the wpa_gui window using the cross in the top corner. This won't disconnect you from the network, although you'll need to reload wpa_gui by double-clicking on its desktop icon in order to disconnect or change networks.

CONFIGURING WIRELESS – TERMINAL

If you're planning on using your wireless Pi for sensing or serving, the chances are you don't want to have to run a graphical user interface and configure the wireless network through the wpa_gui software. In this case, configuring the wireless network at the terminal is preferable, and can be set so the network is automatically connected every time

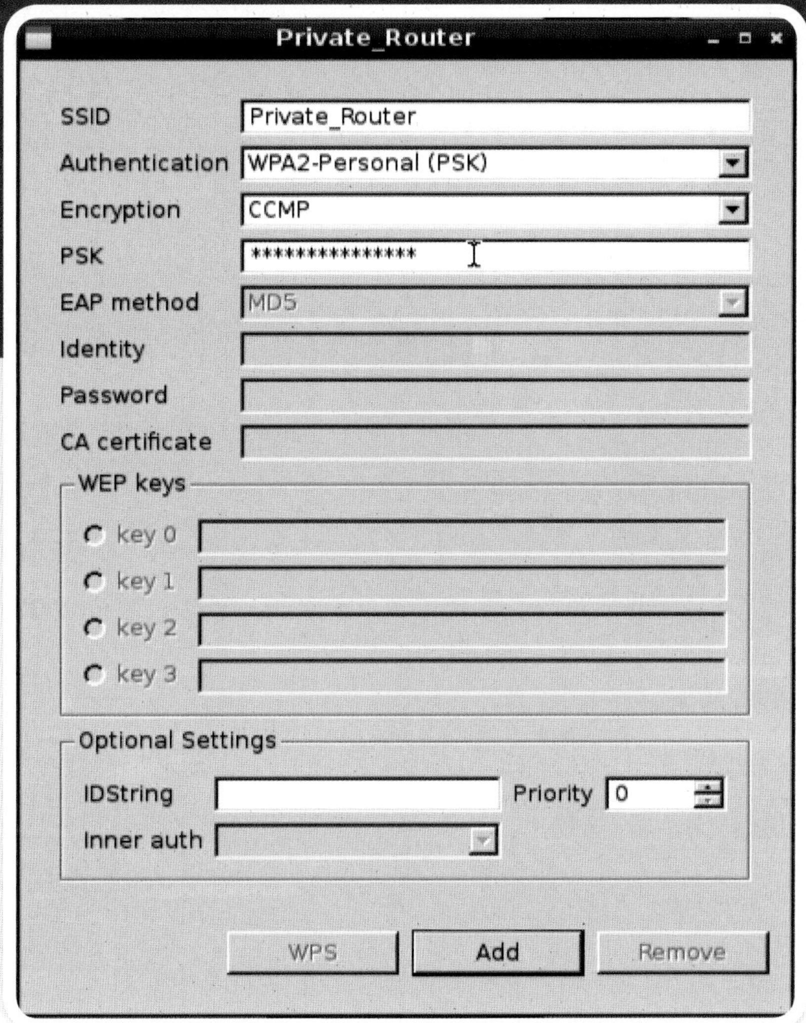

Supply details of any encryption type in use.

the Pi boots, allowing for completely independent operation without a display, keyboard or mouse.

Connect your wireless dongle to your Pi and type the following command at the terminal:

```
sudo iwlist scan | less
```

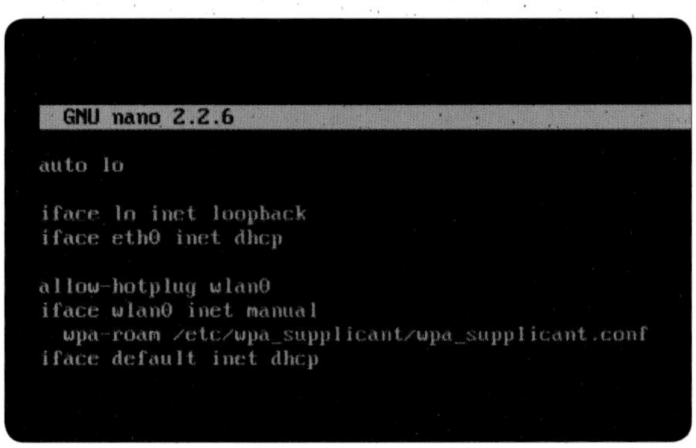

GNU nano 2.2.6
auto lo
iface lo inet loopback
iface eth0 inet dhcp
allow-hotplug wlan0
iface wlan0 inet manual
wpa-roam /etc/wpa_supplicant/wpa_supplicant.conf
iface default inet dhcp

The Pi's network configuration is controlled by a file called /etc/network/interfaces.

This will tell the Pi to scan for available wireless networks using any USB dongle it can find, then send the output to the less application. This pauses on each screenful of information, allowing you to scroll through with the arrow keys or Space. Your network should appear towards the top of the list. Verify that you can see its network name, or SSID, and quit less with the Q key. If you see no entries in the list, your USB dongle may not be supported by the Pi.

The Pi's network configuration is controlled by a file called /etc/network/interfaces, which lists all the network interfaces available to the system and how they should be used. If an interface isn't listed in this file, it's unavailable for automatic use, although it's still possible to use the network interface manually by configuring it directly at the terminal with tools like iwconfig and ifconfig.

In previous releases of Raspbian, it was necessary to edit the /etc/network/interfaces file when connecting a wireless dongle. In its more recent release, this has been made unnecessary, with the default configuration already set to support a single wireless adapter. All you need to do is modify the wireless network list by editing the following file:

```
sudo nano /etc/wpa_supplicant/wpa_supplicant.conf
```

The wpa_supplicant.conf file is somewhat inaccurately named; although most commonly used to control connection to WPA and WPA2 protected networks, the file also holds the keys for WEP networks. All versions of this file start the same way, so type the following to begin:

```
network={
        ssid="YourSSID"
```

Fill in the SSID of your network between the quotes. This is also known as the "network name", and is the friendly name that appeared when you ran the network scan earlier. If you're running an unencrypted wireless network – which is an extremely bad idea from a security point of view – you can finish the file by typing in the following lines:

```
        key_mgmt=NONE
}
```

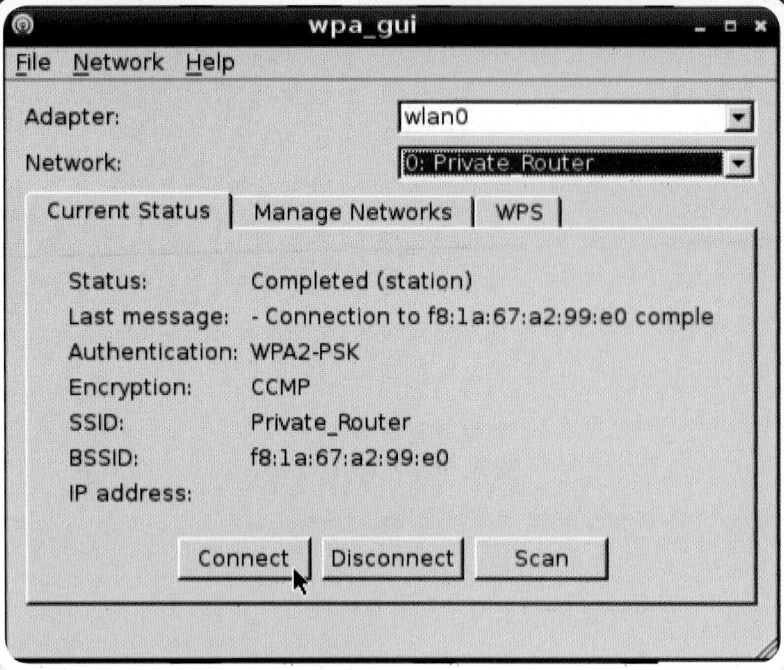

The name of your saved network appears in the Network box.

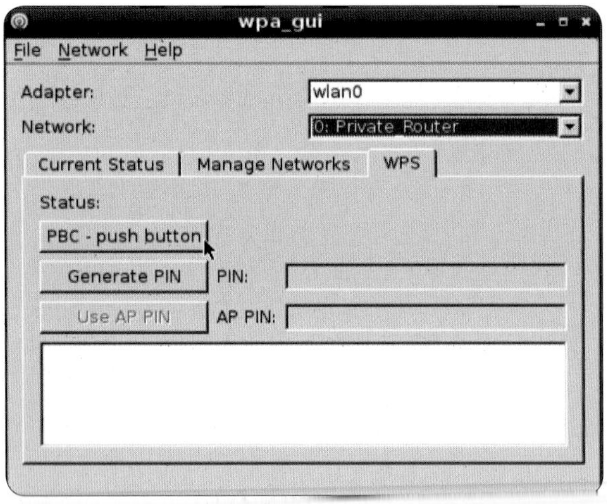

Automatically configure the network's encryption type.

If you're using a WEP network – an older encryption standard, which should really be replaced with a WPA2 encryption scheme as soon as possible, as it's extremely easy to break with little effort – you should instead type the following:

```
        key_mgmt=NONE
        wep_key0="YourWEPKey"
}
```

Put your WEP encryption key between the quotes. If you have more than one key – WEP networks support up to four independent network keys, any one of which may be used to authenticate with the network – you can add those using wep_key1, wep_key2 and wep_key3; normally, a single key is enough to connect to a WEP network.

If you're using a WPA or WPA2 network – the newest wireless encryption standard, considered significantly more secure than WEP – then instead you need to type the following to finish the file:

```
        key_mgmt=WPA-PSK
        psk="YourWPAKey"
}
```

Note that "WPA-PSK" should be used regardless of the network being WPA or WPA2. Place your WPA encryption key between the quotes.

If you want the Pi to be able to automatically connect to multiple wireless networks, repeat the process by adding new network definitions for each network. Note, however, that the Pi can only connect to a single network, chosen automatically based on signal strength, at a time unless you add additional USB dongles. Save the file with Ctrl+O, and exit Nano with Ctrl+X.

The wireless network will only be brought up automatically when the network stack is reloaded, usually when the Pi reboots. To begin using it instantly, type the following to bring the wireless interface live:

```
sudo service networking
restart
```

It can take a few seconds for the Pi to finish connecting to a wireless network, so be patient. When the connection is up, you should be able to use the network as normal. If you want to test the connection, try typing the following command to send a test packet to the *PC Pro* web server:

```
ping -c 1 www.pcpro.co.uk
```

You'll receive confirmation that the packet was received back from the web server, along with an indication of how long the trip took. If your wireless signal strength is poor, you may find that the connection is erratic. Try moving the Pi closer to your wireless access point or router, or look for USB dongles that include RPA-SMA connectors for external antennas.

SETTING A STATIC IP

If you want to use your Pi as a server, it's a good idea to set it up with a static IP address. This makes it much easier to find on the network. Configuring a static IP on a wireless connection is much the same as the process used on a wired network, detailed in the Privacy Router project, and can be performed in two ways: setting up a static IP address reservation on your router or setting a static IP address directly on the Pi.

wlan0 Scan completed :
Cell 01 - Address: 00:62:2C:26:4F:DE
Channel:1
Bit Rates:1 Mb/s; 2 Mb/s; 5.5 Mb/s; 11 Mb/s; 6 Mb/s
9 Mb/s; 12 Mb/s; 18 Mb/s
Bit Rates:24 Mb/s; 36 Mb/s; 48 Mb/s; 54 Mb/s
Mode:Master
Extra:tsf=0000002d1c9d267c
Extra: Last beacon: 30ms ago
IE: Unknown: 000E507269766174655F526F75746572
IE: Unknown: 010882848B960C121824
IE: Unknown: 030101
IE: Unknown: 0706474220010D14
IE: Unknown: 2A0100
IE: IEEE 802.11i/WPA2 Version 1
Group Cipher : TKIP
Pairwise Ciphers (2) : CCMP TKIP
Authentication Suites (1) : PSK
IE: Unknown: 32043048606C
IE: Unknown: 2D1AAC011BFFFF000000000000000000000000008000000000000000000
IE: Unknown: 3D160100010000000000000000000000000000000000000000
IE: Unknown: 4A0E14000A002C01C800140005001900
IE: Unknown: 7F080100000000000040
IE: Unknown: DD180050F2020101800003A4000027A4000042435E0062322F00
IE: Unknown: DD0900037F01010000FF7F
Cell 02 - Address: 12:62:2C:26:4F:DE
Channel:1
Frequency:2.412 GHz (Channel 1)
Quality=41/70 Signal level=-69 dBm
Encryption key:off
ESSID:"BTWiFi-with-FON"
Bit Rates:1 Mb/s; 2 Mb/s; 5.5 Mb/s; 11 Mb/s; 6 Mb/s
9 Mb/s; 12 Mb/s; 18 Mb/s
Bit Rates:24 Mb/s; 36 Mb/s; 48 Mb/s; 54 Mb/s
Mode:Mastelo Interface doesn't support scanning.
eth0 Interface doesn't support scanning.
r
Extra:tsf=0000002d1c9c67e8
Extra: Last beacon: 30ms ago
IE: Unknown: 000F42545769466692D776974682D464F4E
IE: Unknown: 010882848B960C121824
IE: Unknown: 030101
IE: Unknown: 0706474220010D14
IE: Unknown: 2A0100
IE: Unknown: 32043048606C
IE: Unknown: 2D1AAC011BFFFF000000000000000000000000008000000000000000000
IE: Unknown: 3D160100010000000000000000000000000000000000000000
IE: Unknown: 4A0E14000A002C01C800140005001900
IE: Unknown: 7F080100000000000040
IE: Unknown: DD180050F2020101800003A4000027A4000042435E0062322F00
IE: Unknown: DD0900037F01010000FF7F
Cell 03 - Address: F8:1A:67:A2:99:E0
Channel:6
Frequency:2.437 GHz (Channel 6)
Quality=69/70 Signal level=-41 dBm
Encryption key:on
:

Configuring the wireless network at the terminal.

Setting up static IP addresses on the router is the preferred option. The client device can continue to use DHCP to receive other network settings, but it will always be given the same address, which will be made unavailable for use by any other device. Configuring your router or gateway for a static client varies depending on make and model. Look in the manual or help file for reference to "static reservations", "static IP" or "DHCP reservations". You'll most likely need to know the Media Access Control (MAC) address of the device you're reserving. You can find this out quickly by typing the following command on the Pi:

```
ifconfig | grep HWaddr
```

If you run the above command on a Raspberry Pi Model A with a wireless dongle connected, you'll see only one entry; a Model B, however, will list two different MAC addresses. One of the addresses, labelled as etho, corresponds to the Model B's onboard Ethernet connection. The other will be labelled wlano, and it's this MAC address that should be used to configure a static wireless IP address.

If your router doesn't support static IP reservations, the alternative is to set a static address on the Pi itself. This is somewhat less ideal, as if done incorrectly can result in collisions, where the Pi and another device try to use the same address.

To set a static IP, you'll need to know the address of your network, the network mask, the address of your router, and where the DHCP scope – the range of addresses it's configured to give out – begins and ends. All this information can be found on your router's configuration pages. With that information in hand, load the Pi's network configuration file in Nano with the following terminal command:

```
sudo nano /etc/network/
interfaces
```

Find the line that reads "iface wlano inet manual" and alter it to:

```
iface wlan0 inet static
```

Then add the following lines beneath:

```
address ip-address
netmask netmask
gateway router-ip
```

Where "address" is the static IP you want to assign to the Pi, which should be either above or below the DHCP scope and not in use by any other device, "netmask" is the network mask for your home network – typically 255.255.255.0 – and "gateway" the IP address of your router. Double-check the settings, then save them with Ctrl+O. Exit Nano with Ctrl+X to return to the terminal.

While the Pi has its new network settings stored, it won't use them until the next time it's rebooted or the networking stack is reloaded. Force the latter with the following command to use the new settings immediately, but be aware that if you're connected remotely via SSH, VNC or similar, you'll lose your connection and need to reconnect using the new address:

```
sudo service networking
restart
```

INTERFACING WITH ARDUINO

Adding an Arduino to your Pi will give you a lot more flexibility when it comes to building electronics projects. We show you how to get started

The Raspberry Pi is an undeniably capable microcomputer, but it lacks the features of a true microcontroller. Its operating system doesn't operate in real-time, its general-purpose input-output (GPIO) capabilities are basic if not expanded via add-in boards, and it requires more power in order to operate. These trade-offs, of course, are balanced by its flexibility, full multitasking operating system, affordability and ease of use.

There's no reason to choose the Pi over a microcontroller or vice-versa, however; the two platforms can coexist and be used to enhance each others' functionality. The open hardware Arduino project is often picked to sit alongside a Raspberry Pi in embedded projects, greatly expanding the Pi's GPIO capability without adding considerable cost to the project. The Pi, meanwhile, offers network connectivity, storage, graphical display output and other advanced functions at a significant saving over adding those same functions to the Arduino in any other manner.

Adding an Arduino to your Pi will give you much more flexibility when it comes to building electronics projects, including the ability to output accurate pulse-width modulated (PWM) signals to control servos, read analogue inputs using the Arduino's integrated analogue-to-digital (ADC) converter, more GPIO pins for larger and more complex projects, support for common 5V logic components, and a large community offering a vast library of pre-written software and support.

WHAT YOU'LL NEED

Expanding the Pi with an Arduino requires the use of a USB port to connect the two, although this can be replaced later with an external power supply for the Arduino and a connection to the Pi's GPIO port. As a result, and because the common reason to add a Pi to an Arduino project is to provide network connectivity, a Model B with its two USB ports is the best choice. You can use a Model A if you control it over the network rather than with a local keyboard or mouse, or if you use a powered USB hub.

You'll also need an Arduino board. There are both official boards from the Arduino Project itself and from third-party manufacturers. The most common is the Arduino Uno (£22, oomlout.co.uk). If you don't already have any electronic components, consider an Arduino Starter Kit (£62, oomlout.co.uk), which comes with an Arduino Uno, a booklet of projects and all the components you need to get started.

You'll also need a USB A-to-B cable to connect to the Arduino Uno. If you've chosen a different model, such as the cheaper Arduino Leonardo, you'll need a different type of cable, which may not be supplied as standard.

INSTALLING THE SOFTWARE

The Arduino is programmed using an open-source package known as the Arduino Integrated Development Environment, or Arduino IDE. This provides a friendly user interface for writing Arduino programs, and allows them to be compiled, uploaded to the Arduino and their output monitored all from a single application. It also comes with a library of pre-written example programs, helping you get a handle on the Processing language on which the Arduino IDE is based.

The Arduino IDE is a graphical package, so to get started load the Pi's graphical user interface, if it isn't already open, with the following command:

```
startx
```

When the desktop appears, open a terminal session by double-clicking the LXTerminal icon. As always with Pi projects, the first step is to update the package list and any outdated software with the following commands:

```
sudo apt-get update
sudo apt-get upgrade
```

When the upgrade process is finished, install the Arduino IDE with the following command:

```
sudo apt-get install arduino
```

The Arduino IDE requires some additional software, which the Apt package manager will automatically find for you; press Y and Enter when prompted to begin the installation. Downloading the software requires an active internet connection, but the Arduino IDE works fine offline once it's installed. When the process has finished, close the LXTerminal window with the cross in the top corner.

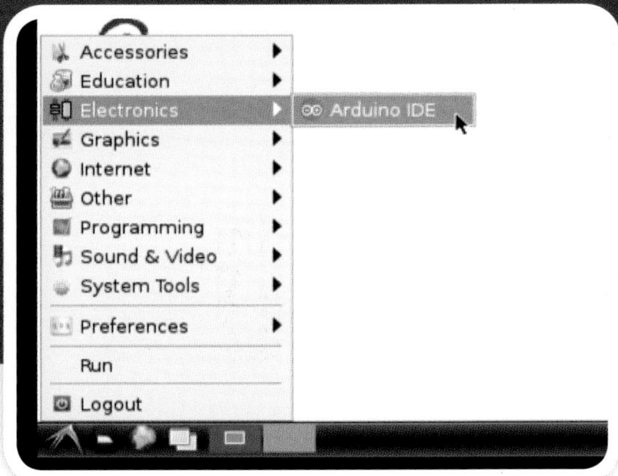

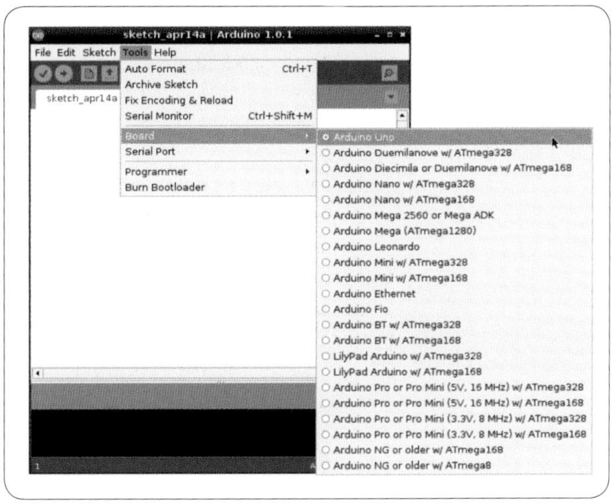

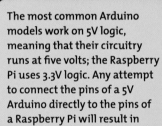

Find your Arduino model in the list and click to select.

WARNING

The most common Arduino models work on 5V logic, meaning that their circuitry runs at five volts; the Raspberry Pi uses 3.3V logic. Any attempt to connect the pins of a 5V Arduino directly to the pins of a Raspberry Pi will result in damage to the Pi. Unless you have additional hardware to swap between the two voltages, or know that you have a specialised Arduino which runs on 3.3V logic, always use the USB cable to connect the Arduino to the Raspberry Pi.

Plug your Arduino into one of the Pi's USB sockets. If you're using a Model A, or a Model B with a separate keyboard and mouse attached, you'll need a USB hub. You'll get no onscreen prompt when the Arduino is connected, but its power light – marked as PWR or ON on the Arduino board, depending on the model and manufacturer – will illuminate. Click the menu button at the bottom-left, choose Electronics and click Arduino IDE to load the IDE itself.

Before you can get using the IDE, you'll need to do some final configuration. When the Arduino IDE loads – which can take a minute or two on a non-overclocked Pi – click on the Tools menu and choose Board. This provides a list of all the different Arduino models that the Arduino IDE can program; find your entry in the list and click to select it. If you can't find your particular model listed, check the manufacturer's website. Many third-party boards require you to choose a similar official model from the Boards menu, while others may need the installation of a special board definition file.

Finally, click on the Tools menu again and select Serial Port. This allows you to choose which port is used to communicate with the Arduino board. All USB-connected Arduino boards have their own USB-to-serial conversion hardware, which shows up in Linux as a virtual serial port, the exact name of which differs from model to model. With only one Arduino connected to a Pi running the standard Raspbian operating system, you'll only have a single entry in this list: ttyUSB0 for older Arduino models, or ttyACM0 for newer models. Click on the entry to select it.

YOUR FIRST SKETCH

Programs for the Arduino are known as Sketches, and are written in a special version of the C programming language known as Wiring. This is an off-shoot of the Processing language originally developed for experimentation and creative computing. Unlike traditional embedded programming languages, Wiring is designed to be as easy as possible to learn by abstracting much of the complexity of writing code for a microcontroller away from the user.

To have a look at a very simple Arduino Sketch, click on the File menu of the Arduino IDE and select Examples followed by 01.Basics. From the list, click on Blink; this will load the Blink Sketch, which is designed to cause an LED built onto the Arduino to flash on and off repeatedly. The Sketch will open in a new window. You can either leave the blank Arduino window open behind the Blink Sketch, or close it with the cross in the top corner.

An Arduino Sketch typically has three main segments: an initial segment where any variables used in the program are initialised; a setup segment, which only runs once each time the Arduino is powered on; and the main program loop, which runs continuously until power is removed from the Arduino. The Blink sketch has all three of these segments, helpfully commented so that you can easily see what each does.

Lines prefaced with two slashes - // - or between a pair of slashes and asterisks - /* */ - are comments, which

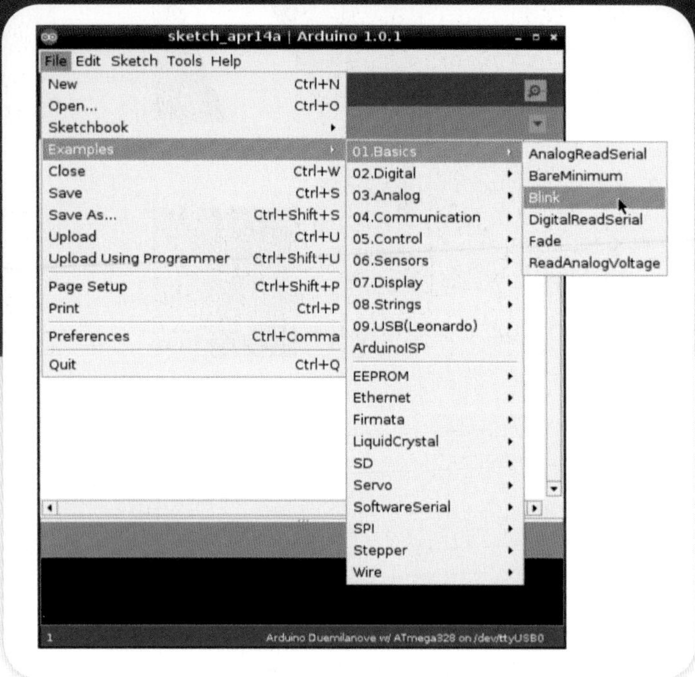

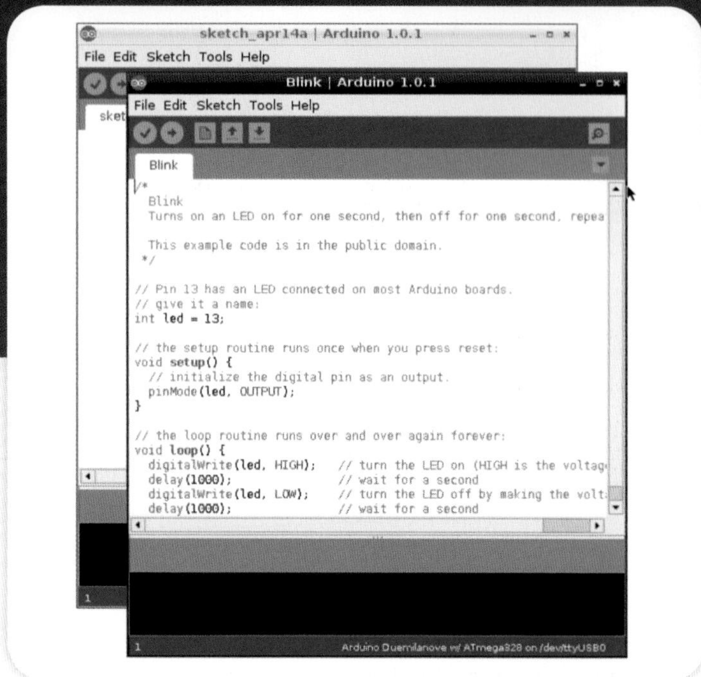

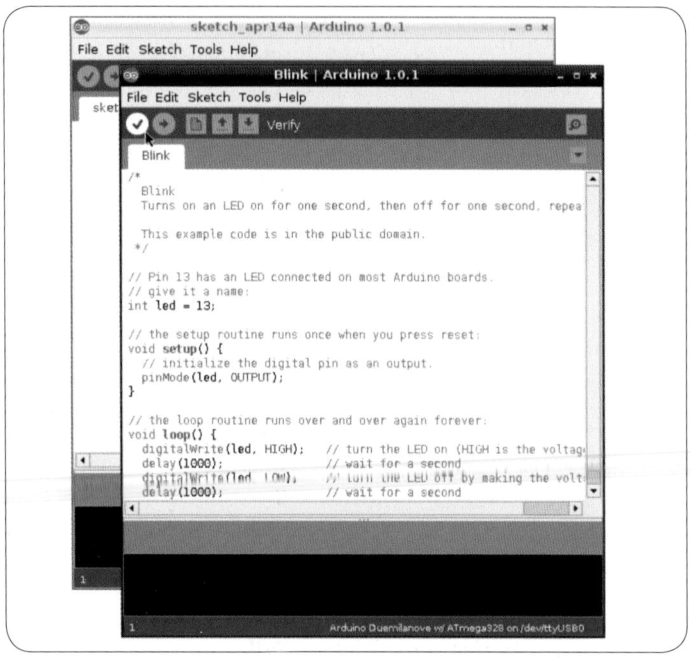

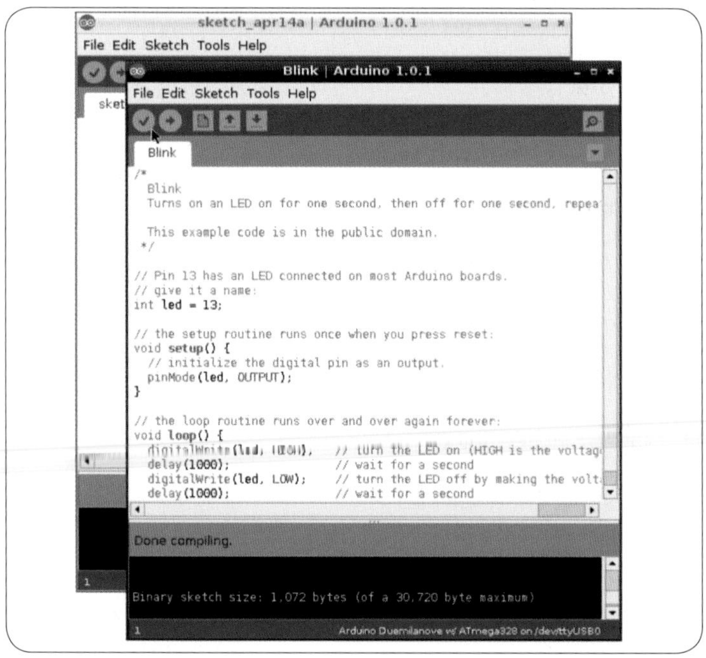

Click on Blink to load the Blink Sketch in a new window.

are ignored by the IDE when it comes to compile the program from human-readable source code into a binary format the Arduino microcontroller can run. The first proper line of the Blink Sketch is:

```
int led = 13;
```

This sets up a new variable called "led", tells the IDE that it's an integer – whole number – and gives it the value 13. If you're used to writing programs in Python or similar languages, you can already see some differences. Where Python allows you to assign values to variables and have it automatically figure out what type they should be, Wiring – based as it is on C – requires you to declare the type of variable in advance. When you begin to write more complex programs, you may use variable types like floating point numbers with decimal places, true or false Boolean types, or strings of text, but in the Blink Sketch the only variable is an integer.

This variable is used to tell the program which pin the LED is connected to. Although this could be defined later in the program, putting it in a variable at the top allows you to

easily change the pin number in the future. Most Arduino models include an onboard LED connected to pin 13, so leaving this variable set to 13 means you'll be able to see the Blink Sketch in action without having to build a circuit yourself.

The next line of the program begins the setup portion of the Sketch:

```
void setup() {
```

Everything between the curly brace on that line and a matching brace on a line below will be run once when the Arduino is powered on. After this, the setup section is ignored until the next time the Arduino is powered on or reset. This is where you can insert code to set up various parts of the Arduino ahead of the main loop. In the case of the Blink Sketch, there's a single entry in the setup section:

```
  pinMode(led, OUTPUT);
}
```

This sets the pin identified by the variable "led" – configured earlier in the program as 13 – as an output. Like the Raspberry Pi's GPIO pins, the Arduino's pins can be configured as either inputs or outputs. Some can also be configured in more advanced modes not supported by the Pi's GPIO pins, like pulse-width modulation (PWM) for controlling a servo or the brightness of an LED, or as analogue inputs for reading sensors. The Blink Sketch uses only a single pin, and the setup portion of the Sketch is then closed by the matching curly brace.

The "pinMode" line, you may have noticed, is indented with a pair of spaces. Unlike Python, which relies on indentation to mark which sections of code are set out in blocks, Wiring and C don't require indentation; the Sketch would work just fine without the spaces there. Indentation in C is purely for the reader, making it easier to see at a glance where blocks of code begin and end without having to search out the matched braces.

The next line of the Sketch begins what's known as the "main loop":

```
void loop() {
```

Unlike the setup portion of the Sketch, which runs only once each time the Arduino is plugged in or reset, the loop – as the name implies – runs continuously. It's possible to make it stop by inserting certain commands within the loop, but it's not common that you would want to do this. It's in the main loop that the work of the Sketch is completed, whether that's waiting for a button press or continuously monitoring a temperature sensor for changes. In the case of the Blink sketch, the main loop is only a few lines long:

```
  digitalWrite(led, HIGH);
  delay(1000);
  digitalWrite(led, LOW);
  delay(1000);
}
```

Plug your Arduino into one of the Pi's USB sockets.

The first line tells the Arduino to turn the pin specified by the "led" variable – set to 13 earlier – on, which in the Wiring syntax means writing a digital value of "high" to the pin. The next line causes the Arduino to wait for a period of time. Unlike the Python time.sleep instruction, delay on an Arduino is measured in milliseconds. Delay(1000), then, is an instruction to wait for one second before continuing.

The next two lines are almost identical to the first two, except this time the pin is switched off by writing a digital value of "low" to the pin. Where a high value provides power to the LED and causes it to light up, a low value removes that power and causes it to switch off. A second delay instruction again pauses the Arduino for a second. Without it, the LED would flash on and off thousands of times a second, appearing as though it's just permanently lit. The final brace closes the main loop; when the Arduino reaches this instruction, it returns to the beginning of the loop once more.

Unlike interpreted languages like Python, which can be directly run from the source code, the Arduino's source code needs to be compiled into a binary format. First, it's good practice to check your code for errors: click the tick symbol at the left-hand side of the menu bar to begin a Verify pass. Verifying your code compiles it, but doesn't try to upload it to the

CHAPTER FIVE

DIY & ADVANCED

The Raspberry Pi has proved extremely popular among makers, hackers, tinkerers and other hobbyists. Its combination of flexible general-purpose input-output (GPIO) capabilities, powerful Linux operating system and integral internet connectivity means it can be used to add capabilities to almost any project without having to spend a fortune.

The uses to which the Pi has been put in the hacker community range from powering near-space photography balloons and coin-operated arcade machines to keeping an eye on homebrew beer.

In this chapter, you'll put into practice some of the more advanced capabilities of the Pi by creating devices ranging from a simple set of traffic lights to a hand-made arcade controller for teaming up with the retro gaming system in the Entertainment chapter, a doorbell that sends you a Twitter message, a simple motor control system and even a printer connected to the growing Internet of Things.

5

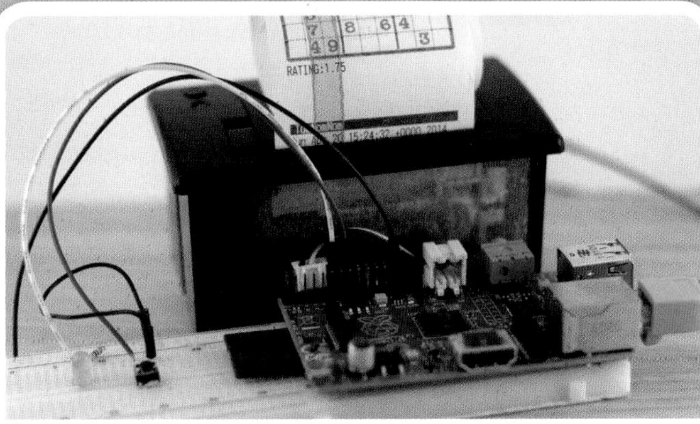

SIMULATING TRAFFIC LIGHTS

Discover how to create a simple set of traffic lights by turning LEDs into output devices for your Pi, then program them to light in the correct sequence

The Pi's General Purpose Input-Output (GPIO) port really sets it apart from a traditional computer, allowing for easy interfacing with various components to build your own intelligent circuits. It can be difficult to know how to get started, but even the most complex of projects are typically built of relatively simple component parts.

This project is great for demonstrating the concepts of computer control to children, but also has a lot to teach adults: it makes heavy use of the Pi's GPIO port to drive a series of LEDs in a pattern reminiscent of traffic lights. By altering the Python source code in a variety of ways, you can change the speed or order of the lights' pattern, or even link them to external triggers such as incoming social network messages and emails, processor load or button presses – once you've got the basics sorted, anyway.

BUILDING THE CIRCUIT

The traffic-light circuit is a simple one, connecting each LED to a different pin on the Raspberry Pi's GPIO header and to the ground pin. All circuits must be connected to a voltage source – in this case, the GPIO pins, which can be switched on and off at your command via Python – as well as a ground, or 0V, connection. Missing one or the other results in an open circuit, which doesn't work. The opposite, where the connection between the voltage source and ground is made too early before the electricity reaches the components of the circuit, is known as a short circuit and is equally useless.

Before you get started, shut down the Pi safely with this command:

```
sudo halt
```

When the process has finished, unplug the power cable and any other cables connected to the Pi. Always switch the Pi off and disconnect the power cable when connecting or disconnecting anything to the Pi's GPIO header. The pins are connected directly to the Pi's BCM2835 processor, and shorting them out by connecting the wrong pin in the wrong place can destroy a Pi in short order. Making sure the Pi is switched off gives you a chance to double-check your wiring before powering it on, and prevents surges when new components are wired into the GPIO header.

Take the breadboard, and orient it so that the central gap runs top-to-bottom. The columns of the breadboard are electrically connected via a metal strip on the underside, separated into two blocks of five by the central gap. If you have a larger breadboard, you may have more blocks or the blocks may have more holes. If you put a component in

WHAT YOU'LL NEED

The ability to make use of the Raspberry Pi's GPIO port in Python requires no additional software if you're using the recommend Raspbian Linux distribution. As a result, a Model A is just as well suited to the task as the more expensive Model B. The latter, however, is a better choice if you're planning on expanding the project to include network-based trigger events such as email monitoring.

You'll also need a breadboard (£3, oomlout.co.uk). This takes the place of a traditional circuit board when building your project, but is reusable: components can be inserted without solder, making it safe for children, and removed quickly if you want to build something else.

To give the Pi something to drive, you'll need at least three light-emitting diodes (LEDs). These can be bought in packs (from £3, oomlout.co.uk) and usually come with the required current limiting resistors to protect them from burning out. If not, you'll also need some resistors (£7.50 for a kit of 500, oomlout.co.uk). For the most common types of LED, 470 Ohm (470Ω) resistors will provide good brightness and long life.

It's a good idea to have a pair of wire-cutters (£4.25, oomlout.co.uk) to trim component leads to size. It's not an absolute requirement, but it will make your final project look neater and helps to prevent accidental shorts between components.

Finally, you'll need some jumper wire (£3.50, oomlout.co.uk) to connect the Pi to the breadboard. Look for wire with a female header at one end and a male header – or supplied conversion pins – at the other. This makes it easy to connect to both the breadboard and the Pi's GPIO header.

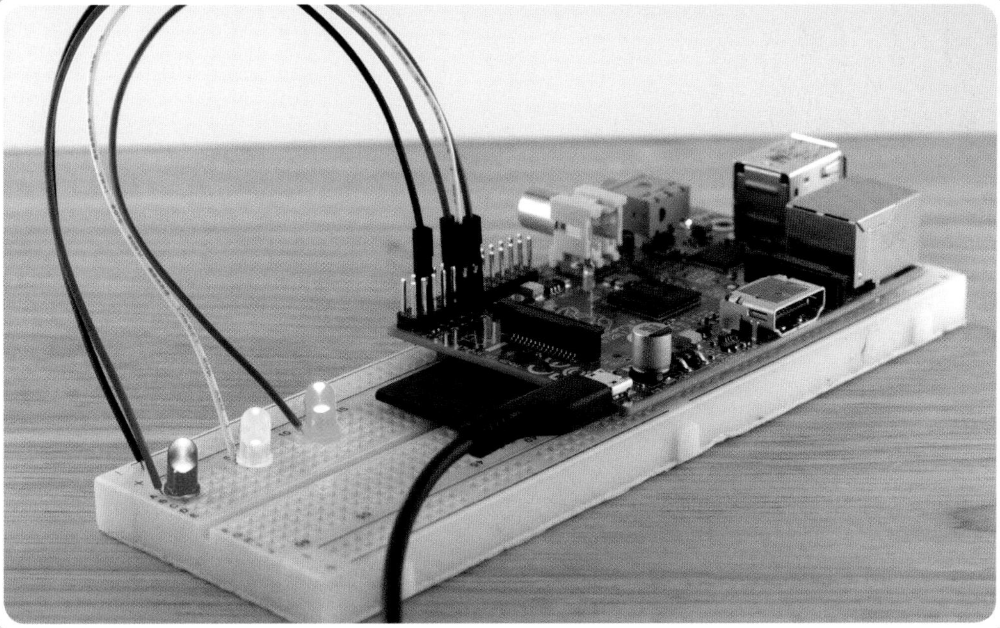

The finished traffic-light circuit in action.

the top-left hole of the first row and another in the next hole along, they will be connected. Move one of the components down to the next row or across the gap at the centre to the next block and that connection will be broken. It's this layout of the breadboard's electrical connections that makes it easy to build complex circuits without excess wiring.

First, take three resistors; these may have been supplied with your LEDs, or if purchased separately should be 470Ω – identified with yellow, purple, brown and gold bands encircling the body of the resistor. Bend the legs at a 90-degree angle from the body a few millimetres out, and snip the remaining wire so that the length after the bend is around the same as the depth of your breadboard. You can skip this step if you don't have any wire-cutters, but be careful: you'll end up with a considerable length of bare lead sticking out from the breadboard, and it can be easy to create a short circuit.

Taking one of the three resistors, place one end into the hole at the far-right of the block of five holes in the second row down, and the other end into the third hole of the blue or black column at the right-hand end of the board. Unlike the rest of the holes, these columns are designed to provide power – red for positive voltage and blue or black for 0V or ground – and are connected vertically rather than horizontally. You'll be using this column to provide a ground connection to the LEDs, without which they won't light up.

Take the next resistor, and place it five holes down at the same angle. Repeat this five holes down again with the third resistor. Resistors don't have an alignment, so it doesn't matter whether the gold stripe is facing to the left or the right when you do this. These resistors are being used as current-limiting resistors. Without current-limiting resistors, the LEDs will attempt to draw as much power from the Pi's GPIO header as possible. This can be damaging for the Pi, and will certainly burn out the LEDs in short order. The resistors act to limit the amount of current each LED can draw, protecting both the LED and the Pi.

Next, take the LEDs. You can use LEDs of all the same colour, but for an authentic traffic-light appearance it's good to have one red, one amber or yellow, and one green LED. Each LED will have two legs: one short and one long. The long leg is the anode, and needs to be connected to the voltage source; the short leg is the cathode, and needs to be connected to ground. If you have wire-cutters, trim the legs of the LEDs now. When doing so, cut at an angle so as to keep one leg longer than the other, to make it easy to see at a glance which leg is the anode and which is the cathode.

The layout of the breadboard's electrical connections makes it easy to build complex circuits without excess wiring

Insert the long leg of the red LED into the second hole from the right of the top row, and the shorter leg into the hole directly beneath, next to the leg of the first resistor. Repeat the process with the amber LED, placing it so the short leg is to the left of the leg of the second resistor; and again with the green LED, with the short leg to the left of the leg of the third resistor. All LEDs are now connected to ground via independent current-limiting resistors, or they will be when you wire the circuit into the Raspberry Pi's GPIO header.

Take your jumper wires, and insert the male end of one into the very top hole of the blue or black column at the far-right of the breadboard. This will provide a connection between the breadboard and ground. The female end should be connected to the third pin on the top row of the Pi's GPIO header, as seen when the board is oriented with the Pi logo the right way up and the HDMI connector at the bottom.

Take another jumper wire, and insert it into the breadboard in the

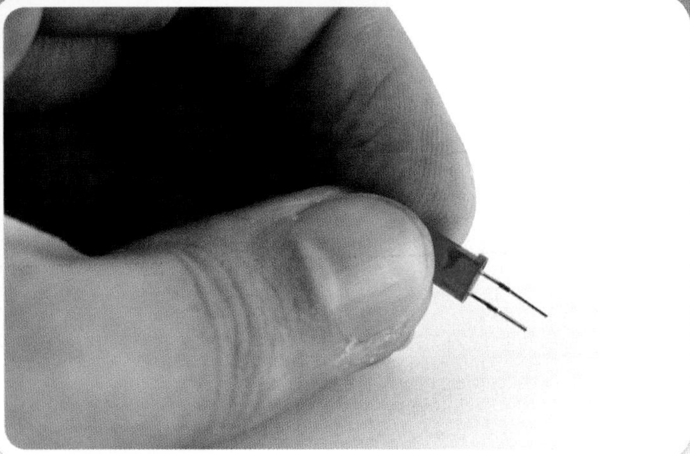

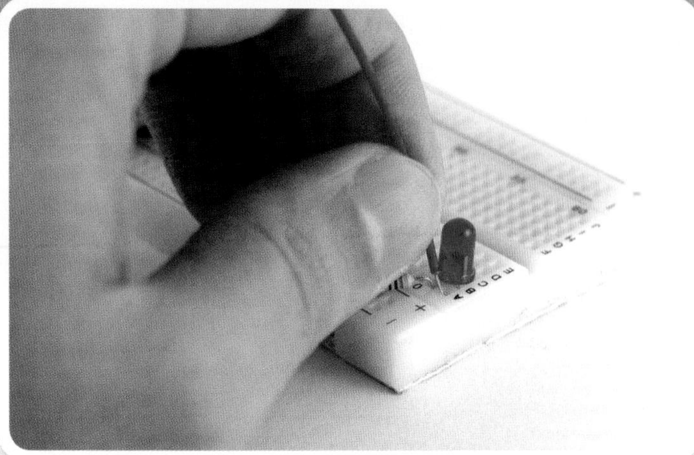

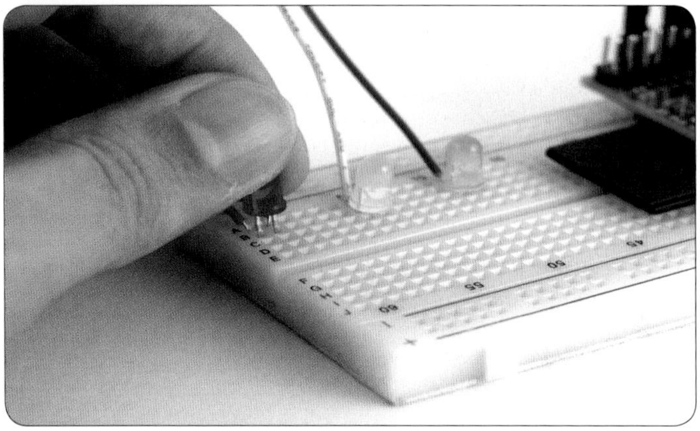

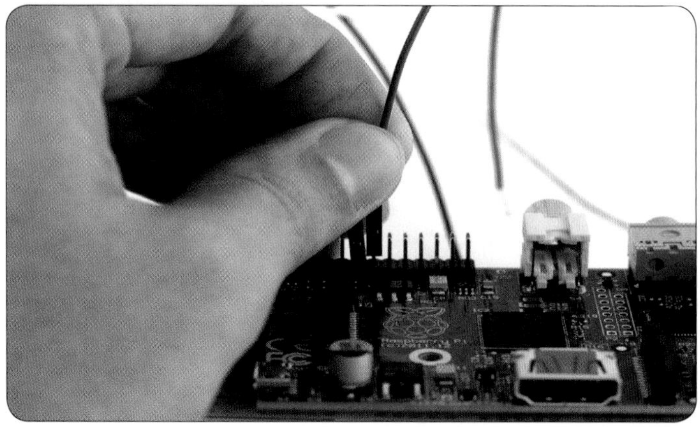

Take time to double- and triple-check your wiring.

hole above the first resistor and directly next to the longer lead of the red LED. Connect the other end to the pin three pins along from the ground wire you just connected on the top row. Place another jumper wire above the second resistor and next to the long lead of the amber LED. Connect the other end to the pin directly below the lead you connected for the red LED on the Pi's GPIO header. Finally, place another jumper wire above the third resistor and next to the long lead of the green LED. Connect the other end to the pin on the bottom row next to the wire for the amber LED.

The circuit is now complete, but before you connect the Pi back up and switch it on take the time to double- and triple-check your wiring. The easiest way to destroy a Raspberry Pi is to connect something to the wrong pin on the GPIO header. Compare the layout of your circuit to those in the diagrams here, and if using untrimmed components make sure none of the leads are touching.

When you're absolutely sure that the circuit is wired up correctly, plug the Pi back into the display, keyboard, mouse and power supply.

WRITING THE PROGRAM

The most popular programming language for the Pi, and the one chosen by the Raspberry Pi Foundation for its educational programmes, is Python. The Raspbian operating system comes with Python along with a library designed to make controlling the Pi's GPIO features as simple as possible. To begin, load the graphical user interface – if it isn't already loaded – with the following command at the terminal:

```
startx
```

When the GUI has loaded, double-click the IDLE icon – not IDLE 3 – to load the Python integrated development environment (IDE). Although it's possible to write Python programs in any text editor, IDLE includes features designed to make your life easier, such as the ability to automatically indent lines where required, saving you having to press the spacebar numerous times, and syntax-sensitive colouring to highlight what each segment of the program does.

IDLE initially loads into an interactive Python shell, where you can type commands and have them execute immediately. To open a blank file to store your more complex traffic-light program, click the File menu and click New Window. When the window opens, click the File menu again and click Save As. Call the file "trafficlights.py" and click Save.

Begin the Python program by typing in the following:

```
#!/usr/bin/env python
```

This is known as the "shebang

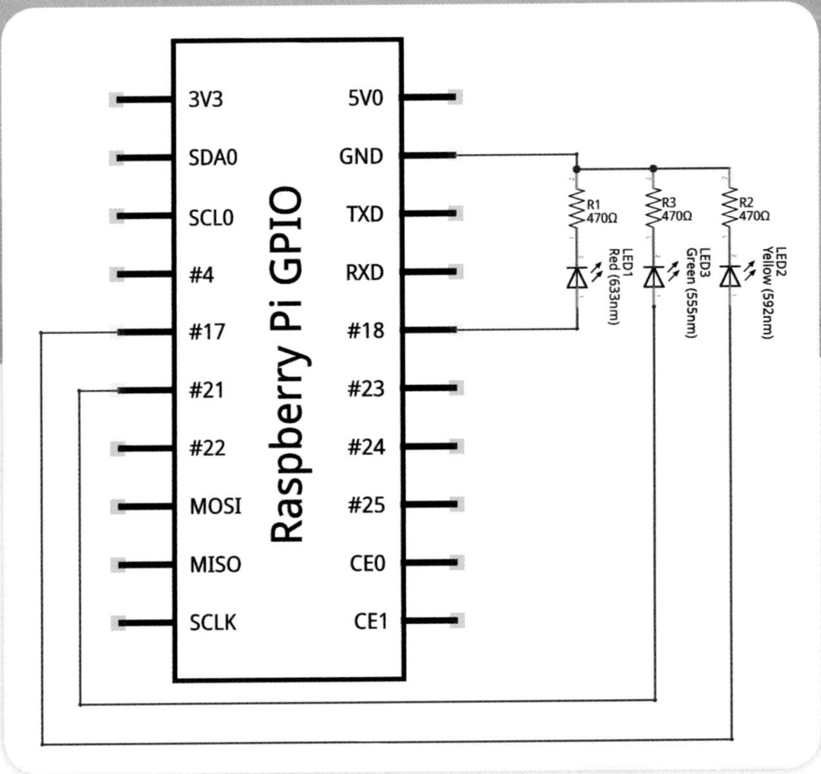

Follow this diagram, and you'll be connected in no time.

line", for the hash and exclamation mark at the start. It's used by the operating system to find the application with which the program should be interpreted if run directly at the terminal. You don't strictly need it for all Python programs – anything that you're planning to run directly inside IDLE, such as a Minecraft script, will work fine without it – but it's a good habit to get into when starting out.

Next, you need to import a pair of libraries, collections of Python code that have been pre-written to make your life easier:

```
import RPI.GPIO as GPIO
import time
```

The first library controls the Pi's GPIO header, while the second provides time-related functionality to Python. You'll be using the first to turn the LEDs on and off, while the second allows you to insert delays within your program. Without those delays, the LEDs would flash on and off so quickly you wouldn't be able to see that they were turning off at all.

You need to tell Python which pins the LEDs are connected to next, so type the following lines:

```
redPin = 18
amberPin = 17
greenPin = 27
```

If you have an original Raspberry Pi Model B Revision 1 board, with only 256MB of memory, you'll need to change the 27 on the last line to 21. If you have a Model B Revision 2 with 512MB of memory or any version of the Model A, leave it at 27. These lines set up variables to hold the pin numbers, making it easy to modify them in future if required. You may have noticed that the pin numbers don't correspond to the physical locations of the GPIO pins themselves. Instead, the numbering scheme used is one internal to the Pi's Broadcom BCM2835 chip.

Now type the following lines to set up the GPIO header:

```
GPIO.setmode(GPIO.BCM)
GPIO.setup(redPin, GPIO.OUT)
GPIO.setup(amberPin, GPIO.
OUT)
GPIO.setup(greenPin, GPIO.
OUT)
```

The first line tells the GPIO library that you'll be using the BCM2835 numbering scheme when referring to the GPIO pins. The remaining lines set up each pin as outputs. This set is required because the GPIO pins on the Pi can act as both inputs and outputs, and you need to choose one of the two functions per pin before you can use them.

Now you can start the program itself, with the following line:

```
while True:
```

This creates an infinite loop; so long as True is equal to 1 – which it always is – the program will continue indefinitely. Without this line, the program would run once and then quit – not a very helpful thing for a set of traffic lights to do. Each line below this one must be indented by four spaces; it's these indentations that tell Python which lines belong to the loop. IDLE, thankfully, takes care of this for you: when you press Enter at the end of that line, the cursor will automatically be moved four spaces in on the next line down and every line thereafter.

You now need to set up the initial state of the traffic lights – red for stop. Type the following lines:

```
    GPIO.output(redPin,
True)
    GPIO.output(amberPin,
False)
    GPIO.output(greenPin,
False)
```

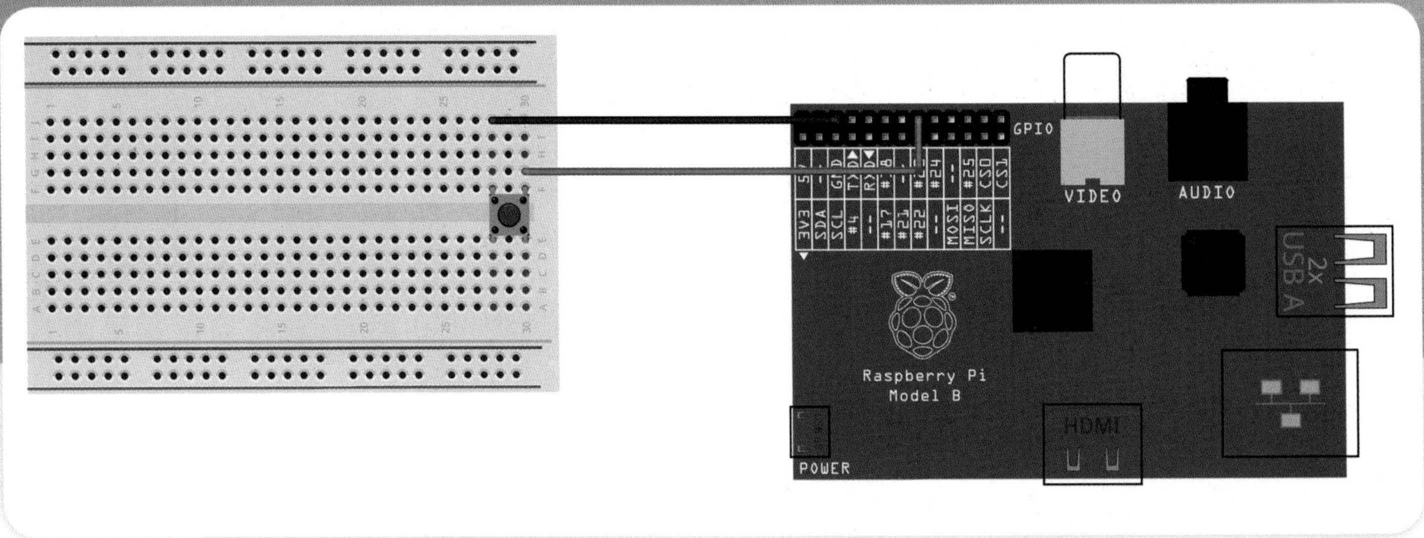

Building the doorbell project using a breadboard.

language picked by the Raspberry Pi Foundation for beginners. A Python program is actually no more than a plain text file, typically given the extension .py. To start coding, create a new file in Nano called doorbell.py using the following command:

```
nano doorbell.py
```

At the top of the file, type the following line:

```
#!/usr/bin/env python
```

This is known as the "shebang" line, named for the hash and exclamation mark at its start. This tells the operating system that what follows should be treated as a Python program. It allows you to call the file directly, as though it were a standalone application, which will come in handy later when you come to automate its startup process. You don't necessarily need it at the start of every Python program you write – especially if it will never be run like an application at the terminal – but it's a good habit to get into.

Next, you need to import a few libraries; these are snippets of commonly used code that you can call from within your program, instead of having to write the code yourself every time you want to use it. Twython is one of these libraries, designed for communicating with Twitter; others let you read the date and time, or communicate over a network connection. The libraries you'll need for this project are imported with the following lines:

```
import RPi.GPIO as GPIO
from twython import Twython
import datetime
```

The first line imports a library designed for accessing the Pi's GPIO header from within Python. The second imports the Twython library for Twitter communication, and the third imports a library designed to handle the system clock, which you'll use to read the current date and time.

Next, you need the keys from your Twitter developer account. Type in the following lines, placing the respective tokens and keys between the single quotes on each line:

```
api_token = ' '
api_secret = ' '
access_token = ' '
access_token_secret = ' '
```

Both the tokens and their respective secrets should be treated as confidential; if you share your code with anyone, remember to take your API details out first. If you leave the keys in place and give away your code, the recipient will be able to easily pretend to be you and have full access to your Twitter account even without knowing your password.

A failure to properly indent lines is the most common reason for a Python script to return an error

You now need to tell the Pi how you're intending to use its GPIO header. In the case of this project, you're going to be using one of its pins as an input. This is Pin 16, which is identified within the Broadcom BCM2835 process as GPIO 23. Type the following lines to configure the GPIO access:

```
GPIO.setmode(GPIO.BCM)
GPIO.setup(23, GPIO.IN,
pull_up_down=GPIO.PUD_UP)
```

The first line puts the GPIO library into a mode where you can label the pins you're using with the GPIO numbers rather than physical locations, which avoids confusion when dealing with Model B Revision 1 boards and their unique layout. The second line sets GPIO 23 to an output, and turns on an internal pull-up resistor. Normally, when wiring a switch into a device like the Pi, you'd need a resistor between the pin and ground to provide a high signal, which the device can contrast with the low signal created when the switch is triggered. The Pi's internal resistors, when activated with the

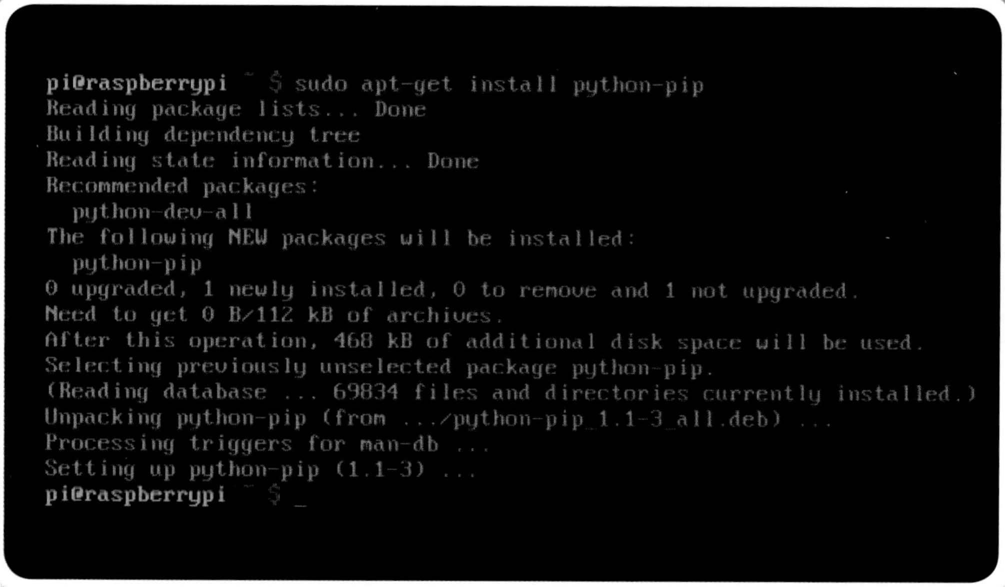

above instruction, provide this functionality without the need for external components.

pi@raspberrypi ~ $ sudo apt-get install python-pip
Reading package lists... Done
Building dependency tree
Reading state information... Done
Recommended packages:
python-dev-all
The following NEW packages will be installed:
python-pip
0 upgraded, 1 newly installed, 0 to remove and 1 not upgraded.
Need to get 0 B/112 kB of archives.
After this operation, 468 kB of additional disk space will be used.
Selecting previously unselected package python-pip.
(Reading database ... 69834 files and directories currently installed.)
Unpacking python-pip (from .../python-pip_1.1-3_all.deb) ...
Processing triggers for man-db ...
Setting up python-pip (1.1-3) ...
pi@raspberrypi ~ $ _

The final piece of setting up your doorbell script is telling Twython your keys and assigning it the friendly name "twitter", by calling it with the following line:

```
twitter = Twython(api_token,
api_secret, access_token,
access_token_secret)
```

Now it's time to start writing the main portion of the script. Because a doorbell that only works once isn't much use, you're going to need an infinite loop. This is a special loop that returns to the beginning every time it finishes, never to end without external intervention. Type the following to begin the loop:

```
while True:
```

This rather odd-looking instruction tells Python to check the value of the built-in function True; if the value of True is 1, the loop runs. Because True is always equal to 1, the loop always runs, creating the infinite loop you need to keep the doorbell operating. Next, type the following line:

```
    try:
```

Note the four spaces at the start: Python relies on indentation like this to know which lines are intended to form part of the loop and which lines fall outside it. A failure to properly indent lines is the most common reason for a Python script to return an error, so always make sure you've double-checked that each line is indented correctly.

The "try" instruction tells Python to set up exception handling; this means that, while the main loop will run forever, if you cancel it manually with a Ctrl+C keyboard combination, Python will generate an exception and run a piece of code you'll set up later; this lets the program exit cleanly, and returns the GPIO port to normal.

Next, start the program proper with the following two lines:

```
        print "Waiting for
doorbell..."
        GPIO.wait_for_
edge(23, GPIO_FALLING)
```

These lines are indented by eight spaces: four for the initial infinite loop, and four more to show they come under the "try" instruction. The first simply prints a message to the terminal so you know the program is running. The second actually looks for the doorbell's switch being pressed.

Pip is a package manager for the PyPI.

The "wait_for_edge" portion of the instruction tells Python to pause the program there until activity is detected on the GPIO 23 input. "GPIO_FALLING" tells Python that it should specifically look for the pin going from a high state – generated by the internal pull-up resistor – to a low state when the switch is pressed.

Python now knows that you're watching the GPIO 23 input for a trigger, but doesn't know what to do when that trigger is activated. Enter the following lines:

```
        print "Doorbell
detected, sending direct
message."
        twitter.send_direct_
message(screen_
name="yourtwittername",
text="DING-DONG at %s"
%datetime.datetime.now())
        print "Message
sent."
```

The first line, again, simply prints a message to the terminal to aid in debugging. The second uses the Twython library to communicate with Twitter. It's possible to use Twython to perform almost any Twitter task, including sending and receiving messages; here, you're using the "send_direct_message" function. Replace yourtwittername with the screen name of the Twitter user you want to receive the direct messages when the doorbell is activated; this is their username minus the @ symbol.

The second part of the instruction tells Twython what message to send; in this case, "DONG-DONG" followed by a time-stamp of when the message

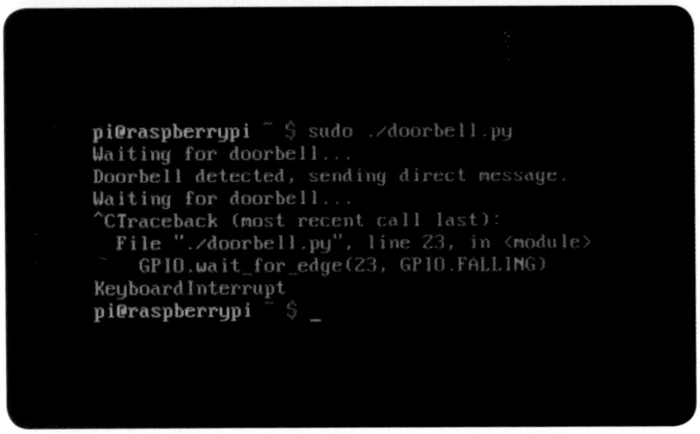

was sent. This is generated using the datetime library you imported earlier, and ensure that every DM sent is unique. Without this, Twitter may reject duplicate DMs if the doorbell is activated twice in quick succession. Note that the Pi is set to Universal Time (UTC) by default, so don't be surprised if the time stamp appears to be an hour out during daylight savings.

pi@raspberrypi ~ $ sudo ./doorbell.py
Waiting for doorbell...
Doorbell detected, sending direct message.
Waiting for doorbell...

That completes the bulk of the doorbell script, but you need an exception rule to match the "try" instruction further up. Type in the following lines:

```
    except
KeyboardInterrupt:
        GPIO.cleanup()
```

These tell Python what to do in the event of an exception, such as you quitting the program with Ctrl+C. The instruction is simple: call the GPIO library's "cleanup" command, which resets the status of all pins on the Pi's GPIO header to their default. This will prevent error messages from appearing next time you run the script, or if you access the GPIO header from a different program later.

Save the file with Ctrl+O, and quit Nano with Ctrl+O.

BUILDING THE CIRCUIT

Connecting a switch to the Raspberry Pi's GPIO header is one of the most simple circuits you can hope for, but that doesn't mean you don't need to take care. The GPIO header on a Pi is extremely fragile, and has no protection against short circuits or devices that try to pull too much current or apply too high a voltage. Because it's connected directly to the BCM2835 processor, damage to the GPIO header can completely destroy a Pi in short order.

Shut down the Pi with the following command at the terminal, and remove the USB power connector and any other cables when the process has completed:

```
sudo halt
```

Orient the Pi so that the HDMI connector is on the bottom, the composite video and analogue audio connectors are on the top, and the Raspberry Pi logo is the right way up. This places the GPIO header at the top-left of the board, with Pin 1 in the bottom-left corner of the header. You're going to need to count which pin is which very accurately, so be sure you know how the GPIO port is numbered: Pin 1 at the bottom-left, Pin 2 directly above it, Pin 3 on the bottom row to the right of Pin 1, Pin 4 on the top row to the right of Pin 2, Pin 5 on the bottom row to the right of Pin 3, Pin 6 on the top row to the right of Pin 4 and so forth.

Count to Pin 16, which is the eighth pin from the left on the top row.

When using the GPIO library in Python, you need full super-user privileges.

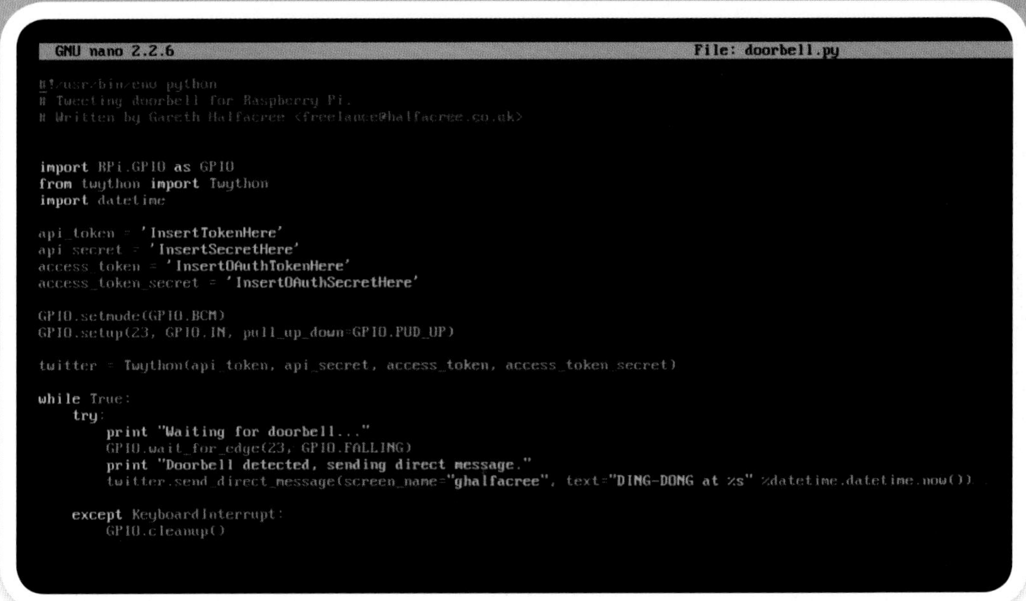

GNU nano 2.2.6 File: doorbell.py
#!/usr/bin/env python
# Tweeting doorbell for Raspberry Pi.
# Written by Gareth Halfacree <freelance@halfacree.co.uk>
import RPi.GPIO as GPIO
from twython import Twython
import datetime
api_token = 'InsertTokenHere'
api_secret = 'InsertSecretHere'
access_token = 'InsertOAuthTokenHere'
access_token_secret = 'InsertOAuthSecretHere'
GPIO.setmode(GPIO.BCM)
GPIO.setup(23, GPIO.IN, pull_up_down=GPIO.PUD_UP)
twitter = Twython(api_token, api_secret, access_token, access_token_secret)
while True:
try:
print "Waiting for doorbell..."
GPIO.wait_for_edge(23, GPIO.FALLING)
print "Doorbell detected, sending direct message."
twitter.send_direct_message(screen_name="ghalfacree", text="DING-DONG at %s" %datetime.datetime.now())
except KeyboardInterrupt:
GPIO.cleanup()

It's more convenient to have the doorbell program run every time the Pi is booted

Connect one wire leading from the switch to this pin; it doesn't matter which wire, as the switch simply connects both wires together when it's pressed. Take the other wire and connect it to Pin 6, the third pin on the top row from the right. This provides a ground connection.

Before going any further, double- and triple-check your connections. The switch should be wired to Pin 16 and Pin 6, and touch no other pins. A short on the GPIO header will damage the Pi, so it's certainly worth taking your time and making sure that you've counted the pin numbers right before continuing.

It's worth taking your time and making sure that you've counted the pin numbers right before continuing

When you're sure the circuit is wired correctly, you can plug the Pi back in and let it boot up before logging in again.

RUNNING THE PROGRAM

In order to run the Python program you've written directly at the terminal, you need to let Linux know that it's executable; this is controlled via what's known as the "executable bit," a permission you can set by typing the following command at the terminal:

```
chmod +x doorbell.py
```

When using the GPIO library in Python, you need full super-user privileges. If you attempt to run the program as the Pi user, it will fail with a permissions error. Instead, type the following to run it as the root user:

```
sudo ./doorbell.py
```

After a few seconds, the message "Waiting for doorbell" will appear onscreen. Press the switch, and the program will spring into action, posting a message to Twitter and confirming that action with another message at the terminal. Because it's an infinite loop, the message "Waiting for doorbell" will appear again when the process has completed. Press the switch again, and you'll generate another Twitter message and another confirmation at the terminal.

Log into your Twitter account, and check your Direct Messages. You'll find you have a message from yourself for every time you pressed the switch, each one tagged with the UTC time-stamp generated by the datetime library.

To quit the doorbell program, press Ctrl+C on the keyboard. This will run the instruction in the "except" section, cleaning up the GPIO port and returning its settings to default in order to prevent errors the next time the program is run.

As an embedded creation, it's more convenient to have the doorbell program run every time the Pi is booted. This allows you to install it next to your door without a keyboard, mouse or monitor connected and still have it operate as expected. To do that, you'll need to open the rc.local file in Nano:

```
sudo nano /etc/rc.local
```

Insert the following line into the file, just above the line that reads "exit 0":

```
/home/pi/doorbell.py &
```

There's no need to use "sudo" in rc.local, as everything in the file is run with the permissions of the root user. The ampersand symbol at the end of the line tells Linux that it should run the command in the background. This allows the rc.local script to continue on and bring up the normal login screen, despite the Python program never exiting by itself. Save the file with Ctrl+O and exit Nano with Ctrl+X.

Now, all that's left for you to do is mount the Pi in an unobtrusive location near your door and enjoy the benefits of a 21st-century doorbell.

TWEETING DOORBELL WALKTHROUGH

Follow our step-by step guide to setting up a developer account on Twitter, to allow your doorbell to post messages to your Twitter feed and to set up your permissions

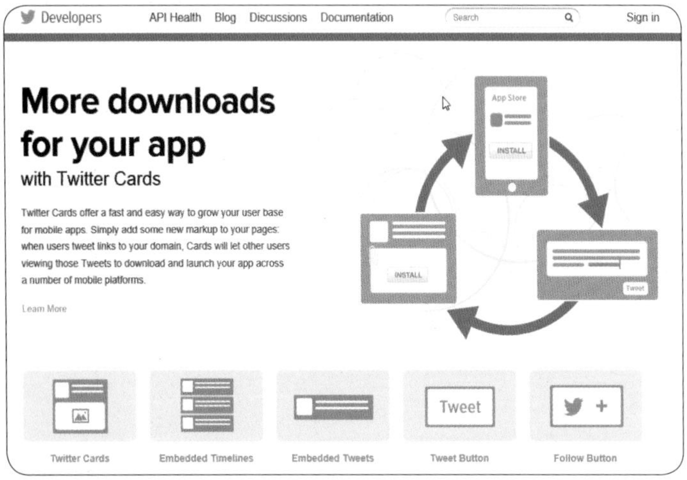

1 You can create as many different applications as you like, all connected to your main Twitter account and with unique keys for each.

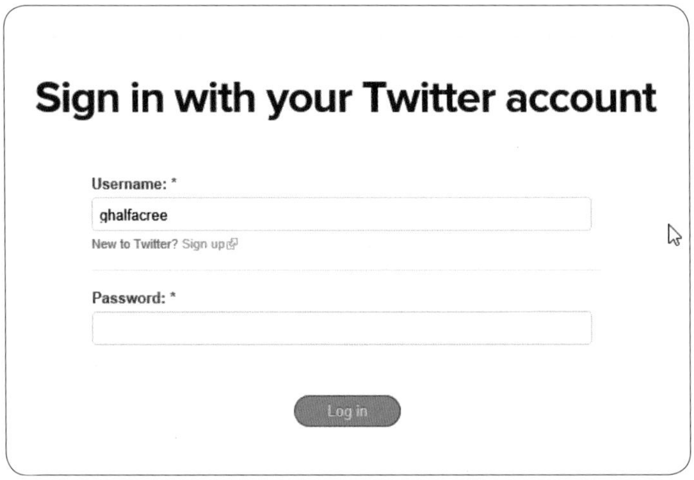

2 You can sign into the development server with your usual Twitter username and password; if you don't have an account, go to twitter.com.

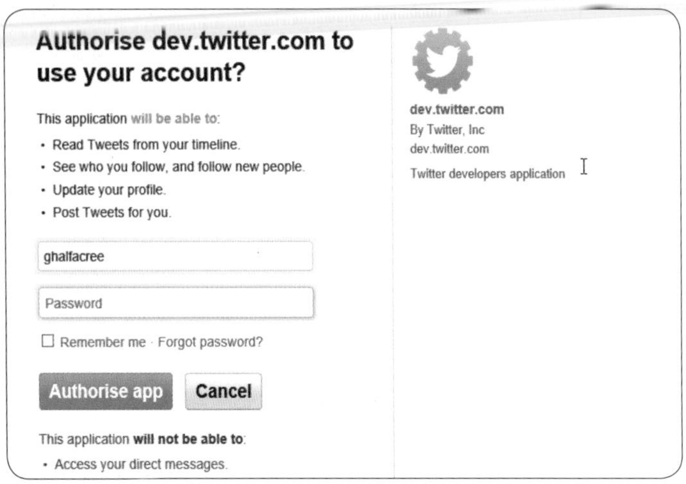

3 Each time you use the Twitter development server, you'll need to re-enter your username and password to give it access to your account.

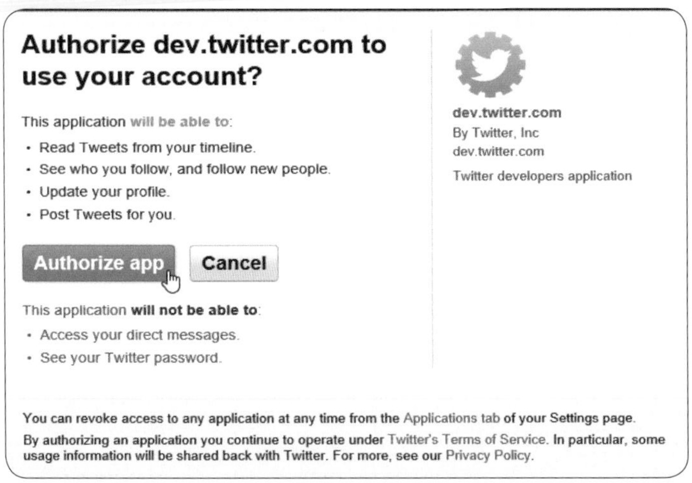

4 Click the Authorise App button to link the Twitter development server to your Twitter account; without this, your app won't be able to post.

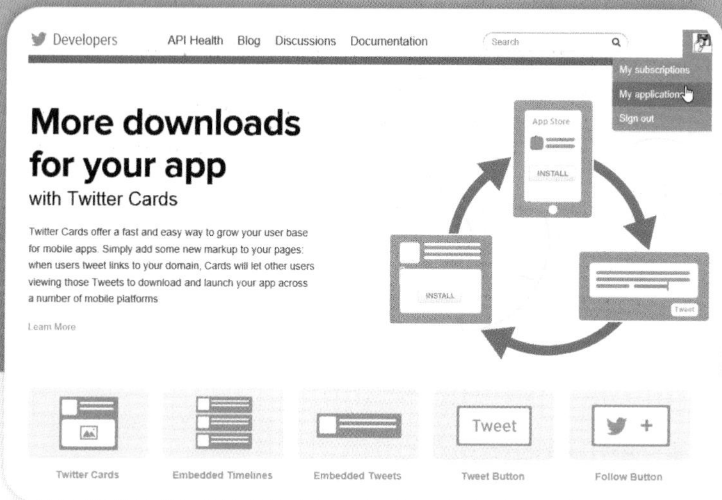

5 Clicking on your Twitter avatar at the top-right of the page gives you a dropdown menu from which you can create new or edit existing apps.

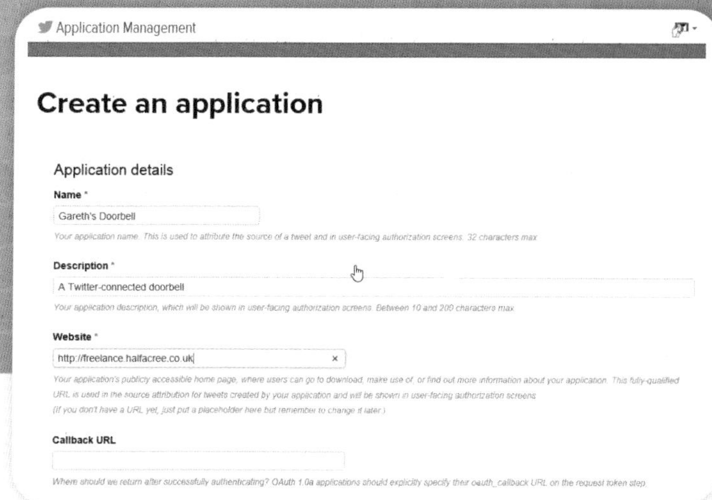

6 Each application has a unique name; if you've already created an app for a previous project, it's a good idea to make a new one here.

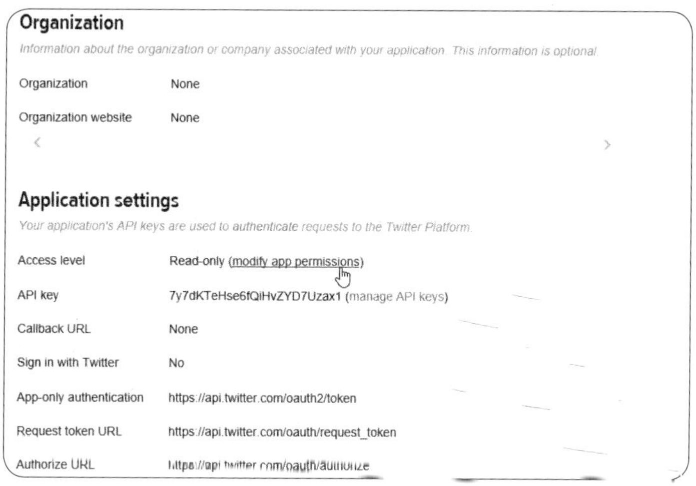

7 The doorbell needs the ability to post messages. Click on Modify App Permissions in Access Level to change from read-only mode.

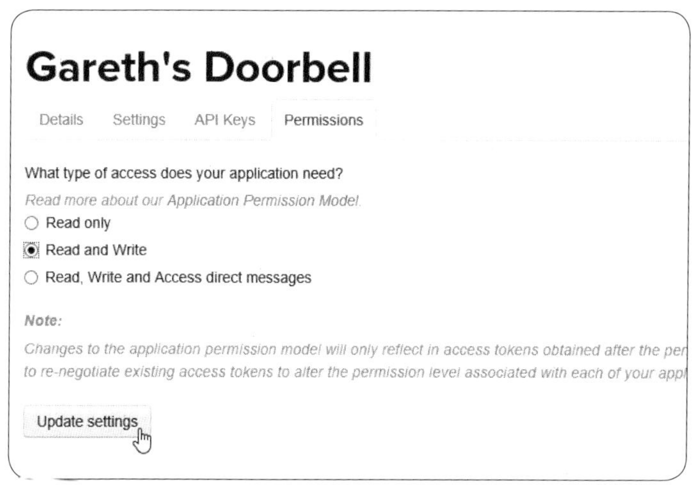

8 The app needs read and write permissions; you can add the ability to access Direct Messages, but it's not required for the doorbell to work.

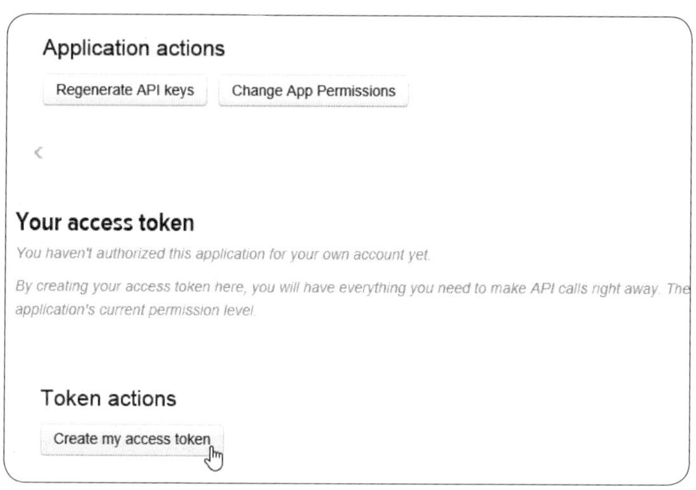

9 You'll need a series of secret keys to give the doorbell app access to your Twitter account; click Create My Access Token to generate these.

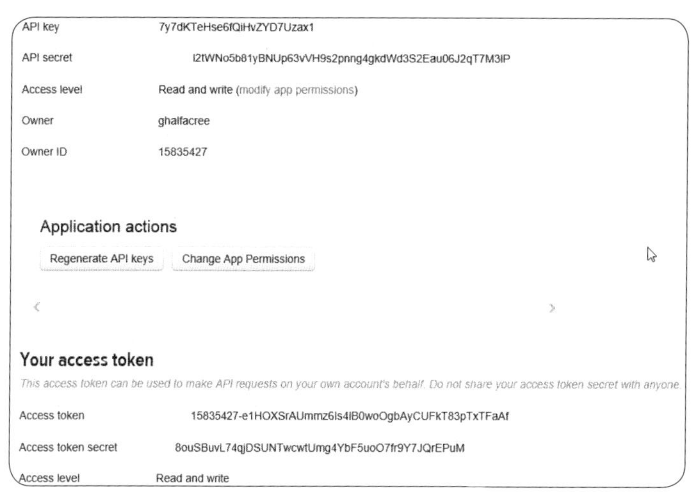

10 Note down the API Key, API Secret, Access Token and Access Token Secret values; keep these safe, as they permit full access to your Twitter account.

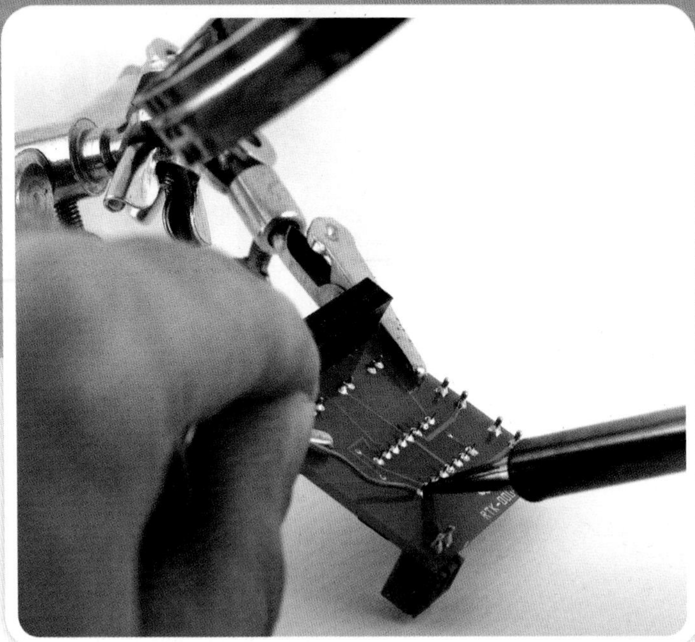

The motors and power supply connect to the Motor Controller Board through the screw terminals.

into the holes marked J2, J3 and J1. You should align these so that the open side, with the visible metal, is facing out from the board; this is where the wires for the motors and power supply will connect. Secure these in place with Blu-Tak, if required, and flip the board over to solder the pins into place.

Some hobby motors come with wire, known as "flying leads", already attached. If yours doesn't, you'll need to solder a pair of wires to the terminals on its back. Using the wire strippers, strip away the insulation from around the ends of a pair of equal-length wires to about a centimetre. Roll the wire in your fingers to bring it to a single point. Insert the end of one wire into the terminal onto the motor, and give it a twist to secure it before soldering it. Use a generous amount of solder to provide good mechanical support. Repeat the process with the second wire.

Before you put away your soldering iron, look closely at your solder points to ensure good contact. Check that there are no shorts, where solder has created a joint between pins. If you find one, melt the solder with your iron to flow it back where it belongs. Also check for "dry joints" or "cold joints": these are bad solder connections, usually caused by one of the two surfaces not getting hot enough during soldering, and will show as the solder "avoiding" either the circuit board contacts or the pins. If you find one, hold the iron against the pin and the circuit board until the solder reflows, then check the quality of the joint again. When all connections have been checked, clean your iron on the sponge, apply another layer of solder to its tip, and disconnect it from the mains to allow it to cool before packing it away.

Finally, take the rectangular chip from the kit by its short edges and align it so that the notch and small circular indentation are to the left before pushing it gently into the chip socket. Make sure to line the legs up with the holes before pushing. If you find that the legs are splayed too widely to fit into the socket, hold the chip with its base facing towards you and gently press one set of legs against the work surface followed by the other set to bend them slightly inwards before trying again.

WIRING THE BOARD

Now you have your Ryanteck Motor Controller Board built, it's time to connect your components to the board. First, gently connect the Motor Controller Board to the Pi's GPIO header. Make sure it's lined up, and that all pins of the GPIO header have been inserted into the female header fully. If it's proving difficult to push, remove the board and check the GPIO header for bent pins; if you find any, straighten them before trying again.

The motors and power supply connect to the Motor Controller Board through the screw terminals at the left and bottom edges. These terminals make it easy to connect and

Before you put away your soldering iron, look closely at your solder points to ensure good contact

disconnect the external components without having to solder, de-solder and resolder the wires each time. The two screw terminals on the left side of the board drive the two motors; the single terminal on the bottom edge is the input for the power supply.

Take the wires coming from your first motor, and insert one into the lower of the two left-hand screw terminals marked M1. Tighten the screw until the wire is snug, and can't

Tighten the screw until the wire is snug, and can't be removed by a gentle tug.

be removed by a gentle tug. Repeat the process with the second wire. It doesn't matter which of the two wires goes into which of the two holes in the screw terminal, as long as they're both connected to the same twin terminal. If you have a second motor, repeat the process for the screw terminal above marked M2; otherwise, move onto the power supply.

Motors can be power-hungry devices, and the Pi's GPIO ports aren't designed to directly drive anything of that type. Although it would theoretically be possible to connect a small, low-power motor to the Pi, once it begins to turn it will likely draw too much power from the GPIO socket and cause the Pi to reboot; worse, larger motors will cause significant and permanent damage to the Pi's BCM2835 processor.

The Motor Controller Board gets around this in two ways. First, it uses a specialised motor control chip known as an H-Bridge to isolate the motors from the GPIO header; rather than the GPIO header switching the motors on directly, it tells the H-Bridge chip to perform that task. Second, the board has a dedicated power input from which the motors will draw their power. This significantly lessens the load on the Pi's GPIO header.

If you've purchased a mains-powered DC adapter, you'll need to cut the connector from the end of its wire and strip the wires back by a centimetre, making sure the adapter is unplugged first, of course. Look for the wire with the red or white stripe on it; this is the positive wire, while the plain back wire is the negative. If you're using a battery holder with wires already connected, the red wire will be positive and the black negative. If the holder has bare terminals, solder a pair of wires on as with the motors earlier.

Take the positive wire from your chosen power supply, twist it so the strands are neat, and insert it into the left-hand hole in the screw terminal marked J1 before tightening the screw. Take the negative wire, twist it as before, and insert it into the right-hand hole before tightening the last screw. Check that the wires are secure with a small tug; if either or both wires spring free, loosen the screws, reinsert them and tighten again.

Note that this power supply is used purely for the motors, and won't power the Pi; you'll still need to connect that to its own battery or mains power supply. Do so now, and connect a keyboard, mouse and display at the same time before connecting the dedicated motor power supply to its power source – either a mains socket or by inserting fresh batteries.

WRITING THE PROGRAM

The Ryanteck Motor Controller Board is designed to be as simple to use as possible, and requires no software or libraries that aren't included as standard with the Raspbian operating system. When your Pi has booted, log in and start the graphical user interface, if it isn't already loaded, with the following command:

```
startx
```

The easiest way to get started with the Motor Controller Board is to program it in Python. Double-click the IDLE – not IDLE 3 – icon on the desktop to load the Python Integrated Development Environment (IDE). Although it's possible to write Python programs in any text editor, IDLE includes features designed to make your life easier, such as the ability to automatically indent lines.

IDLE initially loads into an interactive Python shell, where you can type commands and have them immediately execute. The motor control program is slightly more complex and will require the creation of a blank file. Click the File menu and click New Window. When the window opens, click the File menu again and click Save As; call the file "motors.py" and click the Save button.

Begin the Python program by typing in the following:

```
#!/usr/bin/env python
```

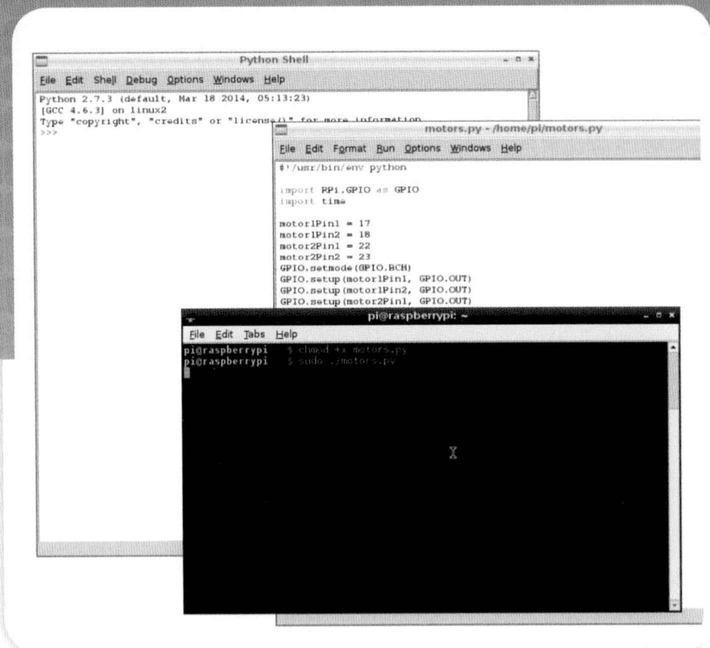

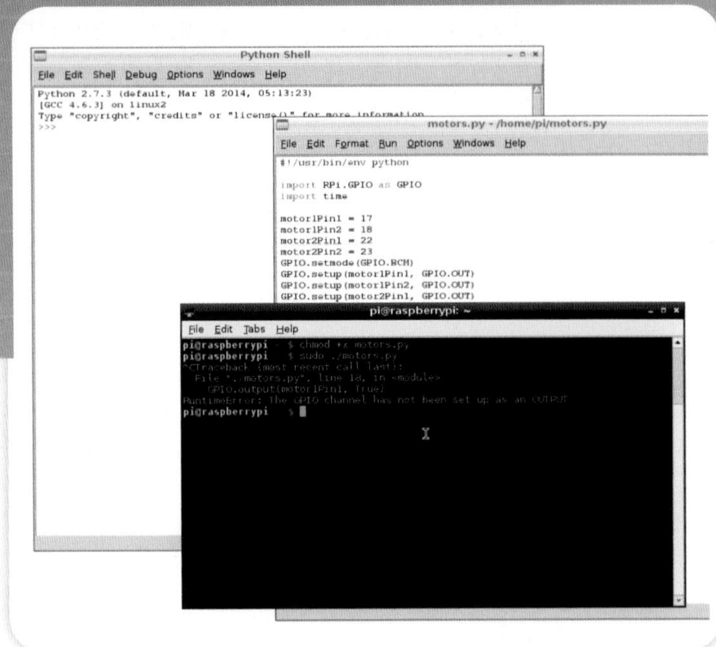

Run the program, and the motors should begin to spin.

This is known as the "shebang line", for the hash and exclamation mark at the start. It's used by the operating system to find the application with which the program should be interpreted if run directly at the terminal. You don't strictly need it for all Python programs – anything that you're planning to run directly inside IDLE, such as a Minecraft script, will work fine without it, but it's a good habit to get into when starting out.

Next, you need to import a pair of libraries, collections of Python code that have been pre-written to make your life easier:

```
import RPI.GPIO as GPIO
import time
```

The first library controls the Pi's GPIO header, while the second provides time-related functionality to Python. You'll be using the first to turn the motors on and off, while the second allows you to insert delays within your program. These delays will allow you to easily see the effect of altering the direction of the motor, as without them the program would change the motor's direction so quickly it would appear to stand still.

Next, you need to set the GPIO header up for use with the Motor Control Board, by typing these lines:

```
motor1Pin1 = 17
motor1Pin2 = 18
motor2Pin1 = 22
motor2Pin2 = 23
GPIO.setmode(GPIO.BCM)
GPIO.setup(motor1Pin1, GPIO.
OUT)
GPIO.setup(motor1Pin2, GPIO.
OUT)
GPIO.setup(motor2Pin1, GPIO.
OUT)
GPIO.setup(motor2Pin2, GPIO.
OUT)
```

The first four lines tell Python which pins each motor is connected to; if you're only using one motor, you can skip the third and fourth lines of the program. The fifth line sets the GPIO library to use the pin numbering scheme internal to the BCM2835 processor. Although this can be confusing, because the BCM2835 pin numbers are different to the physical location of each pin on the GPIO header, it avoids problems when switching between the original Model B Revision 1 and later Revision 2 GPIO pin layouts. The final four lines set each of the GPIO pins to outputs; this particular program requires no inputs. Again, if you're using a single motor you can skip the last two lines.

You now need to write the main portion of the program, starting with an infinite loop that will run the motor until told otherwise. Type the following lines:

```
while True:
    try:
```

The second line sets up an exception so that the program will stop running the motor when you quit it; for more information on exceptions, see the Traffic Lights project. Note that the second line is indented by four spaces; if you're using IDLE, this indentation will be done automatically. Next, type the main part of the program:

```
        GPIO.
output(motor1Pin1, True)
        GPIO.
output(motor1Pin2, False)
        time.sleep(10)
        GPIO.
```

Try connecting fan blades to a motor and have it spin when the Raspberry Pi's processor gets too hot

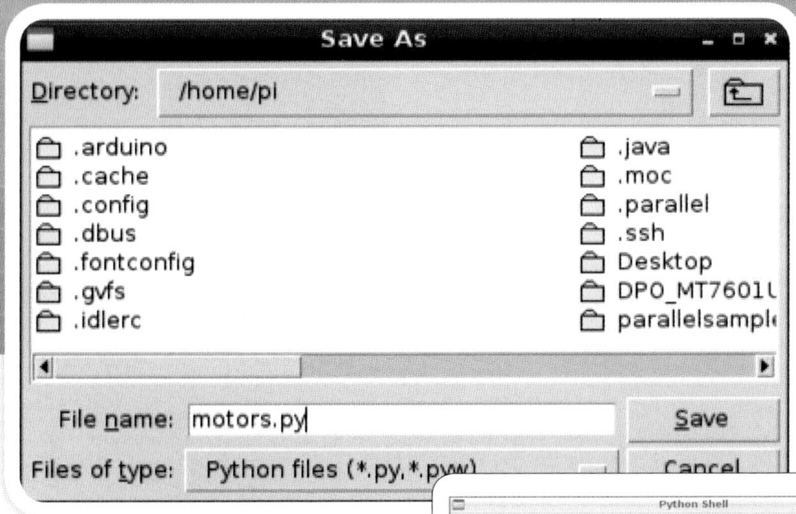


```
output(motor1Pin1, False)
        GPIO.
output(motor1Pin2, True)
        time.sleep(10)
```

All these lines are indented by eight spaces; again, IDLE will do this automatically. The first two lines switch on one of the pins connected to the first motor, then the next line pauses the program for ten seconds. The following two lines swap the pins over, turning the one that was on off and vice-versa before the last line sleeps for another ten seconds. If you have only one motor, skip the next part, only enter these lines if you have a second motor:

```
        GPIO.
output(motor2Pin1, True)
        GPIO.
output(motor2Pin2, False)
        time.sleep(10)
        GPIO.
output(motor2Pin1, False)
        GPIO.
output(motor2Pin2, True)
        time.sleep(10)
```

Finally, you need to finish the exception you began with the "try" line. Type the following lines:

```
    except
KeyboardInterrupt:
        GPIO.cleanup()
```

This ensures that the GPIO port is reset to its defaults when you exist the program, which prevents the motors from running continuously even though the program has been closed. Click on the File menu followed by Save to save your changes.

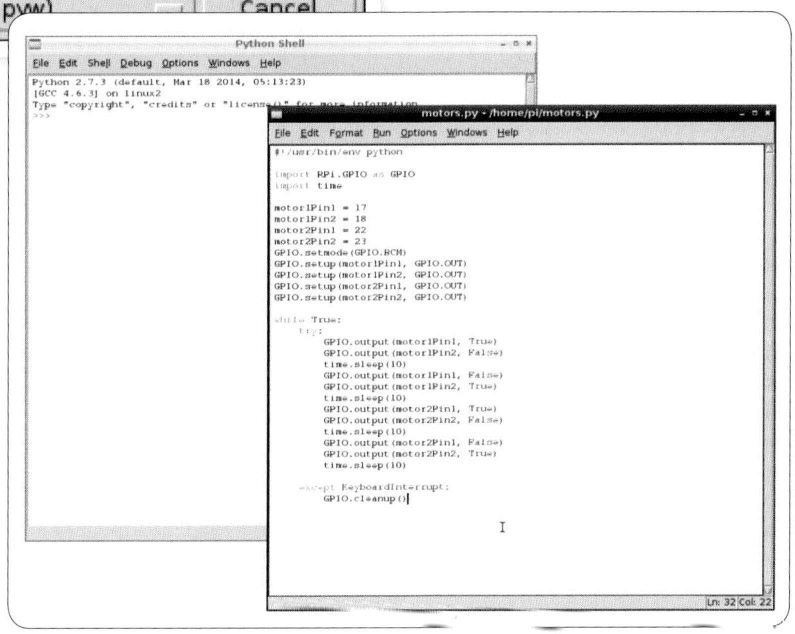

The easiest way to get started with the Motor Controller Board is to program it in Python.

RUNNING THE PROGRAM

Because the motor control program you've written accesses the GPIO port through the bundled Python library, you can't run it from IDLE's Run menu; instead, you need to give it super-user, or "root", permissions. Double-click the LXTerminal icon on the desktop, and type the following two commands:

```
chmod +x motors.py
sudo ./motors.py
```

The first makes the file executable, meaning it can be run like a normal program without calling Python first; the second runs the program itself with super-user permissions. The motors should begin to spin, first in one direction then after ten seconds reversing into the other direction. This will continue for as long as the program runs; to quit, press Ctrl+C. This will trigger the exception you wrote earlier, resetting the GPIO port and stopping the motors.

Using this simple code, you can begin to integrate motor control into your own programs. Try connecting fan blades to a motor and have it spin when the Pi's processor gets too hot, or connect wheels to both and build a Pi-powered robot.

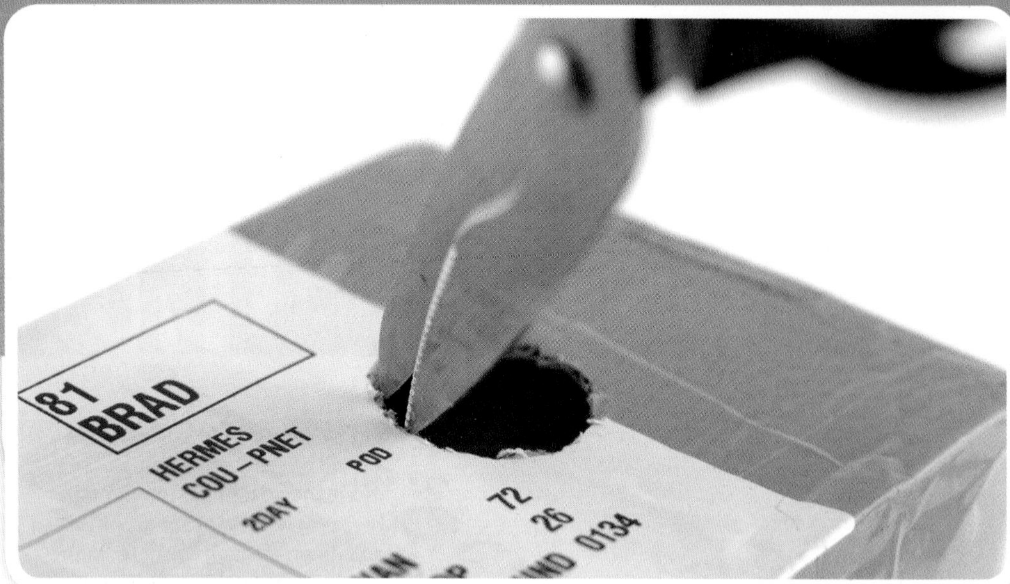

When the hole is cut, push the joystick up through the underside.

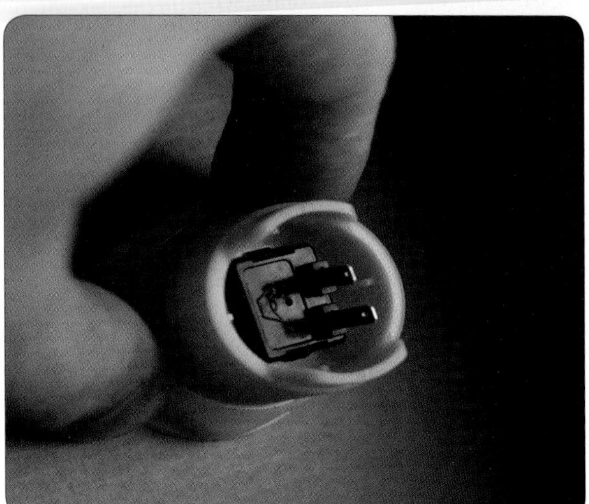

are plenty of GPIO inputs for each direction plus the fire button, there aren't enough ground pins. The solution is to create a common ground connection for all the switches to share; this is already done internally in the Adafruit Arcade Joystick.

Find the ground pin for each switch on the joystick, and attach a length of wire to each. This is best done using spade connectors, which can be crimped onto the end of the wire using an inexpensive hand tool. Strip away the insulation at the end of the wire, give the strands a twist, insert them into the spade connector, place the spade connector into the crimping tool closed side up, and squeeze the tool to create a secure connection between the wire and the connector. Then simply slide the spade connector onto the common or ground terminal of the switch. Alternatively, you can solder the wires to the switches; it's best to remove the joystick from your case to do this, especially if using cardboard or plastic.

Take the other ends of all four ground wires and strip the insulation from their ends by a centimetre or so, then do the same for a final wire – or, if not using a break-out board or terminal blocks, strip one end off a female jumper lead for this last wire. Take all these stripped ends, twist them together, and insert them into another spade connector for crimping. When the wires are all securely crimped into the connector, insert it onto the common terminal – or either terminal, in the case of a two-terminal switch – of the arcade button. This will act as the common ground for all the switches in your game controller.

If you're finding it difficult to crimp all the wires, try using a terminal block instead. This will provide a screw connection for each wire, which can be easier to tighten on the bundle without them slipping out. If using a terminal block, place a spade connector onto a single wire for the arcade button – or solder it to the button, as with the joystick connections, if you're not using spade connectors.

Finally, connect the bare end of the last ground wire to the ground pin of the GPIO header on the Pi. This is the third pin along on the top

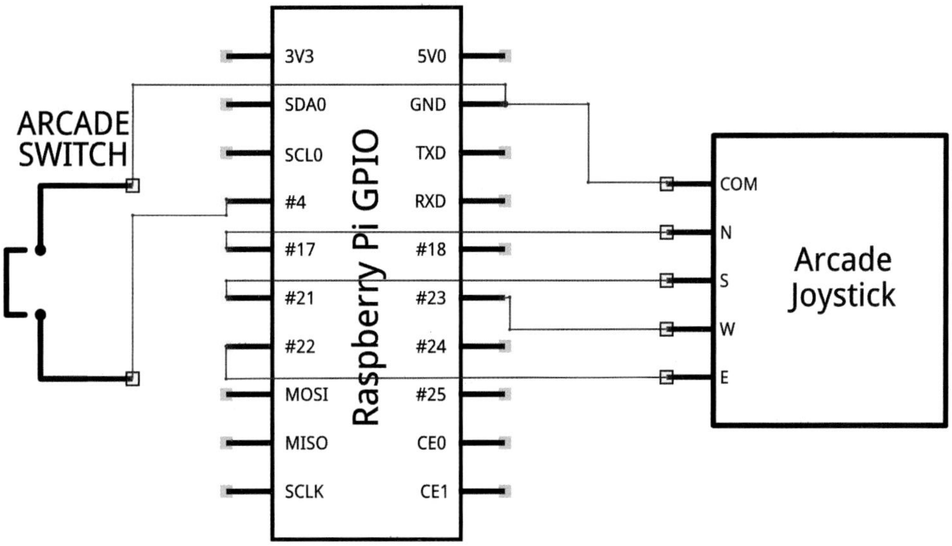

row, with the Pi oriented so that the GPIO header is on the top-left of the board and the HDMI connector on the bottom. Remember that the Pi should always be turned off and fully unplugged from any peripherals when connecting or disconnecting hardware from the GPIO header, or you risk damage to both the hardware and the Pi.

If you're using a breakout board with female headers, you can simply insert the stripped and twisted end of the ground wire into the marked hole

If you're finding it difficult to crimp all the wires, try using a terminal block instead

on the board. Otherwise, you'll need to connect a female jumper lead to the GPIO pin, then join this to the wire you already have. You can either use a terminal block, or solder the stripped end of both wires together.

The last wires you need to connect go to the signal terminal on each switch. In the case of two-terminal switches, this is whichever terminal doesn't already have a wire on it. In the case of three-terminal switches,

Follow this scheme if you have an Adafruit Arcade Joystick.

it's the terminal marked NO, O or NORMALLY OPEN. The easiest way of wiring these up is to strip one end off a female jumper lead and crimp a spade connector on, or solder it to the terminal directly.

Wire the switches in the following order: the switch for North, or Up, should be connected to the sixth pin along the bottom row of the GPIO header; the switch for South, or Down, should go to the pin directly to the right of the North connection on the bottom row; the switch for West, or Left, should go to the pin directly to the right of the North connection on the bottom row; the switch for East, or Right, should go to the pin directly above the West connection on the top row; the switch for fire should go to the pin four from the left on the bottom row.

When all the switches are wired up, double-check for loose connections and to make sure each switch is going to its corresponding point on the Pi's GPIO header. Making a mistake here, by connecting a header to the wrong pin, has the potential to damage your Pi, so it's worth taking the time to make sure that everything is right before moving on. When you're absolutely sure, you can flip the casing the right way up and reconnect the Pi to a keyboard and display before powering it back on.

INSTALLING THE SOFTWARE

Most modern peripherals, like joysticks and gamepads, connect through the USB ports. Because your custom-made controller connects via the Pi's GPIO header, you're going to need some extra software for it to be recognised as a valid input device for gaming. Log into the Pi, and type the following commands at the terminal:

```
sudo apt-get update
sudo apt-get upgrade
```

As always with a Pi project, these two commands download the latest version of the software package list and ensure that any installed packages are the very latest version. Cutting this step out may save you a few minutes now, but don't be surprised if something goes wrong later thanks to an outdated package. When the upgrade has finished, type the following commands:

```
git clone https://github.com/
tuomasjjrasanen/python-
uinput.git
cd python-uinput
```

The first uses the Git tool, designed to allow easy collaboration on coding projects, to download the source code for a Python library called "uinput". This is designed specifically for writing Python programs that can act as a joystick device. The second command places you into the directory containing the uinput library, at which point you can type the following two commands:

```
python setup.py build
```

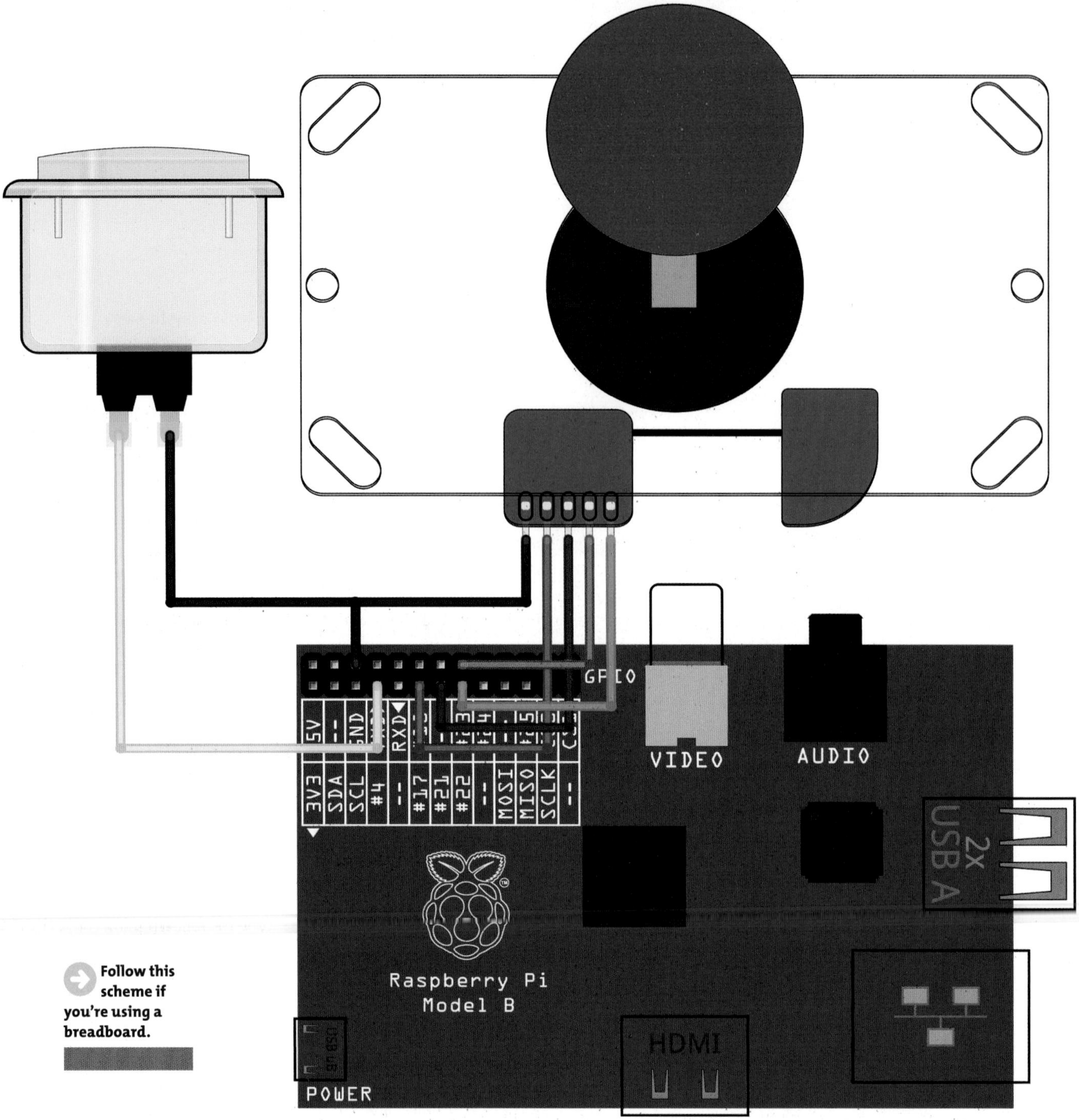

Follow this scheme if you're using a breadboard.

```
sudo python setup.py install
```

The first compiles certain aspects of the library for the Pi platform, while the second installs the library itself – hence the use of the "sudo" prefix, which runs the command as the super-user, or root, account with permissions to make changes to the underlying operating system on the Pi. When installation has finished, type the following commands:

```
sudo modprobe uinput
```

```
cd
curl https://raw.githubusercontent.com/cpswan/Python/master/rpi-gpio-jstk.py > gpiojoystick.py
```

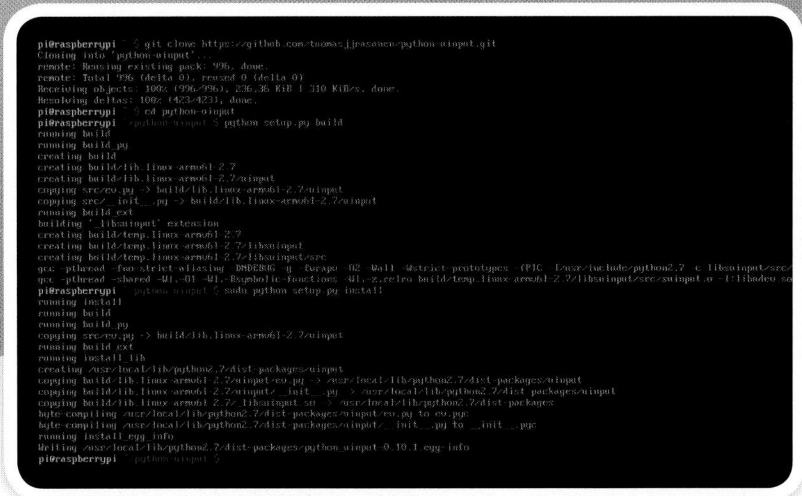

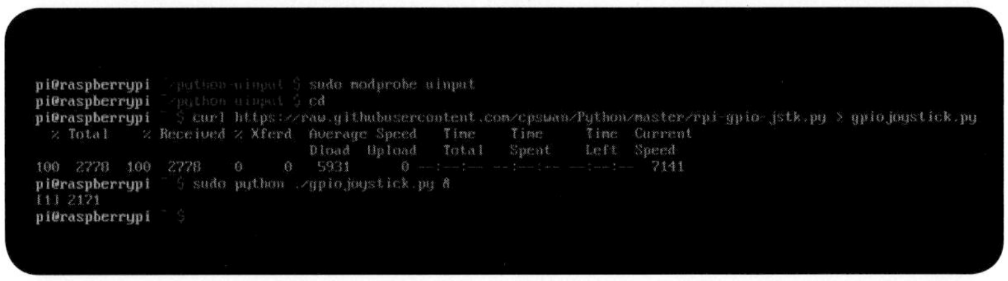

remote: Reusing existing pack: 996, done.
remote: Total 996 (delta 0), reused 0 (delta 0)
Receiving objects: 100% (996/996), 236.36 KiB | 310 KiB/s, done.
Resolving deltas: 100% (423/423), done.

running build
running build_py
creating build
creating build/lib.linux-armv6l-2.7
creating build/lib.linux-armv6l-2.7/uinput
copying src/ev.py -> build/lib.linux-armv6l-2.7/uinput
copying src/__init__.py -> build/lib.linux-armv6l-2.7/uinput
running build_ext
building '_libsuinput' extension
creating build/temp.linux-armv6l-2.7
creating build/temp.linux-armv6l-2.7/libsuinput
creating build/temp.linux-armv6l-2.7/libsuinput/src
gcc -pthread -fno-strict-aliasing -DNDEBUG -g -fwrapv -O2 -Wall -Wstrict-prototypes -fPIC -I/usr/include/python2.7 -c libsuinput/src/
gcc -pthread -shared -Wl,-O1 -Wl,-Bsymbolic-functions -Wl,-z,relro build/temp.linux-armv6l-2.7/libsuinput/src/suinput.o -l:libudev.so

running install
running build
running build_py
copying src/ev.py -> build/lib.linux-armv6l-2.7/uinput
running build_ext
running install_lib
creating /usr/local/lib/python2.7/dist-packages/uinput
copying build/lib.linux-armv6l-2.7/uinput/ev.py -> /usr/local/lib/python2.7/dist-packages/uinput
copying build/lib.linux-armv6l-2.7/uinput/__init__.py -> /usr/local/lib/python2.7/dist-packages/uinput
copying build/lib.linux-armv6l-2.7/_libsuinput.so -> /usr/local/lib/python2.7/dist-packages
byte-compiling /usr/local/lib/python2.7/dist-packages/uinput/ev.py to ev.pyc
byte-compiling /usr/local/lib/python2.7/dist-packages/uinput/__init__.py to __init__.pyc
running install_egg_info
Writing /usr/local/lib/python2.7/dist-packages/python_uinput-0.10.1.egg-info

pi@raspberrypi ~/python-uinput $ sudo modprobe uinput
pi@raspberrypi ~/python-uinput $ cd
pi@raspberrypi ~ $ curl https://raw.githubusercontent.com/cpswan/Python/master/rpi-gpio-jstk.py > gpiojoystick.py
% Total % Received % Xferd Average Speed Time Time Time Current
Dload Upload Total Spent Left Speed
100 2778 100 2778 0 0 5931 0 --:--:-- --:--:-- --:--:-- 7141
pi@raspberrypi ~ $ sudo python ./gpiojoystick.py &
[1] 2171
pi@raspberrypi ~ $

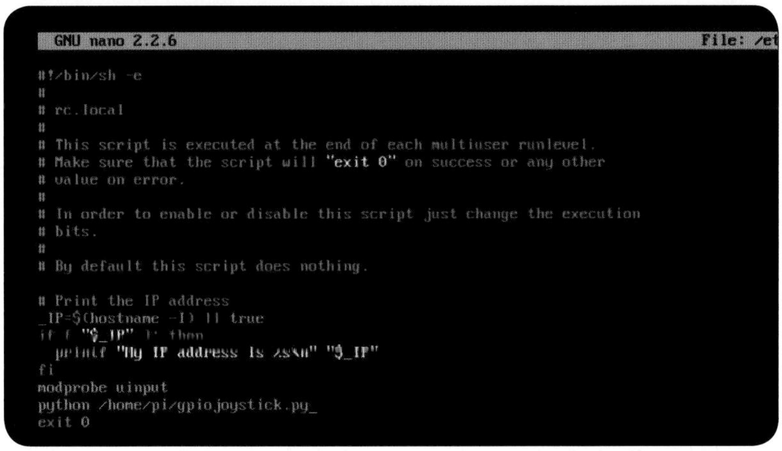

GNU nano 2.2.6
File: /et
#!/bin/sh -e
#
rc.local
#
This script is executed at the end of each multiuser runlevel.
Make sure that the script will "exit 0" on success or any other
value on error.
#
In order to enable or disable this script just change the execution
bits.
#
# By default this script does nothing.
# Print the IP address
_IP=$(hostname -I) || true
if ["$_IP"]; then
printf "My IP address is %s\n" "$_IP"
fi
modprobe uinput
python /home/pi/gpiojoystick.py_
exit 0

Uinput is designed for writing Python programs that can act as a joystick.

The first command installs the uinput kernel module, which is required for the Python uinput library to act as a joystick. The second returns you to your home directory, where the third downloads a Python program written by Chris Swan, based on work by uinput's creator Tuomas Räsänen, designed to read the inputs from the Pi's GPIO header and relay them to the uinput kernel module, where they can be interpreted by a game as joystick inputs:

```
Run the program with the
following command:
```

```
sudo python ./gpiojoystick.
py &
```

This gives Python the super-user, or root, account permissions required to read data from the Pi's GPIO port, and runs Chris Swan's Python program in the background using the ampersand symbol at the end of the line. Without this ampersand, the Python program would run in the foreground and lock up your terminal session, preventing you from loading any games.

At this point, the joystick should be working. Try loading a game, and using the joystick and fire button; they should work immediately. If the joystick doesn't work, check the game you're playing for a configuration menu; joystick control may be switched off. If the directions are reversed, double-check your wiring and, if necessary, move the wires around on the GPIO header to reflect the actual directions, remembering to turn off the Pi and unplug it from all peripherals except the joystick first, of course.

At present, you'll have to run these commands every time the Pi boots up if you want to use the joystick. To automate the process, type the following command at the terminal:

```
sudo nano /etc/rc.local
```

This file is used to run programs as the Pi starts, even before you've logged into the terminal. Move the cursor with the arrow keys so it's above the very last line "exit 0" and type the following lines into the file:

```
modprobe uinput
python /home/pi/
gpiojoystick.py &
```

If you've changed your username from the default "pi", remember to change the path in the last command. This tells the Pi, via rc.local, to automatically load the uinput kernel module followed by running Python with the gpiojoystick.py program, using the ampersand at the end of the line to run the program in the background and allow the boot sequence to continue. Notice that "sudo" isn't required

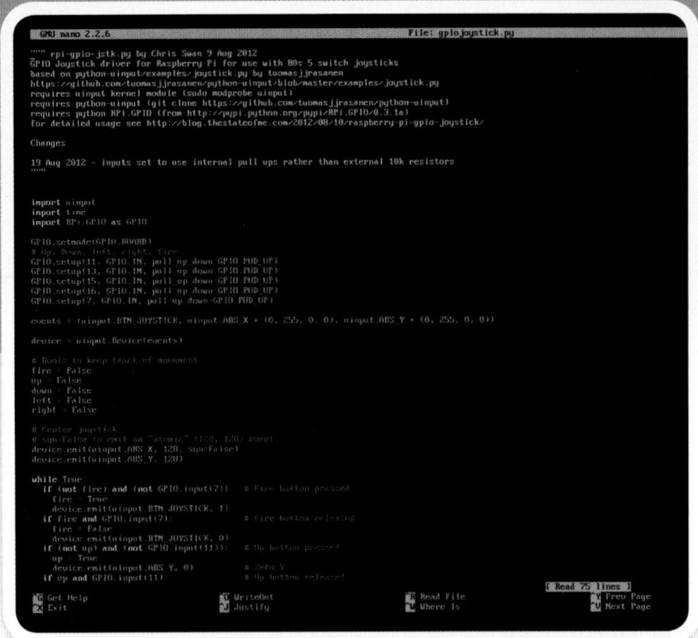

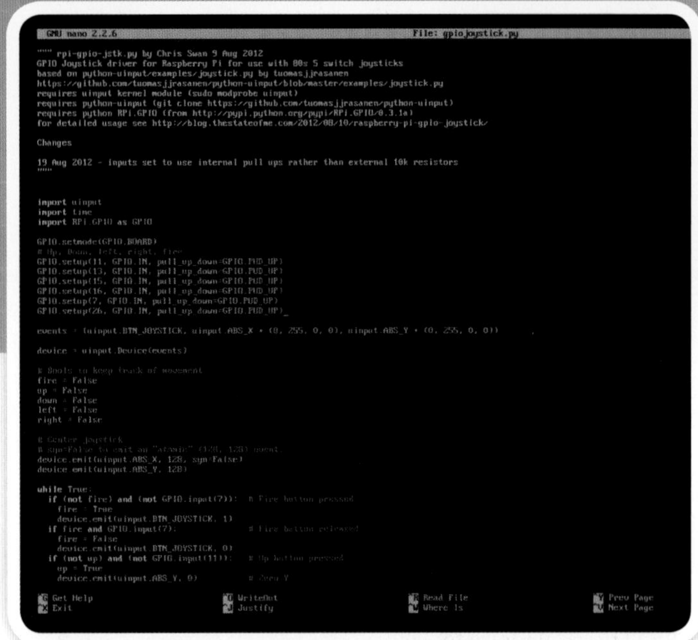

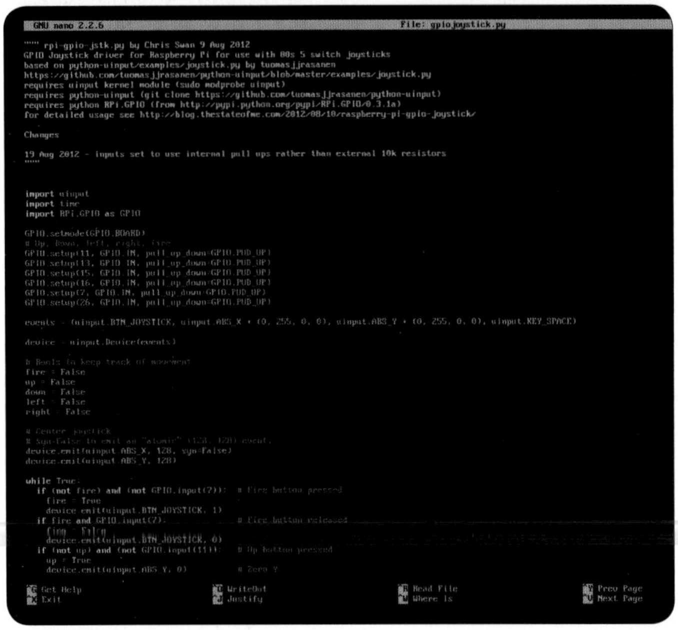

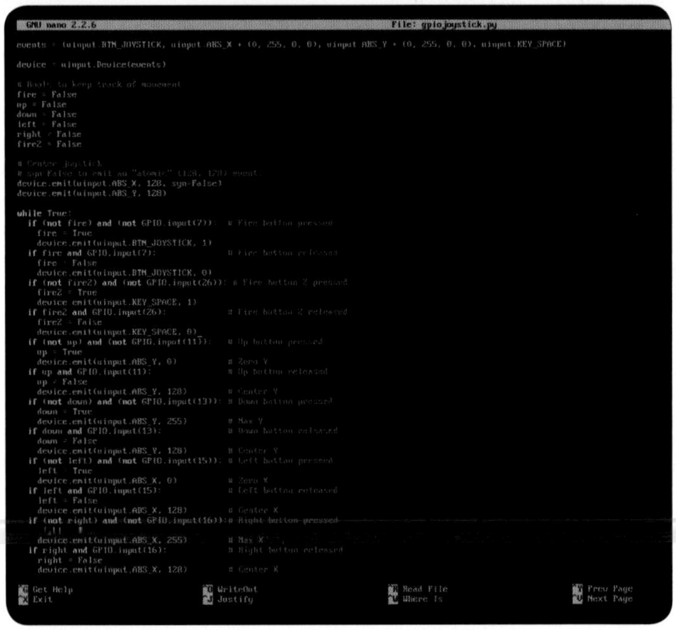

this time. Anything entered into rc.local automatically runs with the permissions of the super-user, or root, account.

Save the file with Ctrl+O, then exit Nano with Ctrl+X. The next time the Pi reboots, it will automatically load both the uinput module and the Python program for translating the joystick inputs. To test this, type the following command to reboot the Pi:

```
sudo reboot
```

It's easy to add an extra button or two to the controller.

UPGRADING THE JOYSTICK

If you want to add an additional fire button or two to the controller, it's easily done. Shut down the Pi with the following terminal command:

```
sudo halt
```

When the Pi has powered off, disconnect the power cable and all peripherals except the joystick and existing fire button. As before, measure out and cut the holes required for however many buttons you're adding, making sure to remove the existing buttons and joystick to prevent any damage to the wires when you're cutting the casing. These new buttons need to be wired into the same common ground connection as all the other switches. You may need to cut your existing spade connector off one of the ground connections to add the new wire or wires in.

Next, find an unused GPIO pin

– try the sixth pin along on the top row, or the very last two pins on the right-hand side of the top row – and wire the switch into this pin. There are enough unused pins on the Pi's GPIO header to add several buttons, so it's perfectly possible to make a more complex controller for fighting games and the like. When the pins are wired in, and you've double- and triple-checked the wiring, you can reassemble the controller and power the Pi back on.

When the Pi has booted, log in and type the following command at the terminal to edit the Python joystick program:

```
nano gpiojoystick.py
```

The program is well documented and laid out, and easy to modify for existing buttons. Use the arrow keys to move the cursor to the bottom of the lines marked GPIO.setup and enter a new line:

```
GPIO.setup(NN, GPIO.IN,
pull_up_down=GPIO.PUD_UP)
```

Replace NN with the number of the pin to which you've connected your button. If you've added more than one new button, add in extra lines for each additional button. Note that the joystick program uses the board numbering, rather than the BCM2835 number, scheme. This means that the numbers you enter correspond to the physical location of the pins on the GPIO header. This starts with Pin 1 in the bottom-left of the header, with Pin 2 directly above it on the top row; the next pin along the bottom row is Pin 3, with the pin directly above numbered Pin 4. This continues through Pin 25 and Pin 26 at the very right-hand edge of the bottom and top rows, respectively.

The Python uinput library only supports a single fire button by default; to add additional buttons, they need to be mapped to keys on the keyboard. Find the line that begins "events" and alter it so that it reads as follows:

```
events = (uinput.BTN_
JOYSTICK, uinput.ABS_X + (0,
255, 0, 0), uinput.ABS_Y +
(0, 255, 0, 0), uinput.
KEY_SPACE)
```

If you're adding more than one button, add additional key bindings before the final bracket; you can try using letters like KEY_H or KEY_X. Next, scroll down to the block with the comment "# Bools to keep track of movement" and add the following line at the bottom of the block:

```
fire2 = False
```

If you have more buttons, add in additional lines, incrementing the number each time: fire3, fire4 and so on. Finally, scroll to the main loop of the program and insert the following lines just above the line with the comment "# Up button pressed":

```
  if (not fire2) and (not
GPIO.input(NN)): # Fire
button 2 pressed
    fire2 = True
    device.emit(uinput.KEY_
SPACE, 1)
  if fire2 and GPIO.
input(NN): # Fire button 2
released
    fire2 = False
    device.emit(uinput.KEY_
SPACE, 0)
```

Replace NN with the pin to which the button is connected, and add more blocks of code – changing the KEY_SPACE and incrementing fire2 to fire3 and so forth – to support additional buttons if you've added more than one. Note that each of the "if" lines is indented by two spaces, and the other lines indented by four. These should match the layout of the existing lines in the program.

To have these new buttons recognised in your game, you'll need to enter its configuration menu to map the keys to in-game events. Look for an option that reads "Controls", "Calibration", "Controller Layout" or "Keyboard Mapping". If set within an emulator itself, the mapping will be carried through all games loaded within that emulator. If set within a game, it will apply only to that game. You now have a fully working custom arcade controller. If you built it in a cardboard housing, you could now consider building something more durable from wood, plastic or metal, or simply enjoy the eye-catching appeal of an upcycled cardboard box. You can also add additional buttons for other purposes: try adding buttons to the top of the controller mapped to KEY_ESC or KEY_PAUSE to exit an emulator or pause a game without having to use the keyboard at all.

INTERNET OF THINGS PRINTER

Program your IoT printer to print out every morning a weather forecast, a puzzle for your commute and even a list of tweets relating to your interests

The Internet of Things (IoT) is moving from a niche technical area to a billion-pound business, with everyone from industry stalwarts like ARM and Atmel to newcomers Microsoft and Intel putting their weight behind the move. Put simply, the IoT is the process of imbuing everyday systems with communications capabilities and a rudimentary "intelligence". Current commercial and volunteer IoT projects range from something as simple as a baby monitor that begins to warm a bottle as a child wakes, to low-cost flood monitoring networks made from cheap microcontrollers communicating in a wireless mesh network.

If you've built the Tweeting Doorbell project, you've already made your first steps into world of IoT. This project goes a step further, pulling information from external sources and printing it into a daily newspaper containing everything from your most recent social networking mentions to a weather forecast, and even a Sudoku puzzle for your to complete on your morning commute. It's a fascinating blend of the modern – a Pi with internet connectivity – and the old-fashioned world of print, and despite its capabilities is a relatively simply project to build.

WHAT YOU'LL NEED

The Internet of Things Printer requires, as its name suggests, an internet connection. As a result, the best choice for this project is a Raspberry Pi Model B. If you want to use the cheaper Model A, be aware that you'll have to budget for a USB wireless or wired networking dongle in order to connect it to the internet.

You'll also need the printer itself (£37.50, oomlout.co.uk). This is an affordable model of thermal printer most commonly used to print receipts. It requires no ink or toner, but instead uses heat to blacken selected areas of special paper, which is supplied on a long roll. Additional rolls can be purchased from office supply stores. These are usually available in varying widths, so make sure to buy 57mm width and 30mm diameter rolls.

The thermal printer requires more power than the Pi can provide, so you'll need to purchase a 5V power supply of 2A or higher current (£8.66, order code PW02884 from cpc.farnell.com). You can wire this into the build by stripping the connector from the end, or purchase a 2.1mm female jack-to-screw terminal adapter (£1.50, shop.pimoroni.com) into which the plug can be inserted.

To finish the printer build, you'll need an LED (£3.50 for 20 assorted, oomlout.co.uk) and a suitable current-limiting resistor (included). You'll also need a push-button switch (£2.50 for five, oomlout.co.uk). To make the process of wiring the printer up as simple as possible, consider using a breadboard (£3, oomlout.co.uk) and female-to-female jumper wires with male headers (£3.50, oomlout.co.uk).

BUILDING THE CIRCUIT

The Internet of Things Printer project uses a simple circuit, using the Pi's General-Purpose Input-Output (GPIO) header to take input from a switch and output to a status LED and the printer itself. Start by unpacking the printer and installing the paper roll. Do this by pulling up the lever at the left-hand side of the printer, below the LED and button, and lifting the flap. Pull the end of the paper roll free, and insert the roll inside the printer so that the free end is closest to you and coming up through the front of the paper. Close the lid of the printer so that it traps the paper at the front, then push firmly until the lever clicks home. If you've purchased a roll of paper too thick to sit in the printer with the lid closed, pull a length off until you've reduced the diameter and allowed the lid to close properly.

Enter the following command at the terminal to safely shut down your Pi:

```
sudo halt
```

Then disconnect it from all peripherals, including the power supply. Turn the printer over; orient it so that on the bottom edge there are two three-pin connectors, one marked DC-IN and one marked TTL. The first is the power input for the printer: as the thermal printer heats up the paper, it draws more power than the Pi could provide through the GPIO port. Connecting a separate power supply to the DC-IN header alleviates

Your finished Internet of Things mini printer.

this problem, providing the thermal printer with enough power to run. The second header, to the right, is the transistor-transistor logic (TTL) serial port for the printer; it's to this port that the Pi will send the data to be printed. Although there are three pins on both headers, you'll only be using two on each.

Find the black and red cable that came with the printer, and insert the end with three holes into the left-hand header on the printer marked DC-IN. The connector is keyed, meaning it will only go in one way: with the black wire to the left and the red wire to the right. Next, take the black, yellow and green wires and connect one end to the header on the printer marked TTL, so that the black wire is to the left and the green wire to the right, with the yellow wire in the middle.

This is the cable that receives data from the Pi, using the yellow wire. It also has a green wire, which would normally be used to send data – such as an alert that there's a paper jam, or that the paper has run out – back to the controlling system. It's important that this green wire is never connected directly to the Pi: the printer runs on 5V logic levels, while the Pi runs on 3.3V. A 3.3V signal from the Pi is high enough voltage for the printer to understand, but a 5V signal from the printer back to the Pi would be too high a voltage and will burn out the Pi's BCM2835 processor. It's possible to reduce the voltage of this wire sufficiently using a resistor, but the program that drives the printer makes no use of bidirectional communication; as a result, it's much safer to leave it disconnected.

The other end of the red and black power wires, from the DC-IN pins on the printer, need to be connected to your 5V power supply. You can do this in a number of ways: you could strip the connector from the end of the power supply and the black and red wires, and solder them together; you could use a breadboard to provide a connection; or you could use a 2.1mm barrel jack connector, into which you've screwed the stripped wires from the printer. Whichever way you choose, make sure that you connect the red wire to the positive side of the power supply and the black wire to ground or negative; reversing the polarity of the connection will damage the printer.

The black and yellow wires from the TTL pins on the printer need to be connected to the Pi's GPIO header. As with the power connectors, there are several ways to achieve this: the easiest is to plug the three-pin connector directly onto the Pi's GPIO header, with the black wire connected to the third pin along the top row and the yellow wire to the pin directly to the left. If doing this, it's vital that you remove the green wire from both ends of the connector by holding the white connector in your hand and pulling the wire firmly upwards. A connection between the green wire and the Pi's GPIO header without a resistor in place will damage the Pi's processor beyond repair.

With the printer connected and the green wire disconnected, it's time to connect the switch and LED. This is most easily achieved using a breadboard: using jumper leads, connect the fifth pin along the bottom row to the blue or black strip running along the edge of the breadboard to provide a common ground connection. Next, insert an LED into the breadboard so that it's in two separate rows; connect a jumper wire from the row with the longer leg of the LED – the anode – to the pin two along from the yellow wire on the top row, five pins along from the left-hand edge of the connector. Take a current-limiting resistor – 470Ω is a good value if one wasn't supplied with the LED – and insert one end into the row with the shorter leg of the LED, and the other end into the blue or black strip running along the edge of the breadboard.

Take a switch, and connect it into the centre of the breadboard, straddling the split in the rows. To the breadboard row in which the top-right leg of the switch is

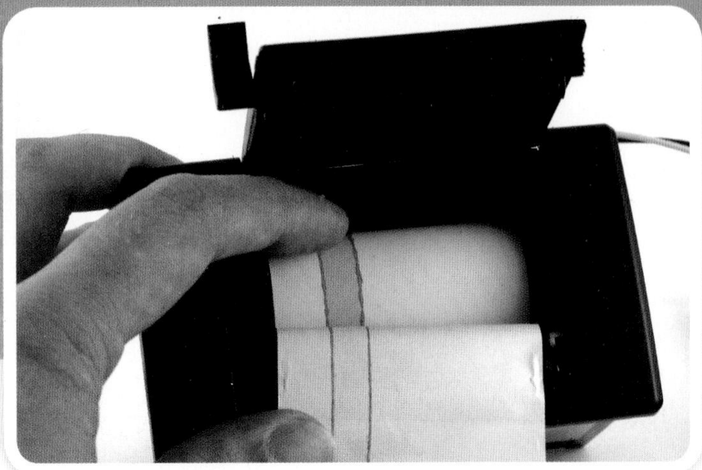

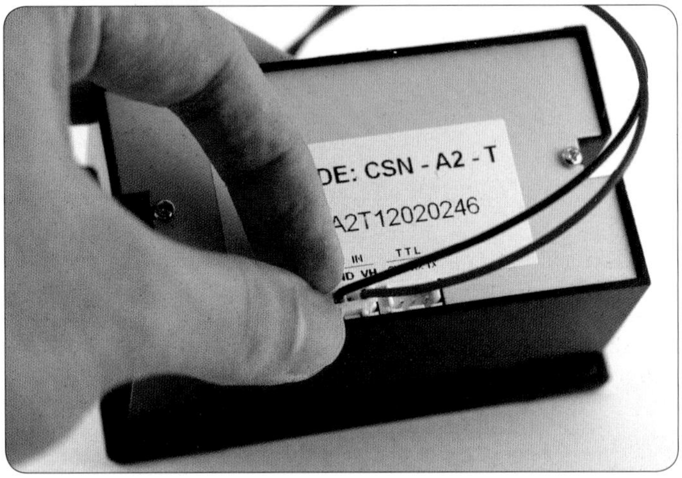

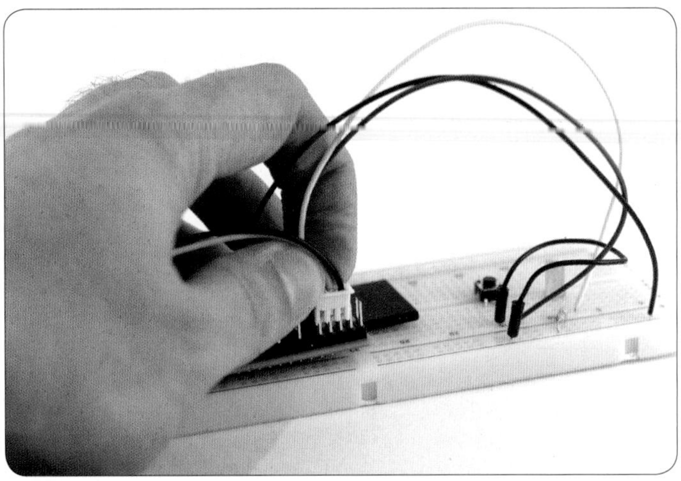

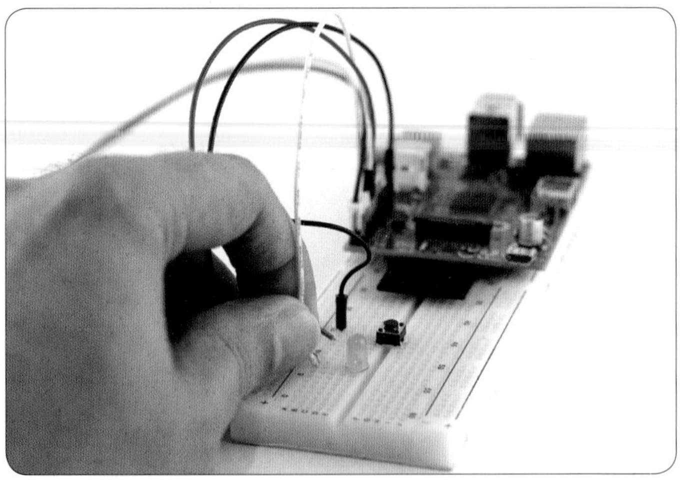

connected, place a jumper wire leading to the pin two along the top GPIO header row from the wire from the LED. Connect another wire from the row where the bottom leg of the switch sits to the blue or black strip running along the edge of the breadboard. This provides the printer's interactivity: the LED will light if it has something to print, while the button will instruct it to print whatever is currently in its memory.

It's easier to connect the switch and LED using a breadboard.

Before reconnecting your Pi to the power supply and its peripherals, take the time to double- and triple-check your wiring: connecting to the wrong pin on the GPIO header will damage the Pi, potentially breaking its processor beyond repair. When you're sure your wiring is correct, plug the Raspberry Pi – but not the

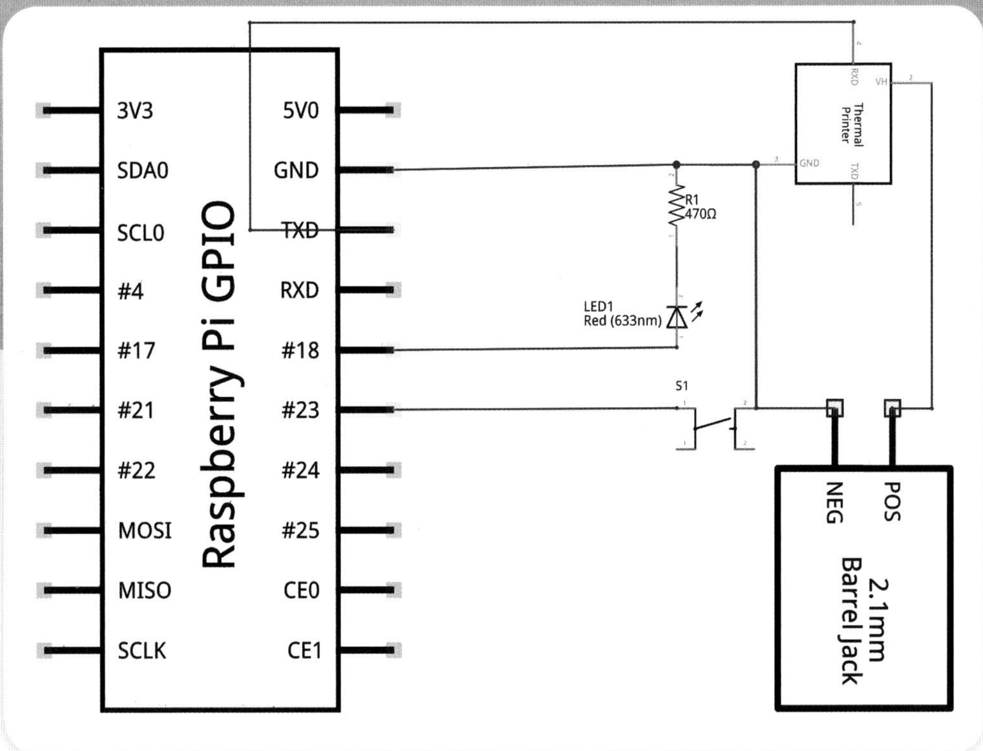

Use this scheme to help you build the circuit.

printer – into a display, keyboard and power supply.

INSTALLING THE SOFTWARE

When the Pi has booted, you need to make some changes to the Pi for it to be able to communicate. Start, as with any Pi project, by ensuring that the Pi's operating system is fully up to date by entering the following commands at the terminal:

```
sudo apt-get update
sudo apt-get upgrade
```

When the upgrade process has completed, install the required software with the following command:

```
sudo apt-get install python-
serial python-imaging
python-unidecode
```

This installs three Python libraries, one for serial communications, one for handling image files, and the last for encoding and decoding text in the Unicode format. This will take a short while to complete. When it has finished, you need to edit some files on the Pi to prevent the printer from printing gibberish as it boots. Start with the following command:

```
sudo nano /boot/cmdline.txt
```

This file contains the options passed to the Pi's operating system kernel as the Pi boots. It controls things like how and where its terminals appear, and at what speed they operate. By default, the Pi uses two of the pins on its GPIO header to provide a serial console. This allows you to connect two wires from a 3.3V TTL serial device and communicate with the Pi without directly connecting a display, keyboard or mouse. Unfortunately, those are the pins the printer uses for its serial communication with the Pi, so you'll have to disable the Pi's serial console. Find the section that reads:

```
console=ttyAMA0,115200
kgdboc=ttyAMA0,115200
```

Delete those two options, but only those two options. Make sure that there's still a single space between every option in the file, then save your changes with Ctrl+O and exit Nano with Ctrl+X. Next, edit another file with the command:

```
sudo nano /etc/inittab
```

Here, find the line at the very bottom of the file that reads:

```
T0:23:respawn:/sbin/getty -L
ttyAMA0 115200 vt100
```

Move the cursor to the start of the line and insert a hash symbol (#); this comments out the line, equivalent to deleting it but in a way that means you can easily reverse the process later. Save the file with Ctrl+O and exit Nano with Ctrl+X.

Finally, you need to install a program for downloading data from the internet and sending it to the printer. A US hobbyist specialist called Adafruit, which sells the same model of thermal printer, has developed just such a tool specifically for the Pi, which has been enhanced for inclusion in this MagBook. To download the enhanced copy, type the following command at the terminal:

```
git clone https://github.com/
ghalfacree/Python-Thermal-
Printer.git
```

This will download the required files into a directory called Python-Thermal-Printer. At this point, you need to reboot the Pi to make the changes to the serial console take effect. Restart the Pi by typing the following command:

```
sudo reboot
```

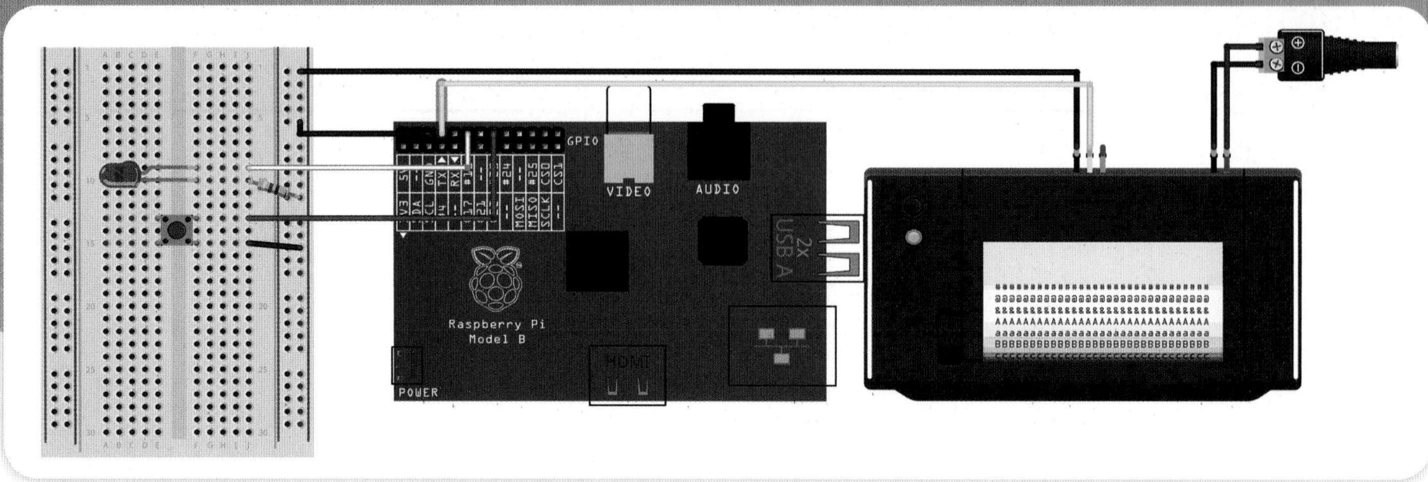

Follow this scheme if you're using a breadboard.

When the Pi has rebooted, you can connect the printer's power supply to the mains. When the printer has been switched on, you can test it by typing the following two commands at the terminal:

```
cd Python-Thermal-Printer
python printertest.py
```

This will print out some images and text demonstrating the capabilities of the printer. As you'll notice, the thermal printer is somewhat limited compared to an inkjet or laser. The graphics are low resolution, and in black and white, although a limited palette of greys is possible using a process known as dithering, where dots of black and white blend together to appear shaded. When the printout has completed, you can tear the paper by holding it at one edge and ripping it across the edge of the printer's slot. Take care not to pull upwards while you're doing this, as you'll forcibly feed unused paper out of the printer and waste it.

If the printer doesn't work, check that the paper is correctly inserted. Next, check that it is, indeed, plugged into its power supply and that the red and black wires are going to the positive and negative of the power supply, respectively. If it still doesn't work, disconnect the power, hold down the button on the top of the printer, and keep it held down while reconnecting the power. This will print out an internal test page. If the internal test page doesn't appear and you're sure the power supply is working and correctly wired, the printer may be faulty. If the internal test page does work, the connection between the Pi and the printer is likely at fault.

CUSTOMISING THE PROGRAM

When the test page has successfully printed, you need to make some changes to the program itself in order to have it recognise your Twitter account. If you've already created a Twitter application assigned to your account for the Tweeting Doorbell or Tweeting Security System projects, you can use the same details here. If not, you'll need to perform the following steps to receive keys for accessing your account.

Start by visiting **dev.twitter.com** in your PC's web browser, and sign in with your normal Twitter username and password. Twitter will then ask you if you want to authorise the Twitter developer site to use your account. Re-enter your username and password, and click the Authorise App button. When the page reloads, click on your avatar at the top-right of the screen and click My Applications in the dropdown box.

You need to install a program for downloading data from the internet.

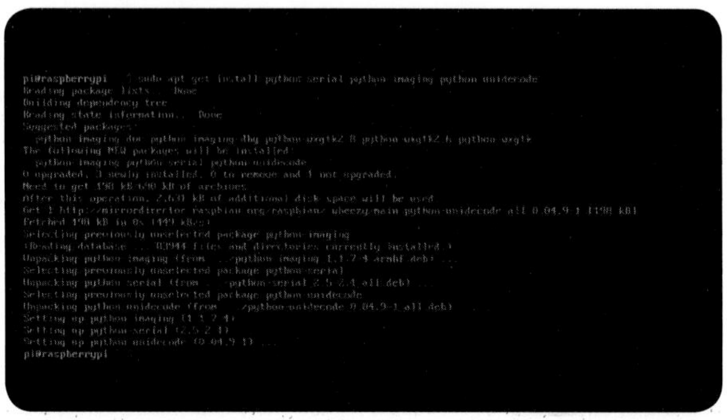

Everything that connects to Twitter using its application programming interface (API) is known as an application, and it requires special keys in order to gain access to your account. Begin by giving your application a name. This has to be unique, so try your name and "Printer". Fill in a description, and link to your website; leave Callback URL blank. Scroll to the bottom, click the tickbox to say you agree to the terms and conditions, and save the changes.

Initially, your application will be created with read-only permissions. This is fine for the printer project, but if you're planning to build anything that posts to Twitter as well as reading from it – such as the Tweeting Doorbell or Security System projects – you'll need to give your application read-write privileges. Scroll down the page to Application Settings and click on Modify App Permissions. Choose Read and Write, then click Update Settings. Click the API Keys tab, then click Create My Access Token at the bottom of the page. The token takes a while to generate, so keep refreshing the page until you see it appear in the Your Access Token section.

This provides you with everything your application needs to access

UNDERSTANDING THE COMMANDS

- **Adafruit_Thermal.py** The library that drives the thermal printer itself; this does not normally need to be changed.
- **README.md** A file identifying the contents of the Git repository; again, this can be ignored.
- **calibrate.py** This file can be used to calibrate the strength of the printer's thermal effect; only use it if you're finding that the printer jams when printing a lot of heavy graphics.
- **forecast.py** The file that downloads the weather forecast data from Yahoo; this should be edited to include your local Where On Earth Identifier (WOEID) for accurate results.
- **main.py** The main part of the printer program; this can be edited if you wish to customise the output by adding or removing modules.
- **printertest.py** A test program; this doesn't form part of the normal output of the printer as generated by main.py.
- **sudoku-gfx.py** Generates the graphical grid for the daily Sudoku puzzle portion of the printout; this doesn't normally need to be changed.
- **sudoku-txt.py** Generates the numbers for the Sudoku puzzle; again, this doesn't normally need to be changed.
- **timetemp.py** Gathers current temperature data for your local area; this should be edited to include the same WOEID as the forecast.py file for accurate results.
- **twitter.py** Searches Twitter for messages matching a query string; this should be edited to include your Twitter API keys and your chosen query string.

Twitter. Make a note of the API Key, API Secret, Access Token and Access Token Secrets; you'll need to fill these in to customise the Internet of Things Printer program itself. Make sure to keep them private; with those keys anybody can access your Twitter account and send messages as though they were you, even if they don't know your password. If sharing your code with anyone else building the same project, remember to remove the keys first!

These keys need to be inserted into the file twitter.py in the Python-Thermal-Printer directory. Type the following command into the terminal:

```
nano twitter.py
```

This will load the file into the Nano text editor. Using the cursor keys, scroll down until you find the section labelled "Twitter application credentials". Find the lines labelled "consumer_key" and "consumer_secret". Fill these in with the API key and API secret from your Twitter developer's page, respectively, inserting the keys in between the single quotes on each line. Remember that these keys provide full access to your account, so if you share your source code with anyone remove the keys first.

You need to edit some of the Pi's files to prevent the printer from printing gibberish as it boots.

Next, scroll down to the line that begins "queryString". This contains the search term that the program will look for when finding Twitter messages to include in its print-out. You can enter anything here that you'd normally search for on the Twitter website: a hashtag, a username, or any key phrase you'd like to see included when the software creates its printout. To print messages that are for your attention from other users, try putting "to:Username" between the single quotes, replacing Username with your Twitter handle minus the @ symbol. By default, the script will search for and print all messages from the Adafruit Twitter account, the original creator of the script.

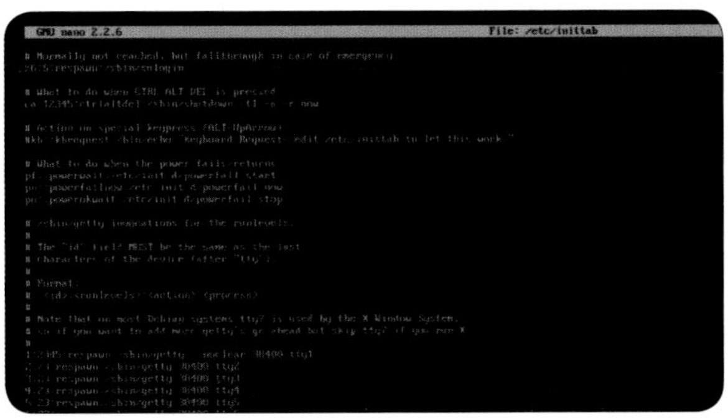

When you've made your changes, double-check that the Twitter keys and the query string are fully enclosed between single quotes, then save the file with Ctrl+O and exit Nano with Ctrl+X. Next, you need to customise the file that prints out a weather forecast so that it picks the weather data from your local area. Open the file for editing with the following command:

```
nano forecast.py
```

Scroll down until you find the line that begins "WOEID". This holds a string known as the Where On Earth Identifier, used by Yahoo for its weather forecasting services. By default, the WOEID in the file is a location in America. To change it to something more useful, you'll need to know the WOEID for your local area. On your PC, visit **weather.yahoo.com** in a web browser. If prompted to share your location with the site, do so; otherwise, enter the name of your nearest city or your postal code into the search bar across the top. When the weather for your local area appears, look at the URL in the address bar for a series of numbers: these represent the WOEID for your location. The WOEID for Leeds, West Yorkshire, as an example, is 26042; for London, it's 44418.

Delete the numbers from between the single quotes on the WOEID line and replace them with your own, as with the below example for Leeds:

```
WOEID = '26042'
```

Make sure that both single quotes are still present, then save the file with Ctrl+O before quitting Nano with Ctrl+X. You'll now need to do the same for another file that downloads the current, rather than future, time and temperature data. Edit the file with the following command:

```
nano timetemp.py
```

As before, look for the line that begins "WOED" and inset your own local Where On Earth Identifier between the single quotes. Save the file with Ctrl+O, and exit Nano with Ctrl+X. That completes the customisation of the printer code; you're now free to run the program itself to see what it can do.

RUNNING THE PRINTER

The program that drives the printer is split up into a range of different files, each one of which handles a different aspect of the overall printout. To get a list of these files, type the following command:

```
ls
```

The file main.py handles most of the heavy lifting, calling each of the subfiles – except for certain files, like calibrate.py and printertest.py, included for manual execution when troubleshooting – as required to build up the entire printout. It's designed to be run in the background; as long as the Pi is switched on, the main.py script should be running in order for it to monitor Twitter messages. The program also works on a timer: at 06:30 every morning, it prints out an entire run of all the linked sub-modules, including Twitter messages, a weather forecast, and a Sudoku puzzle. This provides you with a personalised "newspaper' you can be looking at as you get ready for the day.

You'll need to give your application read-write privileges.

To see this output now, and to leave the main.py program running in the background, type the following command at the terminal:

```
sudo ./main.py &
```

Consider writing your own module to print out new information and integrating it into the main.py program

This terminal command runs the main.py program itself, using the ampersand at the end of the line to tell Linux that it should run in the background and not tie up your terminal. Note that you need to use the sudo command here; the program accesses the GPIO port to monitor the button and illuminate the LED, which requires super-user, or root, permissions.

When the program has run, a welcome message and the Pi's IP address will be printed. This will be followed after a short period by the daily output, including a weather forecast, Sudoku puzzle and recent Twitter messages. The initial printout will take a little while to complete as the program searches the internet for your requested information, then it will begin to spool out of the printer. As before, you can tear the paper off by grasping it at one edge and tearing it against the edge of the printer. Remember not to pull upwards, as you'll end up feeding unused paper out from the roll inside the printer and wasting it.

Having to manually run the program every time the Pi is rebooted is a pain, so to make life easier you can automate the process. Edit the file rc.local with the following

command at the terminal:

```
sudo nano /etc/rc.local
```

At the bottom of the file, just above "exit 0", type the following line:

```
/home/pi/Python-Thermal-Printer/main.py &
```

This will load the main.py program automatically when the Pi powers on, even before you've logged in. The ampersand, as before, makes sure the program runs in the background so the Pi's boot process can continue. Note that you don't need the sudo command here; anything inserted into the rc.local file will run as the root user by default, making sudo superfluous to requirements. Every morning, a printout will be waiting for you with the day's messages, weather and a Sudoku puzzle; providing, that is, the printer is powered on and has enough paper.

USING THE SWITCH AND LED

You may be wondering what the switch and LED are for, if the main.py program creates its printout automatically at 06:30 every morning. The LED is used as a status notification: if it's blinking, that means that the main.py program is currently running and checking Twitter for new messages matching your query string. As these messages come in, they'll automatically be printed. To test this, go to **twitter.com** in your PC's web browser and type in a new message matching your query string. After a minute or two, the message should be printed. If the LED stops flashing, that's a sign that the main.py program has stopped running. You'll need to log into the Pi to find out why, or simply reboot it to get it running again if you've added the command to rc.local.

At any time, you can tap the button once to print out a report of the current time and weather conditions. You can do this as many times as you like; it won't affect the main printout, which will automatically print every day at 06:30 or whenever the Pi is first booted. A longer press on the button will initiate a shutdown sequence of the Pi. This is especially handy if you plan to set up the Pi and printer somewhere they won't have access to a display or keyboard, as it allows you to easily switch off the Pi safely without having to log in and run the halt command.

If you want to build the Internet of Things Printer in a more permanent housing, you can use the mounting brackets provided with the printer. Simply cut a hole in your chosen case the same size as the body of the printer and place it through the hole so that the lip of the printer rests on the surface, then use the screws and brackets provided to secure the printer in place. Cut a hole for the switch and LED – buying an illuminated switch, which includes an integrated LED that can be used for notifications in place of the standalone LED used in this project, is a good idea here as it means only drilling one hole and is easier to mount than a bare LED – and mount them within easy access somewhere you'll see the LED when it's alerting you to new messages.

It's also possible to power the Pi from the same 5V power supply as the printer, to save on mains sockets. If you choose to do so, split the positive and negative connections from the power supply before they reach the thermal printer. Wire the positive side of the supply to the first pin on the top row of the Pi's GPIO header, then wire the negative side of the supply to the last pin on the bottom row of the GPIO header. If doing this, ensure that the power supply has enough amperage to drive both the printer and the Pi. 2A at 5V is the minimum, and if you plan on adding any additional hardware to the Pi it's a good idea to find a 3A or better power supply.

The IoT Thermal Printer program is designed to be easily extensible; open the individual files in Nano or the IDLE Python Integrated Development Environment (IDE) from the graphical user interface and investigate how they work. Consider writing your own module to print out new information – such as the number of emails you have waiting for you, or the time the Pi has been running for without interruption – and integrating it into the main.py program. It's a good way of sharpening your Python skills.

IOT PRINTER WALKTHROUGH

Follow our step-by step guide to setting up a developer account on Twitter, to allow your printer to download and print your Twitter messages

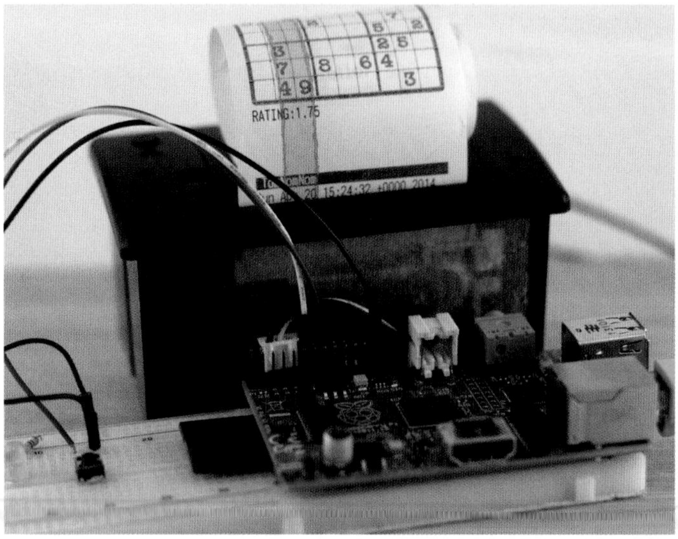

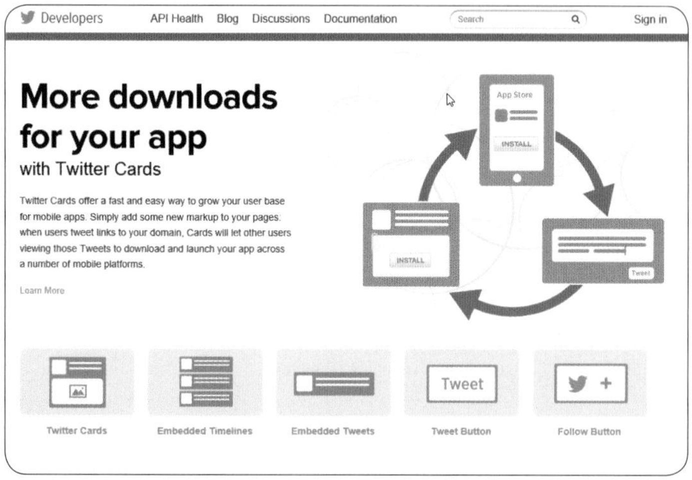

1 **Each app you create should have its own entry in your Twitter Developer account; this keeps things seperated in the event you lose your keys.**

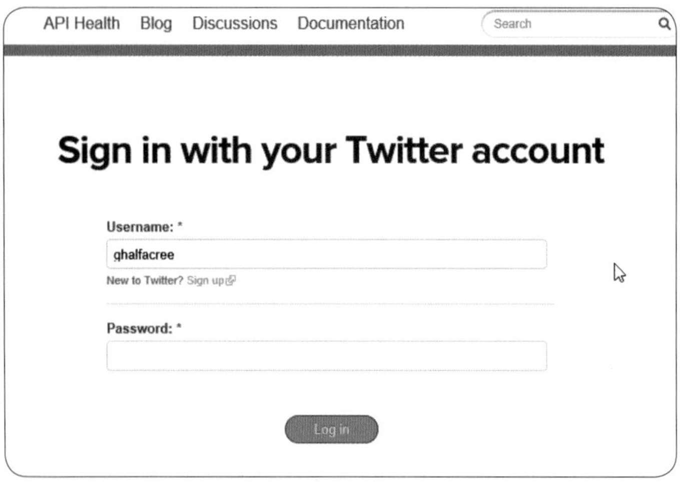

2 **Sign into the Twitter development server with your usual username and password; if you don't have an account, sign up at twitter.com first.**

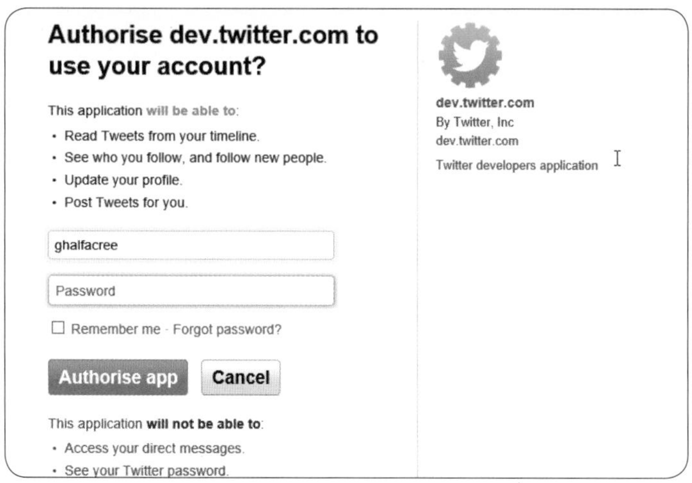

Authorise dev.twitter.com to use your account?
This application will be able to:
Read Tweets from your timeline.
See who you follow, and follow new people.
Update your profile.
Post Tweets for you.
ghalfacree
Password
Remember me · Forgot password?
Authorise app
Cancel
This application will not be able to:
Access your direct messages.
See your Twitter password.
dev.twitter.com
By Twitter, Inc
dev.twitter.com
Twitter developers application

3 **For security reasons, you'll need to authorise the Twitter development server to connect to your account; re-enter your username and password.**

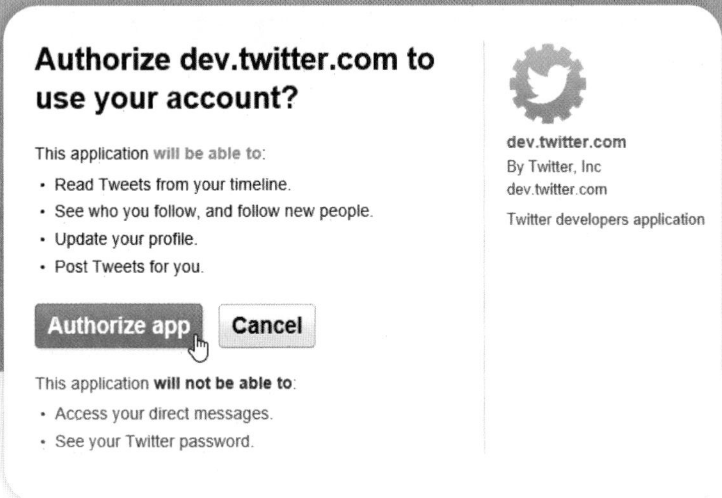

4 Clicking Authorise App will allow the Twitter development server to access your Twitter account, without your app knowing your password.

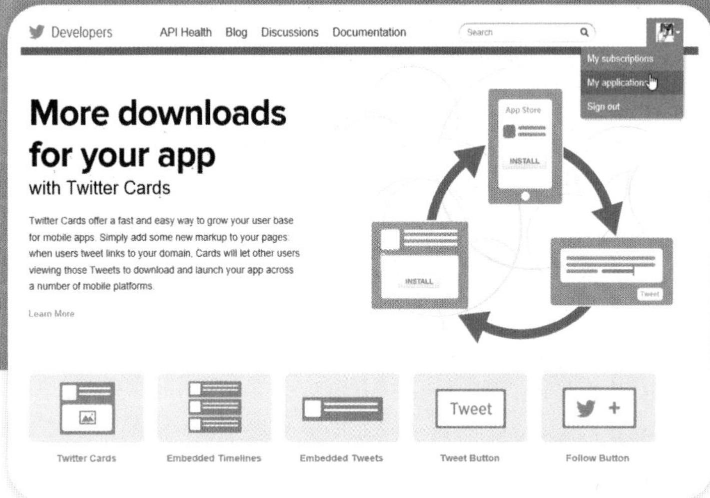

5 A list of your applications is accessible by clicking your Twitter avatar at the top-right of the screen; you can also create new ones here.

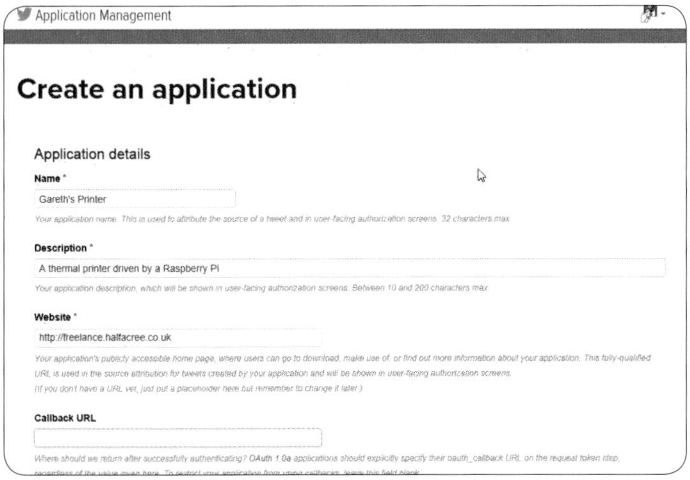

6 Give your new app a unique name; your name plus the word "Printer" is a good way of keeping it globally unique from any other app.

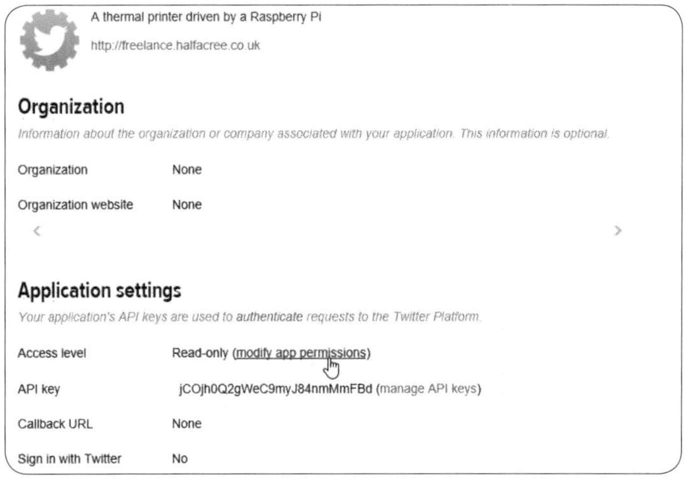

7 Click the Modify App Permissions link in Access Level to grant additional access rights to your application for adding new features in the future.

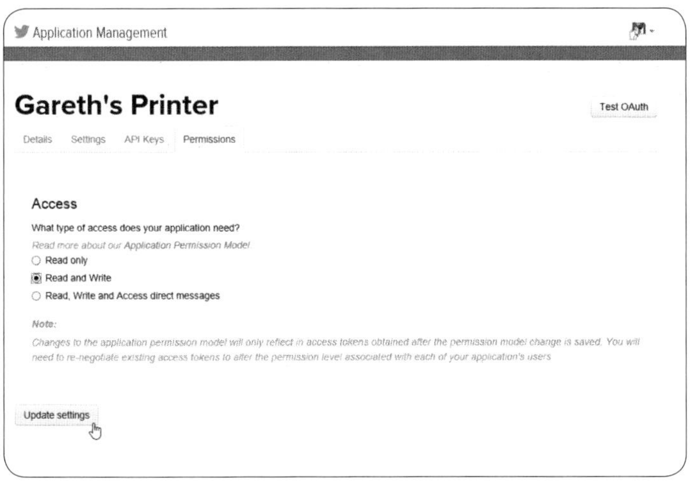

8 Giving your app Read and Write permissions will make it easier to add two-way communication in future, although Read Only works for now.

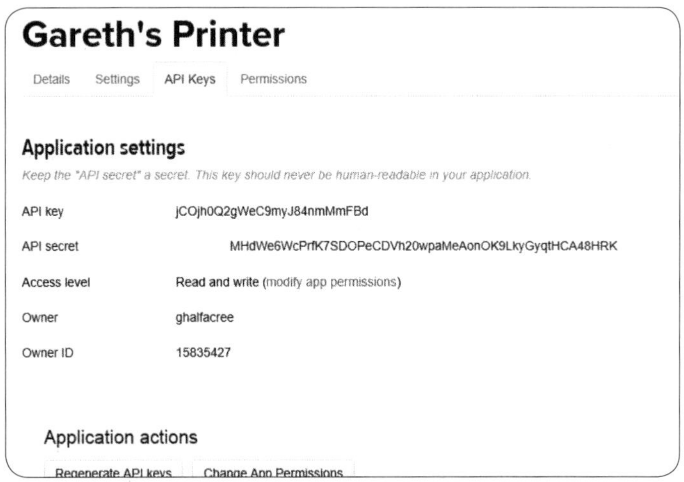

9 Note the API Key and API Secret; you'll need to put these in the printer's Python script to give it access to download and print your messages.

RASPBERRY CLUSTER

Raspberry Pis are small and inexpensive, so it's easier to use them to build a cluster than it would be with PCs. We show you how to get started

The secret of modern high-performance computing – the sort of systems that analyse nuclear physics problems or radio telescope data, or look for the best places to drill for oil – lies in clustering: the combining of the power of hundreds, often thousands, of processors into a single, immensely powerful system. These supercomputer clusters often cost many millions, and occasionally billions, to build, and even more to run, but you can experiment with the same concept at home with little more than a pair or more of Pis.

To temper your expectations: a cluster made up of a hundred Raspberry Pis would struggle to match, let alone exceed, the computational power of an average desktop or laptop computer. It can, however, speed up tasks you're carrying out on the Pi, or simply act as an introduction to the world of clustered computing.

INSTALLING THE SOFTWARE

A true computing cluster works by presenting remote systems – known as nodes – to the local system, where they can be used just the same as a local processor or memory. The most common method is known as the Message Passing Interface (MPI), but outside scientific pursuits it has limited use: programs must be specifically written and compiled to include MPI support.

A better choice for a clustering beginner is to cheat a little using a tool called GNU Parallel. Part of the GNU suite of free software utilities, many of which are bundled with the Linux kernel to make up operating systems such as Raspbian, GNU Parallel automates the process of running multiple versions of a program. It also supports communicating with other nodes over a network, bringing many of the benefits of clustered computing to everyday applications.

As with any Raspberry Pi project, it's important to ensure that your operating system is up to date. Pick one of your Pis – it doesn't matter which – to be the master, then connect this to a keyboard and monitor, and plug all the Pis into the network and power supply. When they've finished booting, log into the master Pi and type the following commands at the terminal:

```
sudo apt-get update
sudo apt-get upgrade
sudo apt-get install
parallel
```

The first two commands download the latest list of software packages and check to see if any software already installed on the system needs upgrading. The third command downloads and installs the GNU Parallel software itself. As standard on Raspbian, this is provided in

WHAT YOU'LL NEED

The definition of a cluster requires that there's more than one of something, so you'll need at least two Raspberry Pis. The Model B is the best choice for clustering, as communication between the individual systems that make up the cluster requires a network connection. You'll also need an SD card with a copy of Raspbian for each Pi in the cluster, but once you've gone through the initial setup process on each you'll only need a single keyboard and monitor. You should also give each Pi a static IP address. See the Privacy-Boosting Router project for details on how to do this.

You'll also need to ensure that all the Pis are connected to the same network. If you're creating a permanent cluster, the easiest way to do this is to buy a dedicated network switch with as many ports as you have Pis. You can also buy a multiport USB power hub at the same time, to reduce the number of mains sockets your cluster will require. Pay attention to the power rating of the USB hub: each Pi will require around 700mA when it's actively processing.

You may want to consider additional cooling for the clustered Pis, such as a heatsink for the memory and processor chips at the centre of the board. This is especially important if you're building a stack of Pis, as the boards in the middle will get hotter than would usually be the case for individual Pis. For larger clusters, fans blowing through the stacks will keep everything running cool.

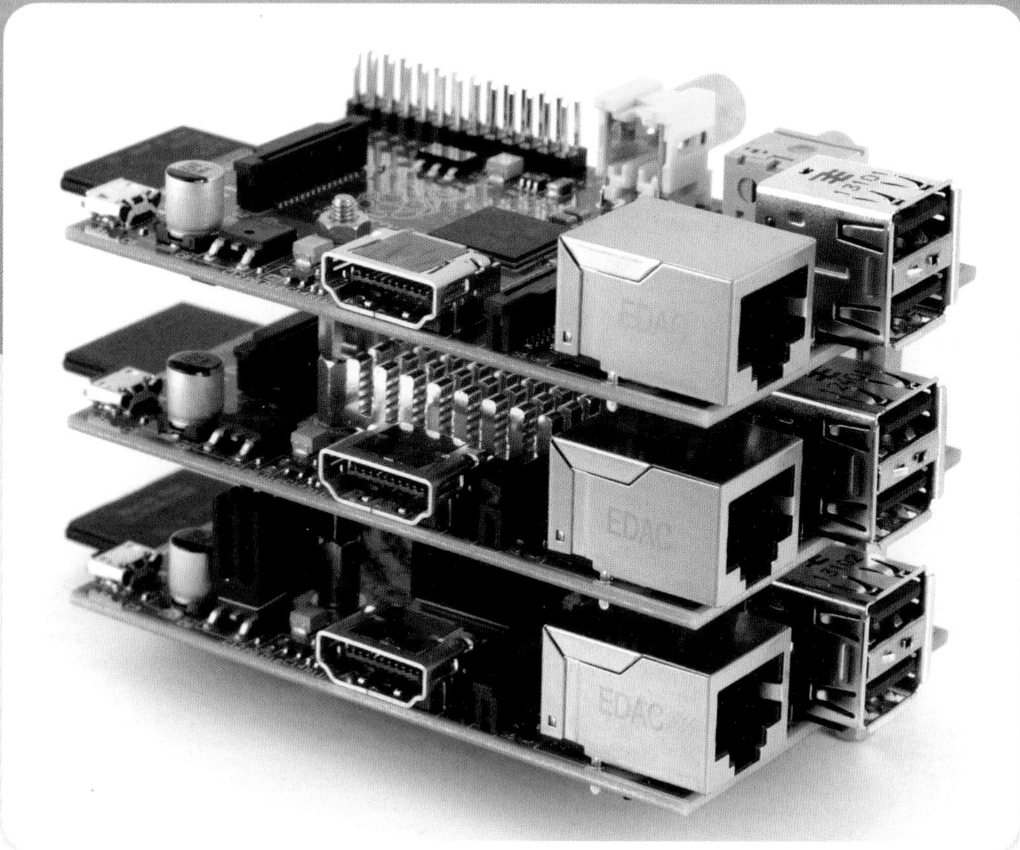

A cluster requires at least two Raspberry Pis.

an outdated compatibility mode, which renders many of its advanced features unusable. To disable this compatibility mode and enable its full capabilities, type the following command to open the GNU Parallel configuration file:

```
sudo nano /etc/parallel/
config
```

This file will have a single line in it, reading "--tollef". This tells GNU Parallel to enable a compatibility mode for an older application of the same name. Delete this line entirely, then save the file with Ctrl+O and exit Nano with Ctrl+X. This will ensure that GNU Parallel runs in GNU mode, the modern default, with all features enabled.

At this point, you've installed GNU Parallel on the master Pi. You'll also need to install it on all the other Pis in the cluster in order for the communication between nodes to take place. You can, if you want, do this by unplugging the keyboard and display from the master Pi and plugging it into the next Pi before repeating this section of the project from the beginning. A more convenient alternative is to connect from the master Pi to the other Pis via the Secure Shell (SSH).

Type the following command in the terminal:

```
ssh ipaddress1
```

Replace ipaddress1 with the IP address of the first Pi in your cluster that isn't the master Pi. This will use the SSH client to create an encrypted connection between the two Pis, using your current username – pi, if you haven't changed it – to log into the second Pi. After a few seconds, you'll be asked for the password; enter it, and you'll be given a terminal on the second Pi. You can now run through the first part of this project again to install and configure GNU Parallel on the second Pi. When you've finished, type the following command:

```
exit
```

This will close your connection to the second Pi and return you to the master Pi's terminal again. Do this for each Pi in your cluster, installing GNU Parallel and editing its configuration file to disable the outdated compatibility mode.

A better choice for a clustering beginner is to cheat a little using a tool called GNU Parallel

SETTING UP THE CONNECTIONS

You now have a number of Raspberry Pis, each with GNU Parallel installed. At the moment, the master Pi doesn't know about the others. If you were to try running a task through GNU Parallel now, it would only run on the master Pi and you'd see no performance advantage. To set up a list of nodes in the cluster, which GNU Parallel can consult when running a task, type the following commands:

```
mkdir ~/.parallel
nano ~/.parallel/sshloginfile
```

The first command creates a hidden directory in your home folder for GNU Parallel's per-user configuration files. The second creates one of these files, a list of network nodes to which GNU Parallel can connect over SSH. Fill in the file with the following lines:

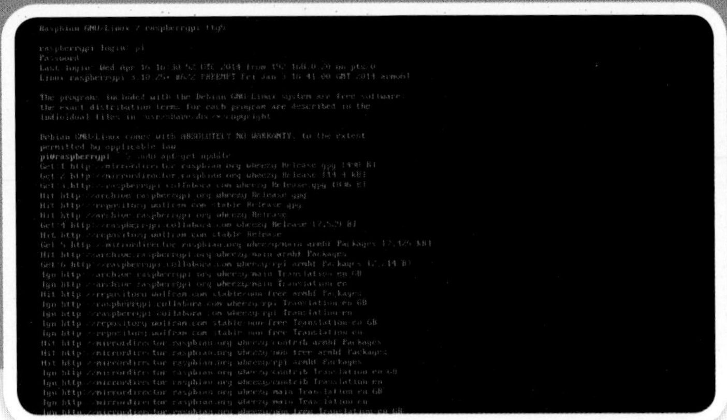

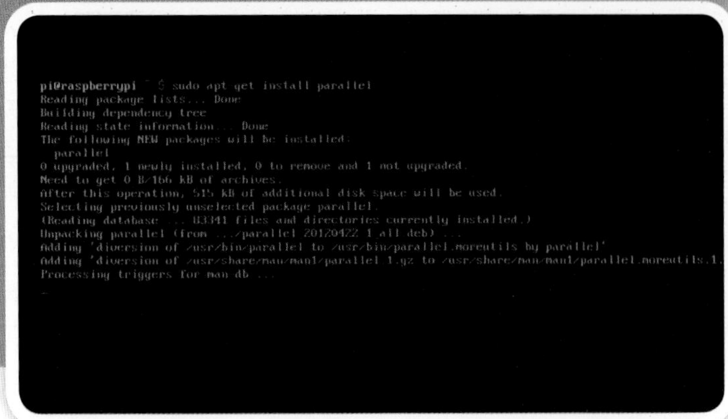

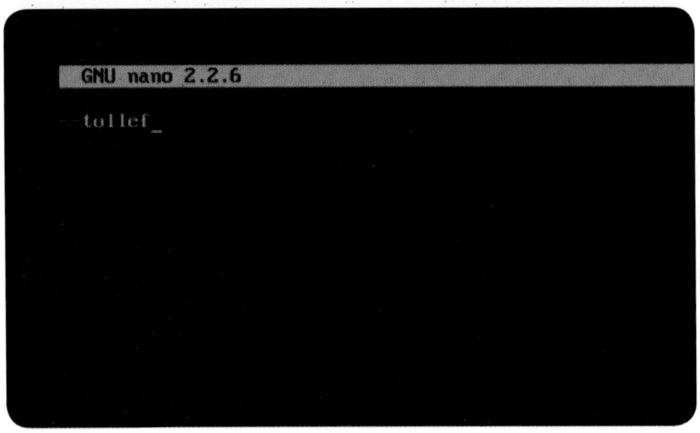

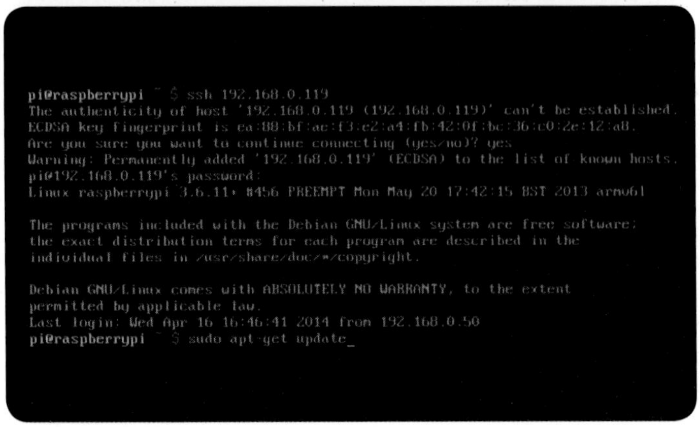

First, install GNU Parallel on the master Pi.

```
1/:
1/ssh -c arcfour ipaddress1
1/ssh -c arcfour ipaddress2
1/ssh -c arcfour ipaddress3
```

The first line tells Parallel that it should treat the local system – specified by the colon symbol – as a node in the cluster capable of running a single job at a time, as specified by the number before the slash. Without this, the master Pi will be used purely to manage jobs running on other systems. The remaining lines detail the systems that make up the cluster.

Each line begins with the number of simultaneous jobs the system can handle. For a Pi, this is 1; the single-core processor can only handle a single task at any given time. If you were adding a modern desktop or laptop to the cluster – which, as GNU Parallel will happily run on any computer capable of running Linux or similar operating systems, you can easily do if you so choose – it could handle as many as 12 simultaneous jobs. Leaving the number and its following slash out will tell GNU Parallel to examine the remote system and run as many jobs as it can find logical processor cores. This doesn't work well on the Pi, which is why you're manually specifying the number for each node.

The second part of each line is a custom SSH command, which uses the -c option to switch from the default encryption cipher to the Arcfour, or RC4, stream cipher. This cipher isn't considered secure enough for general use, but it's extremely fast: file transfers using Arcfour on a Pi can run at around 5MB/s, compared to around 3MB/s for the default AES cipher. This speeds up the transferring of files from node to node when jobs require it.

Finally, each ipaddress should be replaced with the address of a node in the cluster. If you have different user accounts on each Pi, you can prefix its IP address with the username followed by the @ symbol. You can have as many nodes as you like, although the master Pi may struggle to efficiently manage more than a couple of dozen or so. If so, it's possible to use a separate desktop or laptop computer running Linux and GNU Parallel as the master and relegate the master Pi to the status of just another node in the cluster.

Save the file with Ctrl+O, and exit Nano with Ctrl+X. Next, you need to configure the SSH client itself to improve the speed of the connections between nodes. Type the following commands at the terminal:

```
mkdir ~/.ssh/cm_socket
nano ~/.ssh/config
```

The first command creates a new director, which SSH can use for storing information about its active connections; the second loads the per-user configuration file. Type the following lines into the file:

```
ControlMaster auto
ControlPath ~/.ssh/cm_
socket/%r@%h:%p
ControlPersist 1h
```

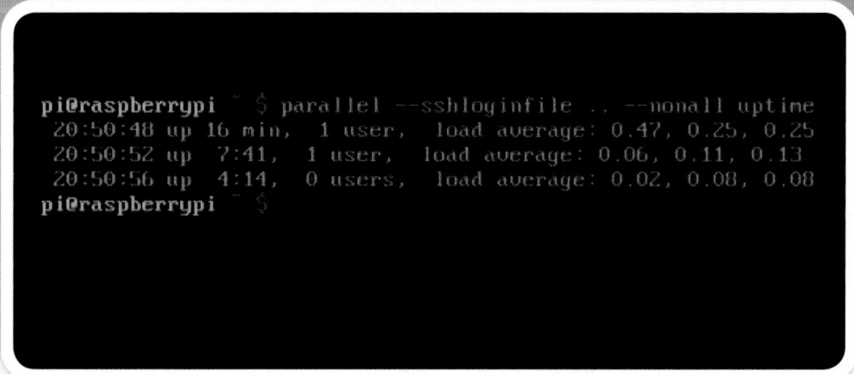

pi@raspberrypi ~ $ parallel --sshloginfile .. --nonall uptime
20:50:48 up 16 min, 1 user, load average: 0.47, 0.25, 0.25
20:50:52 up 7:41, 1 user, load average: 0.06, 0.11, 0.13
20:50:56 up 4:14, 0 users, load average: 0.02, 0.08, 0.08
pi@raspberrypi ~ $

GNU Parallel allows you to run multiple copies of any command on the nodes.

The first line sets up the SSH Control Master option. This allows the SSH client to open a single master connection to a remote system, then channel future connections through it. This eliminates the hand-shaking step normally required for each connection, and can considerably reduce the time it takes to run larger jobs through GNU Parallel. The second line tells SSH where it should store information about the Control Master connections, while the last line tells it to close down any master connections older than an hour.

Save the file with Ctrl+O, then exit Nano with Ctrl+X.

Finally, you need to set up SSH keys so that Parallel can automatically log into each node in the cluster. Ordinarily, you'd need to type your password for every single connection GNU Parallel makes – a time-consuming task that will easily wipe out any performance gains you'll get from running your jobs on the cluster. SSH keys automate the process of logging in; a private key is stored on the master Pi, and used to "unlock" a connection on each node.

To create a private key, type the following command:

```
ssh-keygen
```

Press Enter to confirm the default filename when prompted, and Enter twice when asked for a passphrase to leave the key unlocked.

To copy the public side of the master Pi's private key to each node in the cluster, type this command:

```
ssh-copy-id ipaddress
```

Replace ipaddress with the IP address of the first node. You'll be prompted for the password as normal, then confirmation that the key has been copied will appear. The next time you try to SSH to that node – whether through GNU Parallel or manually – from the master Pi you'll be logged in automatically with no password. This only applies to connections from the master Pi, with any other device on the network having to use a password as normal.

Repeat that command for each node in the system, replacing the ipaddress each time.

RUNNING A PARALLEL JOB

GNU Parallel doesn't work like a traditional clustering system. Where a normal computer cluster would run a specially designed application that splits its workload across multiple nodes in the cluster, GNU Parallel allows you to run multiple copies of any command on the nodes. Each version of the command is independent, which is how GNU Parallel is able to run tasks that would normally only support a single processor on a single host computer across an entire cluster.

The downside to this approach is that it's not possible to use GNU Parallel with jobs that can't easily be split up. Compressing a single large file with gzip, as an example, is a single job and GNU Parallel can't make it run any faster regardless of how many nodes are in your cluster. Compressing multiple files, however, can be run through GNU Parallel; the software will create as many jobs as it can across all nodes, transferring files to and from the nodes where necessary.

To start experimenting with GNU Parallel, type the following command at the terminal on the master Pi:

```
parallel -j N --sshloginfile
.. --nonall uptime
```

Replace N with the number of nodes in your cluster. This simple command loads GNU Parallel and provides it with the list of cluster nodes you created earlier. The --sshloginfile option loads this file, while .. acts as a shorthand way of referring to the default filename. The --nonall option tells GNU Parallel that it should run the following command on all cluster nodes, regardless of whether it would normally need to do so. This option is required to make the final command, uptime, run on all nodes. Uptime has no options and no files to process, so ordinarily Parallel would create only a single job for the task rather than a job per node.

To experiment with true clustering, read the write-up of the cluster created at Boise State University from 32 Pis

When the command runs, there'll be a short delay while GNU Parallel logs into all the nodes. After a few seconds, you'll see a status report from each node in the cluster telling you how long it has been running and

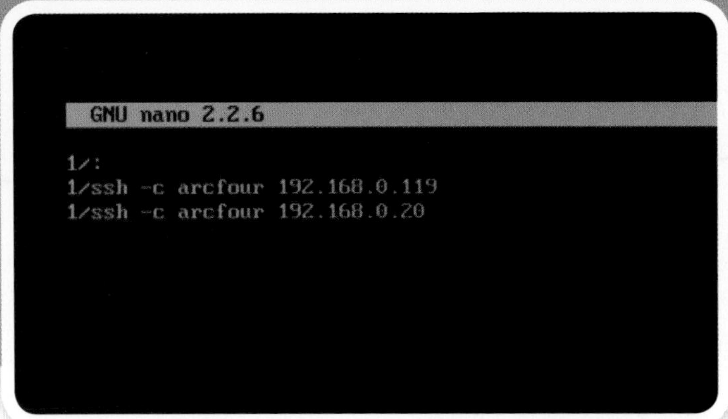

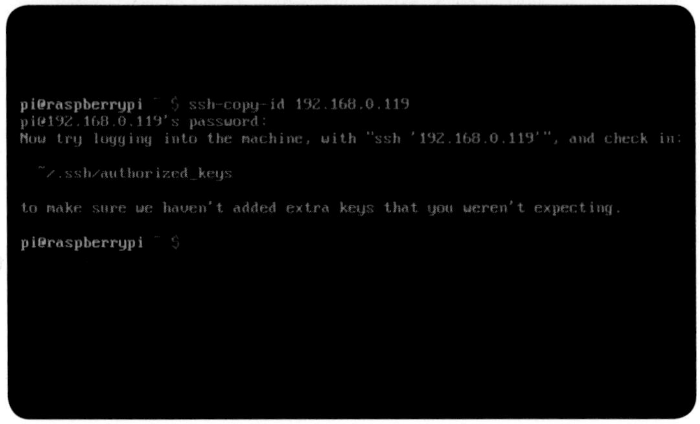

how heavily loaded the system is. That confirms that GNU Parallel is working as expected, communicating with the nodes and running your jobs on each node simultaneously.

pi@raspberrypi ~ $ ssh-copy-id 192.168.0.119
pi@192.168.0.119's password:
Now try logging into the machine, with "ssh '192.168.0.119'", and check in:
~/.ssh/authorized_keys
to make sure we haven't added extra keys that you weren't expecting.
Generating public/private rsa key pair.
Enter file in which to save the key (/home/pi/.ssh/id_rsa):
Enter passphrase (empty for no passphrase):
Enter same passphrase again:
Your identification has been saved in /home/pi/.ssh/id_rsa.
Your public key has been saved in /home/pi/.ssh/id_rsa.pub.
The key fingerprint is:
The key's randomart image is:
pi@raspberrypi ~ $

BIGGER JOBS

GNU Parallel works best when the jobs in question take a long time to run, especially if they're working on small files that can be transferred over the network quickly. The latter is important because the Pi's biggest weakness in clustered systems is its slow network port, which is limited by its connection to the processor through a USB hub.

As you've learned, GNU Parallel works by running a separate version of the command you give it on each node in the cluster. As a result, it requires that any program you run is installed on all nodes in the system. To speed up image processing with the ImageMagick package, for example, requires that ImageMagick be installed on all nodes. You don't need to install it manually, however; using the command format you learned earlier, you can automate the process using GNU Parallel itself. Type the following command at the terminal on the master Pi:

```
parallel -j N --sshloginfile
.. --ungroup --nonall sudo
apt-get install imagemagick
-y
```

Replace N with the number of nodes in your cluster. This command is similar to the one you ran earlier to get status reports from each node, with the exception of the --ungroup option. This tells GNU Parallel that you don't want it to group the output from each node together as it scrolls up the screen. Normally, grouping is a good thing as it makes the output easier to read. In this case, having the commands run faster is better, and grouping slows things down.

Rather than uptime, this time you're running a command through Parallel, which downloads and installs the ImageMagick image processing tools. The -y option at the end tells Apt that you don't want to be prompted during the process, and that it should assume the answer to any given question is yes. This will take some time to complete, but has the advantage that it's running on all Pis simultaneously. There's no need to install the software on one, then another, then another.

When the command finishes running, and you're returned to the terminal on the master Pi, the software is now installed on all nodes. Now you need some files to process, so type the following commands to download and extract a batch of sample images:

```
wget http://freelance.
halfacree.co.uk/downloads/
parallelsamples.tar.gz
tar xvzf parallelsamples.
tar.gz
cd parallelsamples
```

The sample files are all identical: ten images, in Portable Network

It's not possible to use GNU Parallel with jobs that can't easily be split up.

A three-Pi cluster isn't three times faster than a single Pi.

Graphic (PNG) format, showing a Raspberry Pi cluster with three nodes. To demonstrate how GNU Parallel can cut down processing time compared to running on a single Pi, start by running the following command:

```
time parallel mogrify
-antialias {} ::: *png
```

This tells the "mogrify" portion of the ImageMagick package to run an antialias filter across all the images – a time-consuming process. Although you're using GNU Parallel in the command, it's only there for demonstration purposes; without the --sshloginfile option, it will only run the command on the master Pi.

The latter part of the command takes some explaining, and is key to how GNU Parallel commands are formatted. The {} symbols are used as a placeholder for the name of a single file, while the *png wildcard after the three colons tells GNU Parallel which files to pick – in this case, any file that ends in the letters "png" from the current directory. One job will be created for each file, and because you're running GNU Parallel on a single node they'll run one at a time – no faster than if you weren't using GNU Parallel at all.

When the tasks have completed, the "time" command will print out how long the process took to complete. It should take around two minutes and 50 seconds to process all files, giving you a benchmark for seeing how the cluster improves performance.

Next, try running the same image processing task across all nodes in the cluster with the following command:

```
time parallel -j N
--sshloginfile .. --ungroup
--trc {} mogrify -antialias
{} ::: *png
```

Replace N with the number of nodes in your cluster. You'll recognise the --sshloginfile and --ungroup options from earlier; --trc is new. The --trc option is shorthand for three other options that are commonly used together: --transfer, --return and --cleanup. The first option tells GNU Parallel that it should transfer the file that matches the current job to the remote node on which the job is running; the second that it should return the processed file back to the master Pi when the job is finished. The last option, --cleanup, deletes any copies of the files that were created on the individual nodes, leaving only those on the master Pi.

As before, this process will take a while to complete; when it does, you'll again get a printout of the time the jobs took to finish. This time, it should have taken considerably less time: on a three-Pi cluster, a time of just under a minute and 30 seconds should be achievable without overclocking.

You may wonder why a three-Pi cluster isn't three times faster than the single Pi. GNU Parallel comes with overheads: files need to be transferred to the remote hosts for processing and transferred back again afterwards, which takes time. The SSH process by which these transfers are carried out takes up some of the master Pi's processor time, too, slowing it down compared to any other node. If you're building an extremely large node, you may have also noticed an upper limit to the performance improvements you can gain. Because there are ten test files, the GNU Parallel tasks can only be spread across ten individual nodes including the master. If you have more than ten nodes, the remainder will go unused until you repeat the experiment with more files.

If you want to experiment with true clustering, start by reading the write-up of the cluster created at the Boise State University in the US from 32 Raspberry Pi systems. This uses the Message Passing Interface (MPI) technique to create a true cluster, but in doing so makes itself only suitable for specially chosen scientific tasks. A white paper on the topic is available from:

coen.boisestate.edu/ece/files/2013/05/Creating.a.Raspberry.Pi-Based.Beowulf.Cluster_v2.pdf

RASPBERRY PI: NEXT STEPS

Your journey doesn't have to end here. We've barely scratched the surface of what's achievable with the Pi; there are plenty of secrets left to learn

If you've worked your way through the projects in this MagBook, you've earned yourself a good grasp on the capabilities of the Raspberry Pi and how to exploit them. These projects barely scratch the surface of what you can achieve with the low-cost microcomputer, if you're willing to put in some time and effort.

As with any good community, Raspberry Pi enthusiasts are often eager to help each other out and offer their expertise. Likewise, a Pi user should always feel able to ask for help where it's required, even if the solution seems simple. The Raspberry Pi is a relatively new community compared to those for similar endeavours. Just a couple of years ago, everyone was starting from scratch and the majority will still remember taking those first tentative steps to mastery when their Pi arrived in the post.

The secret to success is knowing where to look for help and inspiration, and your journey doesn't have to stop at the end of this MagBook. Try the following resources for hints on how to continue to learn the secrets of the Raspberry Pi.

THE RASPBERRY PI FOUNDATION

A non-profit organisation set up to further the educational promise of the Raspberry Pi, the eponymous Foundation is in charge of the entire project. The Foundation is the only company able to design and build Raspberry Pi boards, which it subcontracts to various local manufacturers around the world. It also creates some official add-on hardware, such as the Raspberry Pi Camera Board and its NoIR variant as seen in the Tweeting Security System project. The majority of this work, however, is left to the Raspberry Pi community itself, with numerous companies such as Pimoroni and Fen Logic springing up to take advantage of the Pi's popularity.

The Raspberry Pi Foundation hosts the official Raspberry Pi Forum, a community-driven gathering of enthusiasts boasting almost a hundred thousand members at the time of writing. Many of these members are newcomers to the project looking for advice on getting their Pi-powered creations operational. Others are highly talented engineers and technicians only too willing to lend a hand to those less experienced than themselves. Members of the Raspberry Pi Foundation's engineering team can sometimes be found posting their own advice, along with announcements of new software releases or board revisions.

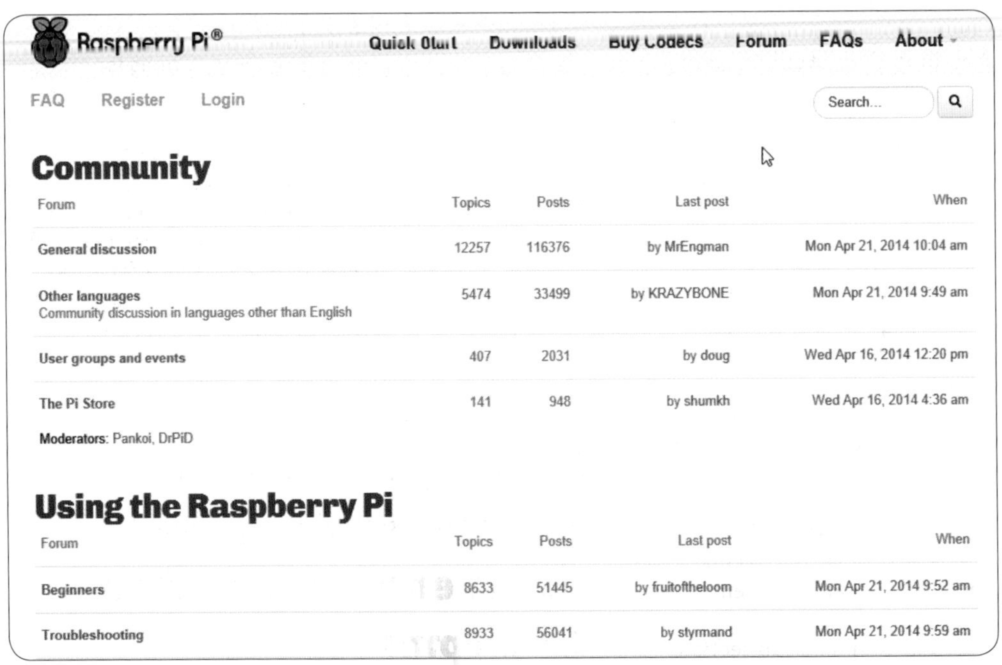

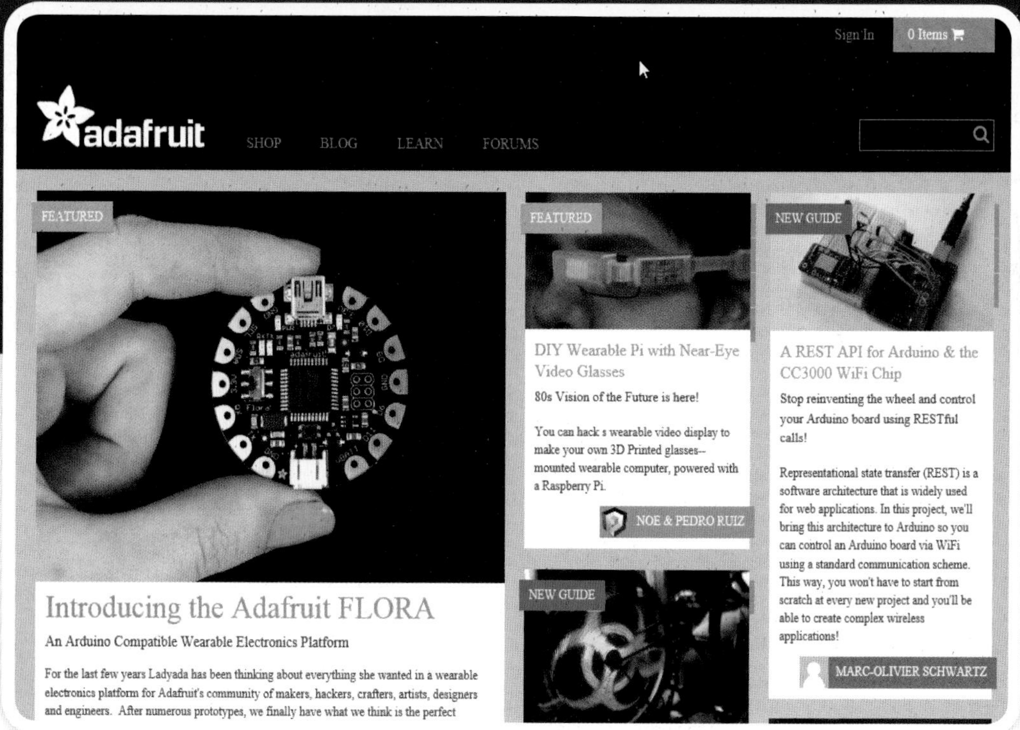

The forum is split into numerous sub-sections, each of which has individual fora for specific topics. A good place to start is the Using the Raspberry Pi sub-section, which has three sub-fora: Beginners, for those without the level of experience gained by following the projects in this MagBook; Advanced Users, for those who've built a project or two and have a good idea of what the Pi can and can't do; and Troubleshooting, for anyone with specific problems or questions they need answering. As it's volunteer-driven and run by the community, don't expect the Troubleshooting forum to act like a commercial customer support service. Provide as much detail when asking your question as possible, and be patient when waiting for an answer. If you solve the problem yourself while waiting, it's good etiquette to reply to your post explaining so, and to detail the steps you took to fix the issue, as that information could be invaluable to someone else having the same problem in the future.

The Programming sub-section offers help and advice for various programming languages and tasks you may want to use with the Raspberry Pi. These are typically more technical than the topics found in the Using the Raspberry Pi sub-section, but just as welcoming to beginners. Sub-fora include sections on Python, Java, C/C++, Wolfram Language and general Graphics Programming. There are also fora on low-level bare-metal programming for advanced users, as well as a section for general programming discussion, a good place for beginners to get a handle on the topic.

As its name implies, the Projects sub-section is dedicated to practical builds. Here, you can ask for advice on building your own projects or browse those created by others for inspiration. Sub-fora include sections for Automation, Sensing and Robotics, custom-build Cases, Gaming, Networking and Servers, and even reviews of Magazines and Books. If you've built a project you'd like to show off, create a topic in the relevant sub-forum; sharing your creations with the world is a great way to encourage further development, and you may receive advice on how to extend its capabilities or make it more efficient.

Sharing your creations with the world is a great way to encourage further development

Other sections of the Raspberry Pi Forum include discussion and help fora for each of the most common operating systems used with the Pi, add-on hardware such as the Camera Board and recently announced industrial Compute Module, and even a trading area where items you no longer require can be sold and other items purchased from community members, typically at a considerable discount over buying the same items new.

The Raspberry Pi Forum is at **www.raspberrypi.org**

ADAFRUIT LEARNING SYSTEM

Adafruit is an American hobbyist electronics company that made a name for itself developing derivative designs and add-on boards for the Arduino microcontroller. When the Raspberry Pi launched, Adafruit was one of the first companies to begin supporting it with add-ons, and that support hasn't diminished in the years since.

Recently, Adafruit has launched a new sub-section to its website called the Adafruit Learning System.

Designed to encourage beginners to get involved with electronics, the Learning System provides step-by-step instructions on how to create a variety of projects ranging from simple single-button circuits to more complex wearable computing devices and intelligent measuring cups.

Many of the projects revolve around kits or components designed and sold by Adafruit, but most can be easily altered for third-party equivalent parts if you can't find a particular Adafruit kit locally. Like the Raspberry Pi Forum the Adafruit Learning System is a great place to browse for inspiration, although not all the projects use the Raspberry Pi.

If you want to build any of the projects that involve Adafruit-specific components, such as the NeoPixel rings and boards, you can order the parts from Adafruit directly. Alternatively, you can find a local reseller; in the UK, the following supply Adafruit components including Raspberry Pi-compatible kits and hardware:

- **pimoroni.com**
- **coolcomponents.co.uk**
- **skpang.co.uk**

The Adafruit Learning System itself is available at **learn.adafruit.com**

MAGPI MAGAZINE

A volunteer-created enthusiast magazine, the *MagPi* offers a monthly look at the most popular projects in the Raspberry Pi world. Available as a free download, or for purchase in print from a number of online retailers, the *MagPi* has been running for over a year and is one of the most popular sources of information surrounding the Raspberry Pi community.

As well as reviews of Raspberry Pi hardware, books and software and interviews with individuals and companies creating new add-ons for the Pi, the *MagPi* offers frequent tutorials ranging from installing new software to building custom hardware. Previous projects found in the *MagPi* include home automation systems, track-based robots and even methods for powering a Pi through renewable energy.

The *MagPi* is written by members of the Raspberry Pi community, and its content can vary from the technical to the extremely simple. Each issue typically has a good range of topics to suit all levels of experience, however, and as a free download it's a good way to keep abreast of the latest developments without having to keep a close eye on the Raspberry Pi Forum. ●

MagPi is available at **www.themagpi.com**

CREDITS

Author Gareth Halfacree
Managing Editor Priti Patel
Production Rachel Storry
Design and layout Billbagnalldesign.com
Digital Production Manager Nicky Baker

MANAGEMENT
Group Managing Director Ian Westwood
Managing Director, Technology John Garewal
Editorial Director, Technology Tim Danton
MD of Advertising Julian Lloyd-Evans
MagBook Publisher Dharmesh Mistry
Newstrade Director David Barker
Chief Operating Officer Brett Reynolds
Group Finance Director Ian Leggett
Chief Executive James Tye
Chairman Felix Dennis

MAGBOOK

21 Brilliant Raspberry Pi projects
ISBN 1-78106-310-9

LICENSING & SYNDICATION
To license this product please contact Carlotta Serantoni on +44 (0) 20 7907 6550 or email carlotta_serantoni@dennis.co.uk.
To syndicate content from this product please contact Anj Dosaj Halai on +44(0) 20 7907 6132 or email anj_dosaj-halai@dennis.co.uk.

Printed in China